STRESS AND THE NURSE MANAGER

by

Peter Hingley

Bristol Polytechnic

and

Cary L. Cooper

*University of Manchester
Institute of Science and Technology*

A Wiley Medical Publication

JOHN WILEY & SONS
Chichester   New York   Brisbane   Toronto   Singapore

Library of Congress Cataloging-in-Publication Data:

Hingley, Peter.
  Stress and the nurse manager.

  (A Wiley medical publication)
  Bibliography: p.
  Includes index.
  1. Nurse administrators—England—Job stress.
2. Nurses—England—Job stress. 3. Health surveys—
England. I. Cooper, Cary L. II. Title. III. Series.
[DNLM: 1. Nursing. 2. Nursing, Supervisory. 3. Stress,
Psychological. WY 87 H663s]
RT89.H56 1986   610.73   86-4090
ISBN 0 471 91022 8

British Library Cataloguing in Publication Data:

Hingley, Peter
  Stress and the nurse manager.
  1. Nurses — Job stress
  I. Title   II. Cooper, Cary L.
  610.73'01'9   RT86

  ISBN 0 471 91022 8

Typeset by Inforum Ltd, Portsmouth
Printed and bound in Great Britain

Contents

Acknowledgements

We would like to thank the nursing staff of the various Health Authorities across the country who have been involved in the various stages of the project. In particular we are indebted to all members of the Authority in which the main survey was undertaken for their active cooperation and support, especially those nurses who gave up their valuable time to take part in the survey and without whom this study would not have been possible. Thanks also to the group of concerned practitioners, in Occupational Health and at Senior Nurse level, whose experiences of the effects of stress helped to provide the original impetus for this study. We would particularly like to thank Phil Harris for his continual support and help throughout the project.

We greatly appreciate the support of the King's Fund and their permission to use material from the original research report, and in particular to Hazel Allen for her cooperation and encouragement over the past few years.

Finally, our thanks to the profession itself, who allowed 'outsiders' to get close enough to share in some of its stresses (and rewards). We hope the material that has emerged from the study will be of practical use in helping to improve the quality of the day-to-day life of the nurse.

Throughout the report we refer to the nurse as 'she' because the large majority of our sample were women. We apologize to our outnumbered male nurse colleagues!

Preface

The consequences of stress are growing in Western culture, as more and more people are suffering from coronary artery disease and many other stress-related illnesses and social manifestations (e.g. divorce, drug-taking). For the individual, stress means 'human suffering'—short-term discomfort and un-happiness, but with the possibility of long-term disease. There is a substantial body of health literature (Cooper, 1983), which documents those effects of relevance in the home and workplace—anxiety, inability to concentrate, irritability, minor physical ailments, etc.

Stress-related illnesses such as coronary heart disease have been on the steady upward trend over the past couple of decades in the United Kingdom. In England and Wales, for example, the death rate in men between 35 and 44 nearly doubled in 20 years and has increased much more rapidly than that of older age ranges (for example, 45 to 54). By the mid 1970s, 41 per cent of all deaths in the age group 35 to 44 were due to cardiovascular disease, with nearly 30 per cent due to cardiac heart disease. In fact, the American Heart Association estimated the cost of cardiovascular disease in the USA at $26.7 billion in one year alone. In addition to the more extreme forms of stress-related illnesses, there has been an increase in other possible stress manifestations such as alcoholism, where admissions to alcoholism units in UK hospitals increased over 33 per cent in ten years; and industrial accidents and short-term illnesses (through certified and uncertified sick leaves), with an estimated 300 million working days lost at a cost of £55 million in social security benefit payments alone.

For a country's employers of manpower, stress also has its costs: absenteeism being one of the more obvious. Stress-related illnesses are second and third in the table of those reasons for short-term sickness absence, which are on the increase in Britain according to the Office of Health Economics. In two decades 'nervousness, debility, and headaches' accounted for an increase of 189 per cent of days off for men and 122 per cent for women; 'psychoneurosis and psychosis' for an increase of 153 per cent for men and 302 per cent for women. Still using 'time off work' as our unit of measurement, we find that stress costs the economy substantially more than industrial injury, and more than strikes. For example, in 1973 approximately 40 million days were lost in

British industry because of 'mental illness, stress and headaches' (as accounted for by NHS health certificates), which is three times the number of days lost by strikes and other forms of industrial action. There are other, less evident, costs of stress to the employer: high labour turnover rates, poor staff morale, and employees who do not find their jobs satisfying, which all increase an organization's costs while reducing its efficiency.

REFERENCE

Cooper, C.L. (1983) *Stress Research: Issues for the 80s.* Chichester & New York: John Wiley & Sons.

CHAPTER 1
The nature of stress: an overview

A review of the literature is presented highlighting alternative approaches to the study of stress. The advantages of an interactionist approach, in which stress is seen as part of a process of transaction between the individual and his/her environment (the 'Person/Environment fit'), are explored in detail. Finally, the research implications of this approach are noted.

DEFINING STRESS

The concept of stress, although generating a considerable degree of discussion and research, is somewhat elusive. It suffers as Seylé, one of the founding fathers of stress research, comments 'from the mixed blessing of being too well known and too little understood'. Because of the lack of a precise and generally accepted definition it is a somewhat elusive concept. As Cox (1978) remarks, 'it is a concept which is familiar to both layman and professional alike; it is understood by all when used in a general context but by very few when a more precise account is required, and this seems to be a central problem.' Indeed, Cassel (1976) comments that the simple-minded invocation of the word stress 'has done as much to retard research in this area as did the concepts of miasmas at the time of the discovery of micro-organisms'.

Almost a quarter of a century ago Cofer and Appley (1964) noted that the then recently popularized concept had all but pre-empted whole areas of existing research which had previously gone under other headings: anxiety, conflict, frustration, crisis, etc. 'Over the last two decades many of the established disciplines have devoted considerable energies to the study of stress, and their interest in both research and application has been wide ranging. It is of concern to psychology and psychiatry, to medicine, physiology, and pharmacology, to sociology and anthropology; each approach reflecting the particular interests and methods of the parent discipline' (Cofer and Appley, 1964). Consequently, the concept itself inevitably reflected the inbuilt disciplinary bias of the researchers involved, and this has resulted in a high degree of conceptual confusion.

1

In the face of such a complex diversity it is a difficult task to present a brief but comprehensive overview of the concept of stress. Yet such an exercise in 'semantic-hygiene' must be attempted if the current state of our knowledge is to be understood. However, any solution offered must be seen as both a compromise and incomplete. It must be seen primarily as a heuristic device rather than a final statement. As such it is dynamic, not fixed, and must be treated as 'a point for debate rather than as an article of faith' (Cox 1978).

OVERVIEWS OF STRESS

A number of ways of classifying the alternative theoretical approaches to the study of stress appear in the literature, and these have been discussed at some length by several authors (Lazarus, 1966; Appley and Trumbell, 1967; Levine and Scotch, 1970; McGrath, 1970; Howarth, 1978). Cox (1978), reviewing the range of alternatives, suggests that it is possible to identify three major approaches. Stress, he concludes, can be seen:

(a) as a *dependent* variable—stress is described in terms of the persons' response to the disturbing situation or environment;
(b) as an *independent* variable—stress is usually described in terms of the stimulus characteristics of those disturbing environments;
(c) as an *intervening* variable—stress is seen as the reflection of a 'lack of fit' between the individual and his environment. In this form stress is studied in terms of its antecedent factors and its effects. Essentially it is seen as an intervening variable between stimulus and response. Although presented here as discrete approaches there is a degree of common ground which they all share. They differ most in where they lay the emphasis in the definitions they propose, and in the methods they adopt.

Hinkle (1973), in a comprehensive review of the literature, takes what is in essence an historical approach. He traces, in some detail, the changes in the use and meaning of the concept:

> Stress, a word derived from the Latin *stringere*, to draw tight, was used popularly in the seventeenth century to mean hardship, straits, adversity, or affliction. Only during the late eighteenth century did its use evolve to denote 'force, pressure, strain or strong effort', with reference primarily to a person or person's organs or mental powers.

The idea of an external pressure seeking to distort or disrupt, and being resisted by the person or object, gained greater currency when it became utilized in engineering and physics. The concept was used both by Boyle (investigating the properties of gases), and by Hooke (the elasticity of springs), in the seventeenth century, though Hinkle credits its earliest precise use to Baron Cauchy early in the nineteenth century.

From these early developments a mechanical model evolved in which 'stress' was seen as 'the internal force generated within a solid body by the action of any external force which tends to distort the body'; 'strain' described the resulting distortion; and 'load' was defined in terms of the external forces at work. We will see that these early explanations, developed within the physical sciences, are still influential in the study of stress today.

STRESS AS A RESPONSE—STRESS AS A *DEPENDENT* VARIABLE

This approach treats stress as the dependent variable to be studied, i.e. it is described in terms of the person's *response* to disturbing stimuli. An early application of this approach to human behaviour, and the idea that stress and strain can result in 'dis-ease', can be seen in the work of Sir William Osler at the turn of the century. He observed that angina pectoris was especially prevalent among members of the Jewish business community. He attributed this, in part, to their hectic life style, and suggested that there was a causal relationship.

living an intensive life, absorbed in his work, devoted to his pleasures, passionately devoted to his home, the nervous energy of the Jew is taxed to the utmost, and his system is subjected to that stress and strain which seems to be a basic factor in so many cases of angina pectoris (Ostler, 1910).

The idea of stress from the environment causing distortion to the object (or disease to the person), and the natural tendency of the person to resist this, can be seen in the work of William Cannon (1935). Utilizing an experimentally based approach his laboratory work centred around the effects of stress upon animals and humans, and in particular upon the 'fight or flight' reaction. Both Hinkle (1973) and Seylé (1976), suggest that the concept was developed from his earlier formulations of the homeo-static properties of living organisms, i.e. the ability to restore to their original state when acted upon by external forces or disturbing agents. Cannon noted the reactions of the adrenal medulla and the sympathetic nervous system when his subjects, both human and animal, experienced a variety of disturbing stimuli. When as a result of these stimuli these physiological changes were occurring, e.g. emergency adrenalic secretions, etc., Cannon concluded that the organism was experiencing stress.

A decade later, in the early work of Hans Selyé, these physiological responses were seen as individual manifestations of a single coordinated stress syndrome. That these same endocrine reactions could be elicited by a wide variety of damaging or alarming stimuli prompted Seylé to postulate a General Adaptation Syndrome (GAS) of somatic symptoms produced by 'non-specific stress' (Selyé, 1946). In effect this was the first scientific attempt to explain the dynamic process of stress-related illness. Of particular importance was the implication that the body's adaptability was finite, and that, under constant stress, exhaustion inevitably resulted.

Seylé suggested that the individual experienced three stages in stressful situations; these make up the General Adaptation Syndrome.

1. The alarm reaction—in which an initial shock phase of lowered resistance is followed by 'counter-shock' during which the individual's defence mechanisms are activated. If the stressor is sufficiently severe and prolonged, resistance may collapse, and death ensues.
2. Resistance—this is the stage of maximum adaptation and, hopefully, the successful return to a state of equilibrium for the individual. However, if the stressor continues, or the defence is ineffective, the individual will move on to the third stage.
3. Exhaustion—this is the final stage in all senses of the word and one in which the adaptive mechanisms finally collapse. The signs of the alarm reaction reappear as the person or animal dies.

The general adaptation syndrome is shown diagrammatically in Figure 1.1.

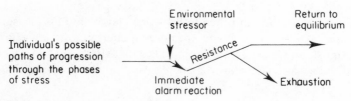

Figure 1.1 Selyé's model of stress.

The idea of 'non-specificity' became particularly influential and only recently has it been seriously challenged. However, there is now growing evidence that the position has been overstated. Mason (1971) has shown that not all noxious physical conditions produce the syndrome. Lacey (1967) argues that researchers have been over-optimistic about the intercorrelations between the various physiological indices of the GAS and that, in his focus upon the body's physiological responses to stress, Selyé has ignored completely the role of the psychological processes at work. More recently researchers have suggested that much of the physiological responses are not directly determined by the actual presence of the stressors, but rather by their psychological impact upon the individual (Cox, 1978).

STRESS AS A STIMULUS—STRESS AS AN *INDEPENDENT* VARIABLE

Definitions which see stress as a stimulus are well established and widely used in the research literature. They rest firmly on models taken directly from the physical sciences and, in particular, the field of engineering. External forces are seen as exerting pressure upon the individual system, and it is suggested that these pressures will give rise to various categories of observable strain depending upon individual makeup, and the severity and duration of the pressure (see Figure 1.2). Methodologically this approach often focuses upon the identification of stimuli which are seen to be diagnostic of stress, and on some attempted measure of their 'toxicity' (see for example the work of Holmes and Rahe, 1967).

Figure 1.2 Physical model of stress. From Cooper and Marshall (1978).

The appeal is two-fold. By using established concepts borrowed from the 'hard' sciences it has an immediate face-validity and general currency. The result is a well recognized, straightforward approach to stress, one reflected in dictionary definitions and in general every-day use. Its popularity is due in part to the fact that 'it allows us to rub shoulders with what is apparently a more clearly formulated discipline, and because it allows us to attempt to measure the stress to which a person is subjected to by the same process as we measure that to which a machine is subjected. Proponents of this view might argue that we can even see at what point collapse occurs. They assume that an undemanding situation is not stressful and is a prescription for maximum well-being' Cox (1978). In this approach explanations must be sought outside 'the person system', a view expressed forcefully by Symonds (1947), who, in a discussion of wartime pilot stress, concludes:

It should be understood once and for all that (flying) stress is that which happens *to* the man, not that which happens *in* him; it is a set of causes, not a set of symptoms.

However, this approach has a number of major weaknesses. Because statements about stressful environments have to be based upon *normative* data (i.e. the stimulus characteristics of that situation which will provoke a stress response from the majority of the population) it employs a broad-based perspective which does not easily account for individual differences. In its defence, and following the mechanical analogy, several researchers have attempted to explain these differences in terms of individual levels of 'built-in resistance' to stress. These, they suggest, may be inherited or learned. Korchin and Ruff (1964), in their studies of American astronauts, suggest that specific personality attributes may contribute to a high resistance to stress, and in particular they draw attention to the importance of early formative experiences in this process. In a similar vein Levine (1967), in a series of studies, showed the effectiveness of 'tempering', or 'stress innoculation', through early training and experience. Animals that had been subjected to stress in early life coped more effectively with later stressful situations than those which had not been subject to such stimulation. From this, and earlier research (Levine 1957), he concluded that infantile stimulation appears to produce more adaptive and variable adult behaviour, and that a person's resistance to stress is partly dependent upon early environment.

But, as Cox (1978) emphasizes, the mechanical analogy is extremely limited when it is applied to human behaviour:

> Men and their organisations are not machines . . . unless the stress/strain relationship in man functions both unconsciously and automatically, we have to accept some intervening psychological process which does mediate the outcome of that relationship. Stress has to be perceived or recognised by man. A machine, however, does not have to recognise the load or stress placed upon it.

In addition, unlike the situation in physics, it is often very difficult, if not impossible, to determine with any degree of certainty what is stressful about specific human situations. Indeed, it has been suggested that:

> Intuition and consensus seem to be the main agents of decision . . . it may be immediately obvious as to what is stressful about stoking a blast furnace, but the stressful aspects of a police control-room operator's job or a teacher's job may not be at all obvious (Cox, 1978).

Consequently, there are major problems of quantification, and the construction of acceptable norms prove particularly difficult. In the final analysis it may be that 'the most important question to ask of experiments on stress, which treat it as an independent variable, is: 'Does stress exist in the eye of the subject or in the eye of the experimenter?' (Cox, 1978).

AN INTERACTIONIST APPROACH—STRESS AS AN INTERVENING VARIABLE

Both of the preceding approaches are based largely on a mechanical Stimulus–Response, view of stress. As far as individual behaviour is concerned they are essentially reductionist in nature, often viewing the person simply as a passive recipient of stimuli from the environment. Such an approach does not account easily for individual differences in either perception or response to stressful events. It seems that neither the study of Stimulus (i.e. environmental variables), nor Response (i.e. the effects on the person), can, in themselves, provide a comprehensive account of the stress phenomena.

Bowers (1973) makes a similar observation in the field of personality studies. In a review of the literature he was able to identify the controlling variables of behaviour, and to categorize them as either personal, situational, or interactional variables. Overall he found that on average 13 per cent of the variance was due to 'person variables', and about 10 per cent was due to 'situational variables'. However Bowers found that the *interaction* between them accounted for almost twice as much (21 per cent) of the variance. In conclusion, he emphasized that any theory must be able to take simultaneous account of both influences, and how they interact, if it is to provide a useful explanation of individual behaviour. A view supported by Mischels (1973), who argues forcibly that any explanation of human behaviour must embrace the three perspectives of 'environmental determinants, person variables, and experiential factors, i.e. the individual's subjective interpretation of events.' One of the earliest, and to some extent neglected, proponents of this approach was Basowitz (1955) who pointed to the interactive nature of the stress response. In particular he emphasized the reaction of the individual as central to any explanation of stress:

> We should not consider stress as imposed upon the organism, but as its response to internal or external processes which reach those threshold levels that strain the physical and psychological integrative capacities to, or beyond, their limits.

Philosophical and conceptual roots

The interactive approach reflects the general development and growth of a more 'individualistic' movement in the social sciences during the post-war period. In sociology, symbolic interactionism and phenomenological explanations of human behaviour highlighted the importance of interaction and the individual's perceptions of his unique social reality. Whilst in psychology a similar concern was evidenced in the work of Maslow, Lewin, and Carl Rogers, and in the growth of a 'humanistic' school of psychology at odds with behaviourist traditions.

Particularly influential in this development has been the early theory-building of George Kelly whose 'Personal Construct Theory' reflected the re-emergence, and growing centrality, of the 'self' in explanations of human behaviour (Kelly, 1955). Kelly vigorously rejected theories which saw man as a collection of conditioned responses, or as the victim of his childhood fantasies. He stressed instead the essential 'problem-solving' nature of all human activity and proposed an alternative model of 'man the behavioural scientist who creates theories, tests hypotheses and attempts to control his environment' (Peck and Whitlow, 1975). In this approach the individual is seen as an active problem-solver (hence 'man the scientist') continually struggling to make sense of the world about him. He constructs theories, tests hypotheses and predictions, and evaluates his experimental evidence in order to make sense of his everyday life.

In Personal Construct Theory Kelly makes the basic assumption that all events are open to *alternatives constructions*. 'There is no absolute truth or objective reality but only ways of interpreting events (constructs), which are more or less useful in advancing our understanding and ability to predict future events' (Peck and Whitlow, 1975). The single fundamental postulate underlying the theory is that 'a person's processes are psychologically channelized by the way in which they anticipate events'. The individual makes sense of his or her world in terms of those 'constructs' that have predictive utility. Thus, in Kelly's eyes, a construct is more than a mere conceptual label; it is at the same time not only a way of ordering present reality but also a way of predicting future events. Individuals will differ not only in the constructs which they use at any particular time but also in the ways in which their 'construct system' is organized. In personal construct psychology it is this unique nature of the structure and organization of an individual's construct system which constitutes their personality.

In addition, the concepts of threat and anxiety are usefully defined in terms of the dynamics of the individual's construct system. Here, again, individual perception is central. Threat is seen as an awareness of 'an imminent comprehensive change in one's core structure'. This would involve the individual's 'core-constructs' which

> subsume the most important aspects of the external world for us and which, when invalidated, produce a feeling of threat. We are threatened when our major beliefs about the nature of our personal, social and practical situation are invalidated and the world around us appears about to become chaotic (Bannister and Fransella, 1980).

Anxiety is caused by the realization that existing constructs are inadequate for understanding and coping with the demands of a particular situation, 'an awareness that the events with which one is confronted lie mostly outside the range of convenience of one's construct system.' As Bannister and Fransella (1980) point out, 'we become anxious when we can only partially construe the events which we encounter, and too many of their implications are obscure', it is the *unknown* aspects of those things that give them their potency.

Again, the individual is seen as playing a pro-active role, and as anticipating probable events. In this respect Kelly's approach highlights the importance of a 'feed forward' loop.

> It implies that you are not reacting to the past as much as reaching out for the future; it implies that you check how much sense you have made of the world by seeing how well that 'sense' enables you to anticipate it; it implies that your personality is the way you go about making sense of the world (Bannister and Fransella, 1980).

Stress, then, can be seen not only as a reaction to an objective failure to cope but also as a reaction to predicted failure.

In conclusion, Kelly's approach to the understanding of human behaviour is firmly anti-reductionist. There is no attempt to explain behaviour solely in terms of underlying physiological or neurological mechanisms, of unconscious or unseen forces, or to fragment the individual's behaviour into various functional systems such as motivation, perception, memory, etc. Rather the individual is seen as reacting consciously to his own interpretation of the world about him, and is engaged in a continuous process of testing out his subjective interpretation against objective reality, i.e. the actual demands of his environment. 'Thus in Kelly's eyes man is not driven by inner urges or controlled by his environment but is at all times actively trying to make sense of his experience' (Bannister and Fransella, 1980). Stress arises when the predictive system proves inadequate in meeting the demands of the situation.

Three proponents of the interactionist approach

Lazarus

Lazarus (1976) presents one of the best-known interactionist explanations of the stress phenomenon. He sees the person, with all his attributes both inherited and acquired, interacting with the environment. Whilst recognizing environmental stimuli, and the effect upon the reacting individual, he emphasizes that it is the *nature* of the relationship of that interaction that is crucial:

> Stress refers, then to a very broad class of problems differentiated from other problem areas because it deals with any demands which tax the system, whatever it is, a physiological system, a social system, or a psychological system, and the response of that system (Lazarus, 1971).

He emphasizes that it is the nature of the *construing* which is all important and, closely following Kelly's ideas of the formation and development of the personal construct system, he states that 'reaction depends on how the person interprets or appraises (consciously or unconsciously) the significance of a harmful, threatening or challenging event'. Like Kelly he sees this process of 'cognitive appraisal' as essentially an individual phenomena:

> The appraisal of threat is not a simple perception of the elements of the situation, but a judgement, an inference in which the data are assembled to a constellation of ideas and expectations (Lazarus, 1966).

Change in any one of these elements is likely to effect the whole 'constellation', and lead to a radical alteration of both perception and response.

Lazarus takes issue with those who see stress simply in terms of environmental pressures. For him 'stress is not simply out there in the environment'. Rather it depends in the final analysis upon the perception of the individual and upon the appropriateness of their physical and cognitive coping abilities. The intensity of the stress experience is determined by the degree of perceived threat, i.e. how well the person feels he can deal with the danger he has identified. Lazarus suggests that if the individual has confidence in his coping abilities then the threat is likely to be minimal. However if the person is unsure of these abilities he is likely to feel helpless and may become overwhelmed by the threatening situation.

The Michigan school

A similar interactionist perspective, in which stress is defined in terms of the relationship between the person and his environment, has been developed at the Institute for Social Research at the University of Michigan. This approach is based on descriptions of motivational processes developed by Lewin (1951) and Murray (1959). The 'Michigan model' starts with objective work situations that may give rise to perceived stress and stress is defined as 'a perceived substantial imbalance between demands and response capability, under conditions where failure to meet demands has important perceived consequences' (McGrath, 1970).

Van Dijkhuizen (1980) reviewing this approach points out that potential stressors will be those elements in the environment, which in the opinion of the person himself (by his perception) influence his daily routine, his psychological and physical health. Examples of these potential stressors might be the nature of relationships with colleagues, role conflict, role ambiguity, workload, etc. He goes on to suggest that stressors are important causes of psychological, behavioural and physiological 'strain'. Strain is used,

> to denote the directly measurable effects of internal stress, being the consequence of the actions of one or several stressors. For instance, high blood pressure, cigarette smoking, high cholesterol level etc. are often pointed to in cardiological literature as important risk factors in ischaemic heart disease (Crawford, 1977).

However, unlike most of the medical research, where these risk factors are treated as isolated variables, the Michigan model, in line with modern interactionist perspectives on personality, takes an integrative view of the stress process in which individual perception plays a crucial role (e.g. French *et al.*, 1974; Ekehammar, 1974; Lazarus and Launer, 1978).

Cox's transactional model

Following in a similar tradition, Cox and his colleagues at Leicester University reject any theoretical explanation which sees stress only in terms of environmental pressures or physiological responses. They suggest that stress can best be described as 'part of a complex and dynamic system of transaction between the person and his environment' (Cox 1978). The approach is eclectic in that it draws both from the stimulus and response based theories, but these are located within a 'transactional' setting which emphasizes the ecological and transactional nature of the phenomenon. This approach sees stress as,

> an individual perceptual phenomenon rooted in psychological processes . . . it treats stress as an intervening variable, the reflection of a transaction between the person and his environment and, like the model offered by Levi and Kagan, it is part of a dynamic cybernetic system (Cox 1978).

This 'dynamic system' consists of five discrete stages (Figure 1.3):

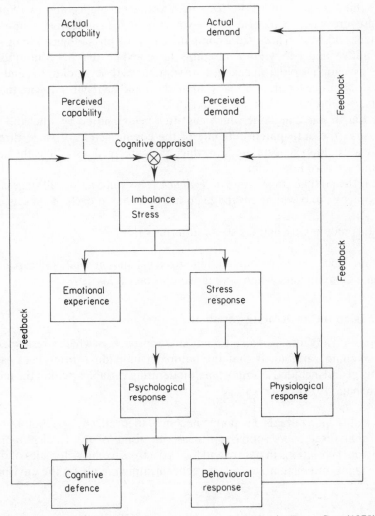

Figure 1.3 Transactional model of stress (Cox and Mackay). From Cox (1978).

1. This first stage arises directly from environmental demands. These include not only external demands but also internal psychological and physiological needs.

2. The second stage is accounted for by the individual's perception of the demand, together with the perception of his own coping abilities: 'Stress may be said to arise when there is an *imbalance* between the perceived demand and the persons perception of his capacity to meet that demand . . . it is essential to realise that the important balance or imbalance is not between demand and actual capability, but between perceived demand and perceived capability. What is important for man is his cognitive appraisal of the potentially stressful situation and of his ability to cope' (Cox 1978).

3. The third stage involves the responses to this imbalance and two kinds of response are suggested. The first gives rise to the subjective (emotional) experience of stress. These are accompanied by both physiological changes and by cognitive and behavioural attempts to allieviate the stressful situation. 'These psychophysiological changes are sometimes thought of as the end point of the stress process but, as already implied, should be regarded as methods of *coping* available to the person' (Cox, 1978).

4. The fourth stage, and one which has often been ignored by other theorists, emphasizes the anticipated outcome of the coping action of stage three. A 'feedforward' loop is postulated, in which the perceived, as well as the actual, consequences are important.

5. The fifth and final stage is one of *feedback*. This will occur at all stages in the stress process, and will affect the eventual outcome at each of these stages.

From this model Cox defines stress in terms of

an imbalance between demand, both external and internal, and capacity in meeting demand, when coping is important (Cox 1978).

Emphasis on the moderating variables

An important advantage of an interactionist approach, in which stress is seen as an intervening variable, is that the nature of individual differences can be recognized and included as important 'moderating variables' within the model. As Marshall (1979) observes:

Once this 'perceptual viewpoint' becomes theoretically acceptable we find that researchers soon seek to ascribe some of the (indisputable) individual variations in nature and levels of stress to characteristics of the individual, rather than, as before, concentrating mainly on the environment.

Reviewing the literature Appley and Trumbell (1967) identify a number of moderating variables, and examine in some detail a range of individual factors in the stress equation which determine an individual's 'vulnerability profile', i.e. those personality traits, demographic factors, physical attributes, past experiences and motivation which determine how the individual responds to perceived stress.

Person–environment fit

Central to interactionist definitions of stress is the concept of the 'person–environment fit' (P–E fit), in which stress is seen as resulting from the 'mis-fit' between the individual and his environment. A number of researchers have shown that the P–E fit is frequently more important than individual or situational differences in explaining behaviour (see Ekehammer, 1974; Bowers, 1973).

The concept is particularly attractive to the researcher as it is comprehensive, it deals with the overall adjustment of the individual to their unique situation, and it has been widely used to explain the relationship between the work environment and individual well-being. 'The basic idea of the P–E fit model is that the individual adjustment consists of the "goodness of fit" between the characteristics of a person and the properties of that person's environment' (French *et al.*, 1982). In the work situation two aspects of 'fit' have been identified:

1. The degree to which a persons' attitudes and abilities meet the demands of the job, and
2. the extent to which the job environment meets the workers' needs, and in particular the extent to which the individual is permitted and encouraged to use their knowledge and skills in the job setting. Stress is likely to occur when the individual's well-being is adversely affected because of a mismatch in either or both of these factors (French, 1974).

INDIVIDUAL DIFFERENCES IN COPING

Problem solving and the use of defense mechanisms

Stress is not only what happens to you, but how you take what happens to you (Lachman, 1983).

French (1974) suggests that when stress arises from the lack of P–E fit the individual will bring into play a number of coping techniques or defence mechanisms. These, he suggests, may be of two types. In the first instance he may use 'environmental mastery', in which an attempt is made to change the work environment in order to increase the degree of fit. The second technique identified is that of 'adaptation', in which the lack of fit is reduced because of change within the individual. For example, if the ward sister is experiencing stress because the number of patients she is having to deal with at any one time is too demanding, she may be able to persuade her superiors to cut down on new admissions in order to reduce the immediate workload (environmental mastery). On the other hand, her stress may be lessened by seeking further training, which may result in her becoming more skilled and effective in dealing with the demands of the job (personal adaptation). She may of course resort to a less constructive response, and employ defence mechanisms which distort or deny the problematic nature of the situation completely.

Using a similar argument, Folkman and Lazarus (1980) suggest that the two main functions utilized during stress and coping are 'problem solving and emotional processing' (see also Lazarus, 1966, 1976; Rachman, 1980). As a problem solving being, 'man the scientist' in Kellyian terms, the individual will employ those active coping strategies which he predicts will lead to a successful conclusion. On the other hand, 'emotional processing' may take place, in which the cognitive meaning of the demands are altered in such a way that they are perceived as less threatening.

Problem solving is recognized in the literature as a crucial stress management skill: 'It is all important. It consists of deliberate, flexible, rational attempts at mastery involving a clearly identifiable sequential process. Each step involving a number of specific skills and abilities' (Jacobson, 1983). As it is essentially a skills-based technique it can be taught, and many of the approaches to stress management focus upon the need to improve problem solving skills (Bailey, 1975). However, attempts at problem solving are not always successful, and 'if active coping strategies fail, then cognitive coping is induced in the form of "denial" or "situational redefinition" ' (Lazarus, 1967). The use of such defence mechanisms are seen by most writers as a negative side of the coping process. In the short term, defences, such as denial, can alleviate a high stress situation, and may help the individual to carry on rather than becoming completely overwhelmed (Jacobson, 1983; Lazarus, 1983a; Baily, 1983a). It has been suggested by several authors that defence mechanisms can provide a vital 'breathing space', giving the health care professional time to come to terms with the real source of the anxiety or pressure.

> Defence mechanisms are ways of coping . . . Short term denial to alleviate anxiety may help the nurse to carry on with nursing. Similarly, intellectualizing the approach to surgery may be of some coping efficacy to surgeons and theatre nurses. Other defense mechanisms such as the employment of suppression, and detachment, may make 'space' for the health professional to mobilize more open forms of problem solving when emotional expression as a means of coping with stress is inappropriate (Bailey, 1983a).

Whereas problem solving is seen by researchers as 'an active, confronting process that gathers and uses new information to respond to a challenging situation', the use of defences aims 'to avoid confrontation with the problem and seeks to maintain a comfortable status by distancing or denying disturbing emotions or information. Problem solving is decision making, whereas the use of defence mechanisms is like a reflex withdrawal from a painful stimulus' (Weisman, 1979). There is general agreement that the continued use of defense mechanisms is in the end self-defeating, as they are likely to inhibit realistic problem solving: 'Used over time, defense mechanisms narrow peoples' vision and prevent them from confronting the problem directly' (White *et al.*, 1974). In the longer term relying solely upon defensive coping is likely to be dysfunctional to the individual (and to the organization) as it leaves the origins and sources of the stress unchanged (Glaser and Strauss, 1965, 1968; Lazarus, 1983a; Stone *et al.*, 1980).

Personality and stress

It can be seen from the interactive model of stress proposed that potential 'stressors' will produce different reactions from different people. Individual variations in perception, coping abilities, and physical and psychological attributes, means that some individuals are more able to cope successfully than others, i.e. they are better able to adapt their behaviour to meet the challenge and engage in successful problem solving activity. Cooper (1978) identifies two main directions taken by researchers examining the relationship of personality and stress. The first has focused upon the relationship between various psychometric measures (particularly the MMPI and the 16 PF) and stress-related diseases (primarily coronary heart disease). The second examines stress-related or coronary-prone behaviour patterns and the eventual incidence of the disease.

Psychometric evidence

Jenkins (1971a, b), in a comprehensive review of the literature, quotes a number of retrospective studies of patients who had developed CHD or related illnesses. Overall, they were found to be more emotionally unstable and introverted than the norm. A number of studies using the MMPI (Ostfeld *et al.*, 1964; Brozek *et al.*, 1966; Bakker and Levenson, 1967; Lebovits *et al.*, 1967; Mordkoff and Rand, 1968; Bruhn *et al*, 1969) indicate that before the onset of their illness CHD patients differed from the normal healthy population on several elements of the MMPI. In particular they scored highly on the 'neurotic triad of hypochondriasis (Hs), depression (D), and hysteria (Hy). Amongst this group the occurrence of manifest CHD increased this tendency even further, and there was evidence of 'ego defence' breakdown. As Jenkins (1971a) concludes, 'patients with fatal disease tend to show greater neuroticism (particularly depression) in prospective MMPIs than those who incur and survive coronary disease'.

Cooper (1978) reports the work of a number of researchers using the 16 PF (Bakker, 1967; Finn *et al.*, 1969; Lebovits *et al.*, 1967). Common to all these studies is the picture of the CHD patient as emotionally unstable and introverted, which closely reflects the findings from the MMPI studies. Cooper comments that 'the limitation of these studies is that they are, on balance, retrospective. That is, that anxiety and neuroticism may well be reactions to CHD or related illnesses rather than precursors of it.' However, Paffenbarger and his associates carried out a *prospective* study in which they were able to link early psychometric data with eventual causes of death (Paffenbarger *et al.*, 1966). They identified a number of significant precursors to fatal CHD, one of which was a high anxiety/neuroticism score.

As part of his classic study of role conflict Kahn (1964) investigated the extent to which that conflict was conditioned by psychosocial factors. He found that the responses of individuals to role conflict were not uniform, rather they were mediated by the personality of the 'focal person' (and also by the quality of his interpersonal relations). In high-conflict situations individuals who tended to be anxiety-prone experienced role conflict as more intense, and they reacted to it with greater tension than those who were not so anxiety prone. Similarly, Kahn found that introverted subjects reacted more negatively to role-conflict than did extroverts. They also reported higher degrees of tension, and a greater deterioration in their interpersonal relationships (Kahn, 1964). Exploring traits of flexibility and rigidity, he found these dimensions of personality were strong mediators in the relationship between role conflict and tension 'with the flexible people accounting for almost the entire tension producing effect of role conflict, and the rigid people reporting virtually no greater tension in the high-conflict situation than in the low' (McMichael, 1978). In a similar vein Gemill and Heister (1972), investigating the relationship between 'machiavellianism' (a tendency to manipulate and control in order to 'win' in interpersonal relationships) and job satisfaction, found that high M scores were highly correlated with high occupational stress and low job satisfaction.

Locus of control

Rotter (1954), an exponent of the 'social learning' approach, has focused upon the question of perceived control in his development of the concept of 'internal/external control' of reinforcement. Rotter maintains that individuals may be classified along an 'internal–external' continuum. At the internal extreme of this dimension are those people who view their behaviour, and what happens to them, as being directly under their control. They see themselves, literally, as masters of their own destiny. At the opposite pole are those who see their behaviour as influenced by events which are completely outside of their control, and due more to chance, fate, and those in authority. The 'internal' person will be more confident that he can bring about changes in his own environment and in his own behaviour, whereas his 'external' counterpart will feel comparatively powerless to produce such changes.

In many ways Rotter's work reflects many of Kelly's ideas. The consequences of a person's behaviour establishes that the same consequences will result from similar patterns of behaviour in the future. Through such a pattern the child learns to distinguish those behaviours that will bring about predictable results from those behaviours that do not. Gradually he will develop a relatively stable attitude, or series of experiences (core-constructs), regarding the locus of control of his own behaviour, i.e. whether the results he observes are due to his own actions or to some other external factor. Rotter suggests that the individual will develop expectancies concerning consequences, over a whole range of specific learning situations. Like Kelly he stresses the essential personal nature of that experience. Because peoples' learning experiences differ, the same situation may be perceived differently by different people. Eventually these expectations become generalized, so that overall the individual feels in control (or otherwise) across a wide range of different situations.

Because of their perception that they are in control of their own destiny Rotter suggests that 'internals' are likely to be more independent, effective, achieving and dominant than 'externals'. Externals on the other hand would feel that they have relatively little real control over their environment and, seeing themselves as being unable to take effective remedial action, they are more likely to feel higher levels of anxiety, and report neurotic symptoms. Research evidence suggests that externals are likely to be more suspicious and dogmatic than internals. They are also likely to be lacking in motivation to achieve difficult goals, and have few aspirations since their efforts are seen as bearing little or no relationship to outcome. 'Purposelessness' and a 'meaningless' existence are also said to characterize the behaviour of people who are clinically depressed, and it has, therefore, been put forward that there should be a relationship between externality and depression (Peck and Whitlow, 1975). Interestingly, Seligman (1973) has proposed a very similar model of depression in terms of 'learned helplessness'. Experimenting on animals within the laboratory setting, he has shown that dogs, subjected to noxious stimuli they are powerless to avoid, develop behavioural and physical symptoms strikingly similar to those found in human depression.

In conclusion the internal/external dimension reflects on the ways the individual perceives his relationship with his environment, and how far he expects his actions to be directly influential in bringing about change.

The internal believes that he has personal control, whereas the external attributes his experiences to fate, luck, or factors beyond his control. Orientation along this dimension results from learning experiences. The internal is more likely to have more aspirations and persistence, to participate in political activity, to be resistant to persuasion, to exert influence over others, and to be independent. The external tends to have the opposite characteristics, refusing to accept personal blame, and being prone to low moods (Peck and Whitlow, 1975).

Locus of control and gender

It has been suggested by several researchers that there is a strong tendency for women to be externalizers, i.e. seeing life events being the result of luck or chance rather than the outcome of their own actions. Men on the other hand, are more likely to be internalizers (Harlan and Weiss, 1980; Davidson, 1983). Thus, women are more likely to attribute success to external forces and failure to their own actions, whereas the opposite is the case for men. Blackstone and Weinrich-Haste (1980) found that young girls attributed their success to luck or extra effort and their failure to their own lack of ability, whereas the pattern was reversed for young boys.

In the management field it has been suggested that an internalized locus of control is an important asset. Successful female managers, unlike the general female population, do not attribute their success to external factors and in this they resemble their male counterparts. Place (1979) reports that an internalized locus of control was seen as an important factor contributing to female managerial success. In his study he found it was likely to be more highly developed in those women who perceived themselves as controlling and mastering their earlier adolescent environment (see also Cooper and Hingley, 1985).

Type-A coronary prone behaviour

The other approach to individual stress differences focuses upon specific patterns of behaviour. Of particular importance is the early work of Friedman and his colleagues in the early sixties (Friedman, 1969; Rosenman, Friedman and Strauss, 1964, 1966). They found that individuals who exhibited certain behavioural traits were significantly more likely to develop coronary heart disease (CHD). These traits were later referred to as 'coronary-prone behaviour pattern Type-A' (high risk of CHD), and were distinguished from 'Type-B' (low risk of CHD).

Type-A behaviour was seen to be characterized by extremes of competitiveness, striving for achievement, aggressiveness, haste, impatience, restlessness, hyper-alertness, explosiveness of speech, tenseness of facial musculature and feelings of being under pressure of time and under the challenge of responsibility. It has also been suggested that people having this particular behavioural pattern were often so deeply involved and committed to their work that other aspects of their lives were relatively neglected (Jenkins, 1971b).

Again, the criticism of these early studies were that they were retrospective in nature, but this methodological weakness was overcome in the classic Western Collaborative Group Study in the mid-sixties (Rosenman et al., 1964, 1966). This was a prospective study of over 3400 men, free of CHD, who were rated Type-A or B after intensive psychiatric interviews. After two and a half years it was found that Type-A men between the ages of 39 and 49, and 50 and 59, had 6.5 and 1.9 times respectively the incidence of CHD than their Type-B peers. In addition the Type-A group had elevated serum cholesterol levels, elevated beta-lipoproteins, decreased blood clotting time, and elevated day-time excretion of norepinephrine. The same relationship between behavioural patterns and CHD was observed after a four and a half year follow up period had elapsed. Many other studies have since supported these findings (Bortner and Rosenman, 1967; Zyzanski and Jenkins, 1970; Caplan *et al.*, 1975; Cooper, 1985).

French and Caplin (1970), reviewing the evidence of psychosocial factors in heart disease, remark that 'such a wealth of findings makes it hard to ignore Type-A as a relevant syndrome'. Cooper (1976), emphasizing the importance of personality traits as an intervening variable in the stress equation, concludes: 'It can be seen therefore that psychometric and behavioural data on individual differences play a crucial role in the person–environment fit paradigm and ultimately in the manifestation of stress-related disease.' Consequently any attempt to understand the 'stress equation' must be able to take into account these complex personality variables.

CONCLUSIONS

In conclusion it is argued that approaches to the understanding of stress which rely on explanations couched only in terms of environmental pressures or behavioural outcomes, cannot satisfactorily explain the individual factors within that relationship. A comprehensive model of stress must be able to account for these individual differences, both in the perception of and in the responses to stressful situations. In Cox's (1978) view the issue is clear:

The interactionist model is a psychologically based approach and explicitly deals with these factors in a way in which the other approaches do not and cannot satisfactorily deal.

From a personal point of view an interactionist approach has two major attractions to the authors, the first philosophical and the second theoretical. On the one hand it is humanistic in nature, and challenges the essentially reductionist standpoint of the other approaches. Interactionist explanations see stress as a product of the relationship between man and his environment, and emphasize the individualistic nature of that experience. Unlike alternative approaches the person is placed very firmly in the centre of the 'stress equation'; an equation in which the individual is seen as continuously reacting to, and acting upon, his environment. As such it is a much more optimistic view of human functioning, as the individual is seen as creating and moderating his own environment and destiny. Secondly from a theoretical point of view, an interactionist approach is particularly attractive as it can incorporate both personal and environmental systems within a single explanatory model. Operationally this is advantageous to the researcher as it can encompass more of the available data on stress than either of the alternative approaches considered in this chapter.

REFERENCES

Appley, M.H. and Trumbell, R. (1967) *Psychological Stress*. New York: Appleton-Century-Crofts.

Bannister, D. and Fransella, F. (1980) *Inquiring Man*. London: Penguin.

Basowitz, H., *et al*. (1955) *Anxiety and Stress*. New York: McGraw-Hill.

Bowers, K.S. (1973) Situationalism in psychology: an analysis and a critique. *Psychol. Rev.*, **80**: 307–335.

Cannon, W.B. (1935) Stresses and strains of homeostasis. *Am. J. Sci.*, **189**: 1.

Caplan, R.D. and Jones, K.W. (1975) Effect of workload, role ambiguity and Type A personality on anxiety, depression and heart rate. *J. Appl. Psychol.*, **60**: 713–719.

Cassel, J.C. (1976) The contribution of the social environment to host resistance. *Am. J. Epidemiol.* **104**: 107–123.

Cofer, C.N. and Appley, M.H. (1964) *Motivation: Theory and Research*. New York: Wiley.

Cooper, C.L. and Marshall, J. (1978) *Understanding Executive Stress*. London: Macmillan.

Cox, T. (1975). The nature and management of stress. *New Behav.*, **2**: 493.

Cox, T. (1978) *Stress*. London: Macmillan.

Crawford, L. (1977) *Pathology of Ischaemic Heart Disease*. London: Butterworth.

Ekehammar, B. (1974) Interactionism in personality from a historical perspective. *Psychol. Bull.*, **81**: 1026.

Eysenck, H.J. (1984) Lung cancer and the stress personality inventory. In Cooper, C.L. (ed.), *Psychosocial Stress in Cancer*. Chichester: Wiley.

French, J.R.P., Rogers, W. and Cobb, S. (1974) A model of person–environment fit. In Coelho, G.W., Hamburgh, D.A. and Adams, J.E. (eds), *Coping and Adaptation*. New York: Basic Books.

Friedman, M. and Rosenman, R.H. (1974) *Type A Behaviour and Your Heart*. London: Wildwood House.

Hinkle, L.E. (1973) The concept of stress in the biological and social sciences. *Sci. Med. Man*, **1**: 31–48.

Holmes, T.H. and Rahe, R.H. (1967) The social readjustment rating scale. *J. Psychosom. Res.*, **11**: 213–218.

Howarth, C.I. (1978) Environmental stress. In Howarth C.I. and Gillham W.C. (eds), *The Uses of Psychology*. London: Allen and Unwin.

Kelly, G.A. (1955) *The Psychology of Personal Constructs*. New York: Norton.

Korchin, and Ruff, (1964) Personality characteristics of the Mercury astronauts. In Grosser G.H. *et al*. (eds), *The Threat of Impending Disaster*. Cambridge, Mass: MIT Press.

Lacey, J.I. (1967) Somatic response patterning and stress: some revisions of activation theory. In Appley, M.H. and Trumbell, R. (eds), *Psychological Stress*. New York: Appleton-Century-Crofts.

Lazarus, R.S. (1966) *Psychological Stress and the Coping Process*. New York: McGraw-Hill.

Lazarus, R.S. (1971) The concept of stress and disease. In Levi, L. (ed.). *Society, Stress and Disease*, Vol.1. London: Oxford University Press.

Lazarus, R.S. (1976) *Patterns of Adjustment*. New York: McGraw-Hill.

Lazarus, R.S. and Launer, R. (1978) Stress-related transactions between person and environment. In Pervin, L.A. and Lewis, M. (eds), *Perspectives in Interactional Psychology*. New York: Plenum Press.

Levine, S. (1957) Psychosocial factors in growth and development. In Levi, L. (ed.), *Society, Stress and Disease*, Vol. 2. New York: Oxford University Press.

Levine, S. (1967) Maternal and environmental influences on the adrenocortical response to stress in weanling rats. *Science*, **156**: 258.

Levine, S. and Scotch, N.A. (1970) *Social Stress*. Chicago: Aldine.

Lewin, K. (1951) In Cartwright, D. (ed.), *Field Theory in Social Science*. New York: Harper and Row.

Marshall, J. (1977) Job pressures and satisfactions at managerial levels. *Unpublished PhD Thesis*, University of Manchester.

Mason, J.W. (1975) A historical view of the stress field. Part 1. *J. Hum. Stress*, **1**: 6–12.

McGrath, J.E. (ed.) (1970) *Social and Psychological Factors in Stress*. New York: Holt, Rinehart and Winston.

Mischel, W. (1973) Towards a cognitive social learning reconceptualisation of personality. *Psychol. Rev.*, **80**: 252–283.

Murray, H.A. (1959) Preparations for the scaffold of a comprehensive system. In Koch, S. (ed), *Psychology: a Study of a Science*, Vol. 3, *Formulations of the Person and the Social Context*. New York: McGraw-Hill.

Ostler, W. (1910) The Lumleian Lectures on angina pectoris. *Lancet*, **i**: 696–700, 839–844, 974–977.

Peck, D. and Whitlow, D. (1975) *Approaches to Personality Theory*. London: Methuen.

Rotter, J.B. (1966) Generalized expectations for internal versus external control of reinforcement. *Psychol. Monogr.*, **80** (Whole No. 609).

Selyé, H. (1946) The general adaptation syndrome and the diseases of adaptation. *J. Clin. Endocrinol.*, **6**: 117.

Selyé, H. (1950 *Stress*. Montreal: Acta.

Seylé, H. (1975) Confusion and controversy in the stress field. *J. Hum. Stress*, **1**: 37.

Seylé, H. (1976) *The Stress of Life*. New York: McGraw-Hill.

Symonds, C.P. (1947). Use and abuse of the term Flying stress *Psychological Disorders in Flying Personnel of the Royal Air Force*. London: HMSO.

van Dijkhuizen, N. (1980) *From Stressors to Strains. Research into their Interrelationships*. Lisse: Swets and Zeitlinger.

CHAPTER 2
Sources of occupational stress

In a complex industrial society work occupies a central role in the lives of all its members. It plays a major role in a person's past, it determines his present, and it moulds his future. Not only does it dictate the quality of life-style, but it also provides a major means of personal identity and self-realization. So it is hardly surprising to find that life within complex work organizations can prove to be a great source of stress. In any occupation there will be a large number of potential stressors. It is a complex equation in which individual differences in perception and response will determine the eventual outcome. The resultant cost in terms of physical and mental ill health is a cost borne not only by the individual, but also by the organization in which he/she operates, and by society in general. Neither is it limited to the arena of the work place, as work-induced stress will inevitably feed into the domestic 'system', often affecting the whole quality of family life.

Studies of occupational stress reflect some of the problems of the study of stress in general. In particular, the lack of any integrated framework or generally accepted 'conceptual map' of the field has been identified as problematic. Cooper and Marshall (1976) in reviewing the literature have attempted to integrate systematically the findings regarding sources of organizational stress. They identified over 40 interacting factors that had been identified as potential sources of occupational stress and suggest that these can be grouped into six major categories (Figure 2.1):

1. Factors intrinsic to the job,
2. The role in the organization,
3. Career development,
4. Organizational factors,
5. Relations within the organization,
6. Organizational interface with external world.

The framework of this section is based upon this model.

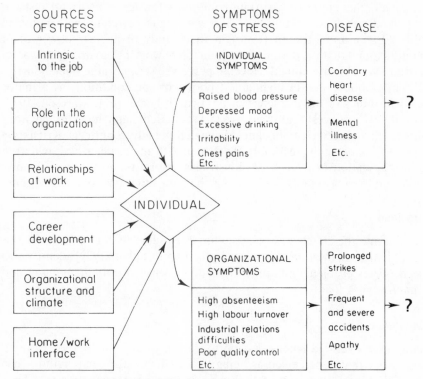

Figure 2.1 Sources of occupational stress.

1 FACTORS INTRINSIC TO THE JOB

The close examination of the very nature of the work task itself and its relationship to physical and psychological well-being was a major concern to many of the early studies in this field, and this can still be seen today in much of the 'shop floor' research. The early classical studies at the Hawthorn Electrical Co. were in this mould and have been followed by numerous studies exploring the relationship between working conditions and stress levels.

Different occupations have their own specific intrinsic stressors, but researchers have identified a number of common patterns which can be seen across a number of different occupations. These include poor working conditions, work overload and underload, shift work, person–environment fit and job satisfaction.

Working conditions

There has been a considerable interest in the relationship of the physical environment and its relation to occupational stress. Kornhauser (1965) found, for example, that unpleasant working conditions, the necessity to work fast and to expend a high degree of physical effort were highly correlated with mental ill health. Otway and Misenta (1980) in their study of nuclear power plant operators found that the design of the immediate working environment was an important variable affecting the level of perceived stress. In the steel industry, Kelly and Cooper (1981) highlighted poor working conditions as a major stressor. Studies of the incidence of physical ill health (e.g. Marcson, 1970; Shepard, 1971) suggest that repetitive tasks and dehumanizing work environments (such as paced assembly lines) have definite adverse effects. Kritsikis *et al.*, (1968), for example, in a study of 150 men with angina pectoris drawn from a total population of over 4000 industrial workers, found that significantly more came from 'assembly line' systems than any other type of environment.

Work load

Research into the effects of work load has been substantial as it is an obvious potential stressor in all occupations. French and Caplan (1973) identify two aspects of this problem and argue the need to consider both *quantitative* and *qualitative* work load.

Quantitative

Quantitative overload means 'having too much to do'; qualitative overload means work that is perceived as being 'too difficult' (the same authors also suggest that work *underload* can also be seen as a potential stressor). They found that objective quantitative overload was strongly linked to stress symptoms (particularly cigarette smoking), and that those subjects with more phone calls, office visits, meetings, etc. per unit of time were found too to have a significantly higher level of stress symptoms than those experiencing lower levels of demands. In a study of 100 young coronary patients, Russeck and Zohman (1958) found that over 25 per cent had been working at two jobs, and an additional 45 per cent had worked in jobs in which they were so overloaded that they had to spend at least 60 hours a week to keep up with the demand. They observed that a pattern of prolonged stress preceding the coronary attack was evident in at least 91 per cent of the cases, but that similar stress patterns could be observed in only 20 per cent of the control group.

A substantial investigation by Margolis *et al.* (1974) on a representative sample of employed persons found that work overload was significantly related to a number of stress symptoms. In particular, they point to escapist drinking, absenteeism, low work motivation, and lowered self-esteem. The results from these and similar studies (Cooper and Smith, 1986) indicate that quantitative overload is indeed a potential source of stress in the workplace and can affect both personal health and job satisfaction. In a study of British police officers, for example Cooper *et al.* (1982), it was found that work overload was a major stressor. In particular, indicators of mental depression were linked to perceived overload and a general feeling of a lack of control.

Qualitative

There is also evidence that in some occupations there are problems of 'qualitative' overload. French *et al.* (1965) looking at work overload in a large university found that qualitative work overload was significantly correlated to low self-esteem amongst academic staff members. Unlike their administrative colleagues, the researchers found that the greater the 'quality' of the work demanded the lower the self-esteem. Several other studies have reported an association between qualitative overload and physiological symptoms of stress: Friedman *et al.* (1958), with tax accountants facing annual deadlines; Dreyfuss and Czackes (1959) with medical students performing examinations under observation.

In reviewing the field French and Caplan (1973) identify at least nine separate symptoms of physical and psychological strain arising from the various forms of work overload: job dissatisfaction, job tension, lowered self-esteem, threat, embarrassment, high cholesterol levels, increases in heart rate, skin resistance and the incidence of smoking.

Underload

Again, as with work overload, there is a quantitative and qualitative aspect to this phenomenon. Either there is not enough to do ('quantitative underload'), or the level of the task is undemanding ('qualitative underload'). Job underload is often associated with repetitive, routine and unstimulating work situations (e.g. assembly line production), and has been linked with ill health (Cox, 1980). Inherent in certain occupations (police, hospital accident departments) are long periods of reduced activity (work underload), with the likelihood that this pattern will be disrupted by emergency situations (work overload). McCrae *et al.* (1978) found that these sudden changes in the level of demand can have particularly detrimental effects on health. Low levels of demand resulting in boredom and general disinterest have been found to reduce the worker's response to emergency situations (Davidson and Veno, 1980). However, the interactive nature of the relationship of the job and employee must be emphasized. Work overload, whether of a quantitative or qualitative nature, cannot be viewed in isolation, but only as part of the 'person–environment fit' equation, where individual perception and capabilities determine the final outcome.

Shift work

Several major occupational studies have identified shift work as a common occupational stressor. Selyé (1976) in a review of the field, points to links to changed neurophysiological rhythms such as blood temperature, metabolic rate, blood sugar levels, mental efficiency and levels of motivation; all of which, he suggests, can lead to stress-related disease. In a study of air traffic controllers, Cobb and Rose (1973) found four times the prevalence of hypertension and more mild diabetes and peptic ulcers among their subjects than in a control group of airmen. Although a cluster of related variables was identified, shift work was the major source of stress.

As with other potential stressors shift work will affect different individuals in different ways. Selyé (1976) notes in his conclusion that most investigators agree that shift work becomes physically less stressful and that the person will gradually adjust to the conditions. However, this is more likely to apply to fixed shift work patterns. In the case of rotating shifts this adjustment is less obvious and stress levels are likely to be correspondingly higher. In both patterns, a common cost is 'an exclusion from normal social activities' which can result in social and emotional isolation.

Person–environment fit and job satisfaction

A particularly/potentially valuable development in the field of occupational research is based on the work of Caplan *et al.* (1975) and the concept of person–environment 'fit' (P–E fit). In the work situation, P–E fit can be defined as the interaction between an individual's psychosocial characteristics and the objective environmental conditions (McMichael, 1978). An indication of the 'closeness' of fit can be obtained by comparing the amount/degree of a particular job factor (e.g. work load) preferred by an individual with the actual amount in the working environment. Caplan's overall hypothesis is that stress will occur if there is a lack of P–E fit and that this can lead to physical and psychological ill health and a lack of job satisfaction.

2 THE ROLE IN THE ORGANIZATION

Occupational stress can also arise because of the role the individual plays within the organization. Kahn (1964) and his colleagues working at the University of Michigan have focused in particular upon the effects of role ambiguity and role conflict.

Role ambiguity

Role ambiguity arises when the individual does not have sufficient information about the nature of the role itself. It manifests itself in a general confusion about appropriate objectives, a lack of clarity regarding expectations from the 'role set', and a general uncertainty about the scope and responsibility of the job itself. Consequently, the individual is often unable to meet the legitimate expectations of his role. Kahn *et al.* (1964) found that men who suffered from role ambiguity were more likely to experience lower job satisfaction, a greater incidence of job-related tension, greater feeling of futility and lower levels of self-confidence.

French and Caplan (1970) found that role ambiguity was related to a cluster of similar symptoms, including low job satisfaction and feelings of threat to mental and physical well-being. They also established links with physiological indicators such as increased blood pressure and higher pulse rates. Further research by Margolis *et al.* (1974) found a number of significant relationships between symptoms or indicators of physical and mental ill health and role ambiguity. In a national study, they found that depression, lowered self-esteem, life and job dissatisfaction, low work motivation, and intention to leave the job were seen as being of particular importance. However, as Cooper and Marshall point out, the evidence has its limitations for, although statistically significant correlations were not high, 'as one can see these were not very strong relationships (contributing at most 2.5 per cent of the variance), indicating that although "lack of role clarity" may well be a potential stressor at work, on its own it may not be a substantial one.'

Role conflict

Role conflict can be of two kinds. The first, 'internal' role conflict, will occur when two or more roles occupied by the individual are in conflict (i.e. manager versus union rep, or mother versus worker). The second, 'external', role conflict occurs when the demands and expectations of the 'role set' are incompatible. The most common example would be when a person is caught between the demands of two or more members of his role set who demand different kinds of behaviour.

In both cases the person occupying the role is torn between conflicting expectations and is likely to experience anxiety and stress. Kahn and his colleagues found that men who suffered from high levels of role conflict were likely to experience lower job satisfaction and higher levels of job-related stress than colleagues who had lower levels of role conflict (Kahn *et al.*, 1964). French and Caplan (1970) found that the mean heart rate for individuals in their sample was strongly related to the perceived level of role conflict. Shirom *et al.* (1973), in a large study of Israeli males drawn from various occupational groups, found that there was a significant relationship between role conflict and coronary heart disease (CHD), but that this was only true for the white-collar workers in the sample. Additional comparisons between the subgroups within the sample led the researchers to conclude that as they moved from the more manual occupations towards the white-collar groups (i.e. clerical, managerial and professional), occupational stress was more likely to be caused by problems of identity and other interpersonal dynamics than by the physical conditions of the work. Cooper and Smith (1986) in their review of the literature conclude that less physical occupations, such as managerial, clerical and professional, are more prone to stress related to role conflict.

Mettlin and Woelfel (1974), using the Langer Stress Symptom questionnaire with a sample of high-school students, found that subjects who had a more extensive and diverse communication network were more likely to experience a higher degree of role conflict. Organizational roles which are at 'system boundaries' and in which individuals are 'link-pins' between two systems, i.e. between departments or between the organization and the outside world, are likely to involve more extensive networks and, therefore, potential higher levels of role conflict. Kahn *et al.* (1964) hold that such roles are likely to be particularly stressful, a point of view supported by a number of research findings; Margolis and Kroes (1974), for example, found that foremen (a potentially high conflict-prone 'boundary role') were seven times more likely to develop ulcers than shopfloor workers.

Responsibility for people

A potential stressor associated with the organizational role and of particular concern to the 'caring' professions is the responsibility for *people* rather than *things* (i.e. equipment, finance, etc.). In an early study Wardwell *et al.* (1964) found that those in his sample who were responsible for people were signifi- cantly more likely to develop CHD than those responsible for things. French and Caplan (1970) found that responsibility for people meant that more time was spent interacting with others, attending meetings, working alone and in trying to meet more numerous deadlines. They found that responsibility for people was significantly related to heavy smoking, diastolic blood pressure and serum cholesterol levels—the more the individual had responsibility for 'people' rather than 'things' the higher was each of these CHD risk factors. In a study of the American police force, Kroes (1976) sees the responsibility for people and their safety as a potentially significant occupational stressor. A similar pattern has been found in studies of air-traffic controllers. For example, Crump *et al.* (1980) isolate responsibility for people's safety and lives as a major occupational stressor.

The problems of internal role conflict within the caring professions is well illustrated in Cooper, Mallinger and Kahn's study of American dentists. They found that the variables which best predicted abnormally high diastolic blood pressure among their sample were factors central to the professional role. In particular, they found a high level of conflict between the idealized 'caring/ healing' role and the actual reality of 'an inflictor of pain'. In addition, the carrying out of non-clinical tasks such as administrative duties and building up a practice, clashed with a commitment to a 'people-based profession'.

Other role stressors

Like work underload, having too little responsibility in the work role can lead to stress (Brook, 1973). Cooper and Marshall in their review of the field also point to lack of participation in decision making, lack of managerial support, having to keep up with increasing standards of performance and coping with rapid technological change as other potential role stressors identified in the literature 'but often with little supportive evidence'.

3 RELATIONSHIPS AT WORK

A third major potential source of occupational stress concerns the nature and quality of relationships at work. Working relationships occur at three levels; with superiors, with colleagues, and with subordinates. The sources and quality of stress are likely to be different for each level. The quality of working relationships is seen by many behavioural scientists as being a central and crucial factor in determining individual and organizational health (e.g. Greenburg, 1980; Cooper, 1983; Cooper and Smith, 1986).

French and Caplan (1973) define poor relationships as 'those which include low trust, low supportiveness, and low interest in listening to and trying to deal with problems that confront the organisational member'. They found that mistrust of work colleagues was positively related to high role ambiguity. This was likely to lead to inadequate communications between individuals and to 'psychological strain in the form of low job satisfaction and to feelings of job-related threat to one's well-being'. Wardwell and Bahnson (1973) found a positive relationship existed between perceived workload, serum glucose, blood pressure and smoking levels for those who reported poor relationships at work. Whilst amongst those who had good relationships, work stress was not found to be related to these heart disease factors.

Cooper and Melhuish (1980) in a study of senior British executives discovered that their major problems were seen in terms of interpersonal relationships. It was found that certain personality traits (e.g. extraversion, toughmindedness, etc.) and the quality of relationships at work were central to increased risks of high blood pressure. 'They were particularly vulnerable to the stresses of poor relationships with subordinates and colleagues, lack of personal support at home and work, and the conflicts between their own values and those of the organisation.'

Positive relationships and support systems established in the work place also appear to have more general effects. In an American study of the effects of unemployment by Kasl et al. (1975) it was found that perceived stress resulting from unemployment produced much higher cholesterol levels, increased depression and illness among those with low social support, while those with higher levels of support seemed to be protected from these consequences.

The centrality of interpersonal relationships to the task of management is well illustrated in Minzerg's (1973) study of the manager's use of time. In an intensive study of a small sample of chief executives in a large organization he found that only 22 per cent of thier time was spent at their desks, compared with almost 70 per cent devoted to face-to-face contacts of one kind or another.

Relationships with superiors

Buck (1972), using the Fleishman leadership questionnaire, found that workers who felt that superiors were low on 'consideration' (a factor within the questionnaire associated with 'friendship, mutual trust, respect, and some degree of warmth between superior and subordinate') reported more feelings of job pressure. These revolved around the lack of helpful criticism and feedback, favouritism of others, 'pulling rank' and taking advantage whenever the opportunity presented itself. Buck concludes that 'considerate behaviour of supervisors appears to have contributed significantly inversely to feelings of job pressure.' It is interesting to note that Cobb and Rose (1973) found that air traffic controllers got greater help and social support from friends and colleagues than from those in supervisory positions within the organization.

Cooper and Davidson (1982) found, in a large UK study of female managers, that 'lack of support from boss' was one of their major stressors, leading to job dissatisfaction and ill health among women executives.

Relationships with subordinates

One of the key functions of any managerial role is the supervision and support of subordinates. Obviously this involves 'process' skills and depends in a large part on the quality of interpersonal relationships. Caplan (1971), in a study of the incidence of CHD amongst administrators, engineers, and scientists, found that for those who reported poor relationships with their subordinates there was a positive relationship between role ambiguity and serum cortisol levels (an indicator of physiological arousal related to heart disease as well as to stress reactions).

Relationships with colleagues

Researchers have identified two potential sources of stress in this area. On the one hand, there is the possibility of stress caused by rivalry and competition. In highly competitative managerial situations, it is likely that shared problem solving or other cooperative approaches will be inhibited because of the fear of appearing weak. The second aspect is a lack of adequate 'peer support' in difficult situations. Much of the American literature stresses the potential of isolation as an added source of strain in the life of top executives, and our own studies have identified a similar pattern in top UK executives (Hingley and Cooper, 1983).

Morris (1975) presents a useful amalgamation of all these three relationship factors into a single model which he terms the 'cross of relationships'. He acknowledges the differences between relationships on each of the various dimensions, but he feels that the prime task of the manager is to be able to bring all four into a 'dynamic balance' in order to be able to minimize and deal successfully with the inherent stress of his role.

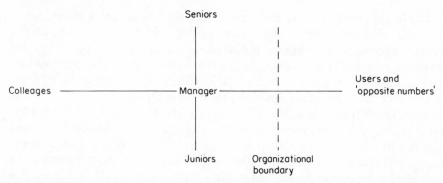

Figure 2.2 The cross of relationships. From Morris (1975).

However, in spite of the importance that relationships in the work situation receive in the literature, it is an area in which there is a scarcity of empirical evidence. As Cooper (1978) remarks, 'despite its obvious importance and the inclusion of "relationship" measures in many multivariate studies, there is little "in depth" research available in this area.'

4 CAREER DEVELOPMENT

Marshall (1977) identifies two major clusters of potential stressors in this area:

(1) lack of job security, i.e. fear of redundancy, obsolescence, forced early retirement, etc.;
(2) status incongruity, i.e. under- or over-promotion, frustration at having reached the career ceiling, etc.

Career progression is of great importance to most workers. Promotion up the career ladder not only determines material rewards, but also provides enhanced status and new challenges. It is usually at middle age and middle management levels that career progression becomes problematic, for it is at this stage that many managers find their progress slowed and sometimes halted completely. Constandse (1972) refers to this phase as "the male menopause' and found, like Levinson (1973) that the manager is likely to suffer his fears and disillusionment in 'silent isolation', unable to share his anxieties with either his work colleagues or his family.

Cooper (1978) suggests that the fear of obsolescence and failure resulting in demotion is likely to be strongest in those who believe they have reached their 'career ceiling', and that most will suffer some erosion of status before they retire. However, this is not solely a male phenomenon. Career development blockages are particularly evident among women managers as a recent study by Cooper and Davidson (1982) reveals. They found that women managers are still found clustered in low status managerial jobs and are, therefore, prone to the frustrations linked to blocked career promotion.

McMurray (1973), on the other hand, in a syndrome he lables 'the executive neurosis', describes the over-promoted manager as grossly overworking in order to keep up with the job and to hide his insecurity. He stresses the negative consequences of this and the cost to both the individual and the organization. The rapidity of technological change and its effects on most occupational areas means that the individual cannot rely on pursuing a single career during his working life. More likely he/she will change career at least once or twice in a life time, facing the inevitable trauma of career termination, retraining and re-entry into a new occupational area. Such change inevitably brings uncertainty, and research suggests that older workers are particularly vulnerable as they tend to place a high value on stability (Sleeper, 1975). Unless managers adapt to face these new and changing conditions, stress arising from this area of 'career development', particularly in later life, is likely to become an increasingly common phenomenon.

Position within the organizational hierarchy must also be considered. The levels of middle management seem particularly vulnerable; senior managers appear to be under stress less frequently than middle managers. Persons at or near the top have more power and control over their sources of stress than individuals at a lower echelon, they are also more likely to have fulfilled their career aspirations. Kay (1974) identifies the role of 'middle manager' as being particularly liable to high levels of stress. Independent of the type of employing organization, he found that middle managers are likely to be particularly stressed by (1) pay compression, as the salaries of new entrants increase; (2) job insecurity—middle managers feel particularly vulnerable to redundancy and forced or premature retirement; (3) having little real authority in spite of their high level of responsibility; (4) feeling 'boxed in' and trapped by the organization.

Status congruency (the matching of individual advancement to experience ability) and the cost of incongruency have been well researched in the United States. Arthur and Gunderson (1965) in a study of naval personnel found that promotional lag was significantly related to psychiatric illness. Status incongruency can also occur outside of the workplace. A number of sociological studies have suggested that incongruencies in social status or social class can also lead to stress-related conditions. Shekelle et al. (1969) found that men in their sample whose present social class was substantially different from that of their childhood ran a significantly higher risk of CHD. Kasl and Cobb (1967) found a similar pattern and concluded that parental status stress had 'strong, long-term effects on physical and mental health of adult offspring'. Cooper (1978) notes that more and more evidence is growing that social status stress is a problem in Western, highly mobile society. Wan (1971) reviewing the field of status stress and morbidity concludes that 'role conflict generated from incompatible expectations of a social position may yield psychological disturbances and frustrations which in turn form part of the stress-disease linkage.

5 ORGANIZATIONAL STRUCTURE AND CLIMATE

The very fact of working within an organizational setting can be in itself stressful. The 'organization man' has given up some of his own freedom, autonomy and identity in order to be accepted, and to function within that setting. Researchers have identified a number of potential problem areas that are likely to lead to enhanced levels of occupational stress. Marshall (1977) refers particularly to lack of involvement in decision making, feelings of dehumanization and no sense of belonging, lack of effective consultation and communication, restrictions on behaviour and effectiveness (e.g. through financial restrictions) and 'office politics'.

Of particular interest in this context, is the question of worker involvement and participation and its relation to stress-related conditions. French and Caplan (1970) in their NASA study found that individuals who reported greater opportunities for participation in the process of decision making reported significantly higher levels of job satisfaction, lower feelings of threat, and increased self-esteem, while Margolis *et al.* (1974) in their study of a representative sample of over 1400 workers found that 'lack of participation at work was the most constant and significant predictor or indicator of strain and job-related stress. They found that non-participation was significantly related to a number of health risk factors, such as overall poor physical health, escapist drinking, depressed mood, feelings of low self-esteem, low life and job satisfaction, a low motivation to work, intentions to change job, and absenteeism from work. Kasl (1973) also found that low job satisfaction was related to a lack of participation in decision making, inability to provide feedback to supervisors, and lack of positive recognition for good performance. Neff (1968) highlights the importance of participation and involvement for physical and emotional well-being and suggests that the key question is one of locus of control: 'mental health at work is to a large extent a function of the degree to which output is under the control of the individual worker.'

To summarize, the research seems to indicate that increased levels of worker participation leads to lower staff turnover and more efficiency; where this is low or absent, lower job satisfaction and higher levels of mental and physical ill health are likely to be present.

6 EXTRA-ORGANIZATIONAL FACTORS

A major criticism (and weakness) that has been levelled at research in the field of occupational stress is that it is often extremely 'area-specific', i.e. the examination is often limited to a single aspect of the phenomenon which is then studied in artificial isolation (Wright, 1975). As Cooper (1978) comments: 'despite repeated calls to researchers to acknowledge that the individual "functions as a totality", the practical problems of encompassing the "whole person" in one research plan usually leave those who try with either incomprehensible complex results or platitudinous generalisations. Most studies, then, have only one life area as the focus of interest.'

Yet the effects, and sources, of job-related stress cannot be understood simply in the context of the workplace. The individual is central and must be seen as operating within and across a number of 'systems', the workplace being only one. Cooper and Marshall (1978a) stress this dynamic relationship and highlight the need to take account of the interaction that takes place between systems: 'when investigating the disruption of home and social life as a direct outcome of occupational stress, one has to be aware that there is a feedback loop with stresses at work affecting social life, and vice versa.'

Work/home interface

The individual is likely to be faced with two sources of stress with respect to his family and work. The first is quantitative, and involves resolving conflicting demands of time and commitment. To some extent this problem is inherent at all levels, but two groups can be seen as being particularly vulnerable. Beattie *et al.* (1974) highlight the difficult situation faced by the young executive who, in order to advance his career, must devote extra time and energy to his job to the detriment of his young family. The female worker will face a similar dilemma. More and more women are working full-time, have their own career aspirations, and yet still have to meet domestic commitments. Evidence is growing that conflicting demands from home and work can generate considerable degrees of stress (Davidson and Cooper, 1983). Cooper (1982) argues that this is in part because of the slow moving change in men's attitudes towards female careers. He found 'more and more married women are either divorcing, limiting their family size, or coping with both worlds at the expense of their physical and psychological health.' Married female managers who have young children find themselves less able to relax at the end of the day than male managers do, and are much more susceptible to feelings of guilt, role conflict, work overload, tiredness and ill health (Larwood and Wood, 1977; Bhagat and Chassie, 1981).

The second area is qualitative and revolves around the degree of support provided by the partner. Pahl and Pahl (1971) found that the majority of wives in their middle-class sample saw their role in relation to their husbands job as primarily 'supportive and domestic'. Gowler and Legge (1975) have termed this bond 'the hidden contract', an implicit agreement in which the wife acts as a 'support team' to her working husband. Cooper and Hingley (1985) found a similar pattern in the wives of their sample of top U.K. executives.

Again the upwardly mobile junior executive appears to be particularly at risk. Beattie *et al.* (1974) found that he is likely to fight to maintain a distance between his wife and the organization, paradoxically at the very time in his career when he is most in need of support and understanding. Handy (1975) explores a number of possible 'marriage-role' combinations in his study of British executives. He found the most frequent combination, and most beneficial to the husband, was the 'thrusting male – caring female' pattern. Here the wife's role was highly segregated from the work environment and was focused upon 'separation', 'silence', and 'support'. In this situation, the husband is free to vigorously pursue his career while his wife provides a 'safe haven' to which he can return to relax and recuperate from the demands of the work environment.

However, in the current climate of high unemployment and uncertain economic conditions the tensions the manager brings into the domestic situation are likely to affect the home environment in a way that may not hold to the 'sanctuary' expectation. As Cooper (1983) comments, 'But during a crisis of the sort we are currently experiencing, the problems increase in geometrical proportions as managers strive to cope with some of their basic economic and security needs . . . it may be very difficult, for example, for the wife to provide a kind of supportive domestic scene her husband requires at a time when she is beginning to feel insecure, when she is worried about the family's economic, educational and social future.'

Dual career stress

Another frequent 'marriage role' combination Handy terms 'involved — involved'. Here both husband and wife are pursuing their own careers and the emphasis is upon complete sharing. Although this pattern is potentially more rewarding to both partners, it can demand such a high level of energy and commitment that neither of the roles involved can be successfully fulfilled. Consequently, both husband and wife will bear the cost of failure.

Traditional role expectations, particularly those revolving around male/female responsibilities, may be challenged, leading to feelings of threat and anxiety. Davidson and Cooper (1983) comment that 'women managers report that problems often arise when they overtake their husbands in terms of salary and status. It becomes apparent that some men still view their role of "breadwinner" as being very important in relation to status and esteem.'

CONCLUSION

In conclusion, the 'six element model' of stress provides a useful structure in locating the sources of occupational stress, but it should be remembered that it is being used simply as a heuristic device. The interactive approach emphasises that sources of job stress cannot be fully understood by positing single causative agents such as 'long hours', 'an autocratic boss', or 'unpleasant working conditions'. The reality is a more complex equation; an interaction involving the perception, coping abilities, and personality traits of the individual concerned.

REFERENCES

Arthur R.J. and Gunderson, E.K. (1965) Promotion and mental illness in the Navy. *J. Occup. Med.*, **7**: 452–456.

Beattie, R.T., Darlington, T.G. and Cripps, D.M. (1974) The Management Threshold. *British Institute of Management Paper*, OPN 11.

Bhagat, R.S. and Chassie, M.B. (1981) Determinants of organisational commitment in working women; some implications for organisational integration. *J. Occup. Behav.*, **2** 17–30.

Brook A. (1973) Mental stress at work. *Practitioner*, **210**: 500–506.

Buck, V. (1972), *Working Under Pressure*. London: Staples Press.

Caplan, R.D. (1971) Organizational stress and individual strain: a social–psychological study of risk factors in coronary heart disease among administrators, engineers, and scientists. *Unpublished PhD Thesis*, University of Michigan.

Caplan, R.D., Cobb, S., French, J.R.P., Van Harrison, R. and Pinneau, S. (1975) Job demands and workers' health. US *Dept. Health Educ. Welfare Pub. (NIOSH)*, pp. 75–160. Washington, DC: US Government Printing Office.

Cobb, S. and Rose, R.H. (1973) Hypertension, peptic ulcer and diabetes in air traffic controllers. *J. Aust. Med. Assoc.*, **224**: 489–492.

Constandse, W.J. (1972) A neglected personnel problem. *Personnel J.*, **51**: 129–133.

Cooper, C.L. (1978) Work stress. In Warr, P.B. *Psychology at Work*. London: Penguin.

Cooper, C.L. (1982) *Executive Families Under Stress*, New Jersey: Prentice Hall.

Cooper, C.L. (1983) Identifying stressors at work: recent research developments. *J. Psychosom. Res.*, **27**: 369–376.

Cooper, C.L. and Davidson, M.J. (1982) *High Pressure: Working Lives of Women Managers*. London: Fontana.

Cooper, C.L. and Hingley, P. (1985) *The Change Makers*. London: Harper and Row.

Cooper, C.L. and Marshall, J. (1976) Occupational sources of stress: a review of the literature relating to coronary heart disease and mental ill health. *J. Occup. Psychol.*, **49**: 11–28.

Cooper, C.L. and Marshall, J. (1978a), *Understanding Executive Stress*. Longon: Macmillan.

Cooper, C.L. and Marshall, J. (1978b) Sources of managerial and white collar stress. In Cooper, C.L. and Payne, R. (eds), *Stress at Work*. Chichester: Wiley.

Cooper, C.L. and Melhuish, A. (1980) Occupational stress and managers. *J. Occup. Med.*, **22**: 588–592.

Cooper, C.L. and Smith, M.J. (1986) *Job Stress and Blue Collar Work*. Chichester: Wiley.

Cooper, C.L., Davidson, M.J. and Robinson, P. (1982) Stress in the Police service. *J. Occup. Med.*, **16**: 654–661.

Cox, I. (1980) Repetitive work. In Cooper, C.L. and Payne, R. (eds), *Current Concerns in Occupational Stress*. New York: Wiley.

Crump, J.H., Cooper, C.L. and Smith, J.M. (1980) Investigating occupational stress: a methodological approach. *J. Occup. Behav.*, **1**: 191–202.

Davidson, M.J. and Cooper, C.L. (1983) *Stress and the Woman Manager*. Oxford: Martin Robertson.

Davidson, M.J. and Veno, A. (1980) Stress and the policeman. In Cooper, C.L. and Marshall, J. (eds), *White Collar and Professional Stress*. Chichester: Wiley.

Dreyfuss, F. and Czackes, J.W. (1959) Blood cholesterol and uric acid of healthy medical students under stress of examination. *Arch. Intern. Med.*, **103**: 708.

French, J.R.P. and Caplan, R.D. (1970) Psychosocial factors in CHD. *Ind. Med.*, **39**: 383–397.

French, J.R.P. and Caplan, R.D. (1973) Organizational stress and individual strain. In Marrow, A.J. (ed.), *The Failure of Success*, pp. 30–66. New York: AMACOM.

French, J.R.P., Tupper, C.J. and Mueller, E.I. (1965) Workload of University Professors. *Unpublished Research Report*. Ann Arbor, Mich: University of Michigan.

Friedman, M., Rosenman, R.H. and Carroll, V. (1958) Changes in serum cholesterol and blood clotting time in men subjected to cyclic variations of occupational stress, *Circulation*, **17**: 852–861.

Gowler, D. and Legge, K. (1975) Stress and external relationships—the 'hidden contract'. In Gowler, D. and Legge, K. (eds), *Managerial Stress*. Epping: Gower Press.

Greenburg, H.M. (1980) *Coping with Job Stress*. New Jersey: Prentice Hall.

Handy, C. (1975) Difficulties of combining family and career. *The Times*, Sept. 22, p.16.

Hingley, P. and Cooper, C.L. (1983) The loners at the top: the personality characteristics of key change agents. *New Soc.*, Oct.

Kahn, R.L., Wolfe, D.M., Quinn, R.P. and Rosenthal, R.A. (1964) *Organizational Stress*. New York: Wiley.

Kasl, S.V. (1973) Mental health and the work environment. *J. Occup. Med.*, **15**: 509–518.

Kasl, S.V. and Cobb, S. (1967) Effects of parental status incongruence and discrepancy in physical and mental health of adult offspring. *J. Pers. Soc. Psychol.* Monograph 7, 1–15.

Kasl, S.V. *et al.* (1975) The experience of losing a job: reported changes in health, symptoms and illness behaviour. *Psychosom. Med.* **37**: 106–122.

Kelly, M. and Cooper, C.L. (1981) Stress among blue collar workers. *Employee Rel.*, **3**: 6–9.

Kornhauser, A. (1965) *Mental Health of the Industrial Worker*. New York: Wiley.

Kritsikis, S.P., Heinemann, A.L. and Eitner, S. (1968) Die Angina Pectoris im Aspekt ihrer Korrelation mit biologischer Disposition, psychologischen und soziologischen Emflussfaktoren. *Dtsch Gesundheitswes*, **23**: 1878–1885.

Kroes, W.H. (1976) *Society's Victim—The Policeman*. New York: C. C. Thomas.

Larwood, L. and Wood, M.M. (1979) *Women in Management*, London: Lexington Books.

Levinson, H. (1973) Problems that worry our executives. In Marrow, A.J. (ed.), *The Failure of Success*. New York: AMACON.

Marcson, S. (1970) *Automation, Alienation and Anomie*. New York: Harper and Row.

Margolis, B.L., Kroes, W.H. and Quinn, R.P. (1974) Job stress: an unlisted occupational hazard. *J. Occup. Med.*, **16**: 654–661.

Margolis, B.L. and Kroes, W.H. (1974) Work and the health of man. In O'Toole, J. (ed.), *Work and the Quality of Life*. Cambridge, Mass: MIT Press.

Marshall, J. (1977) Job pressures and satisfactions at managerial levels. *PhD Thesis*. Manchester: UMIST.

McCrae, R.R., Costa, P.T. and Bosse, R. (1978) Anxiety, extraversion and smoking. *Br. J. Soc. Clin. Psychol.*, **17**: 269–273.

McMichael, A.J. (1978) Personality, behavioural and situational modifiers of work stressors. In Cooper, C.L. and Payne, R. (eds), *Stress at Work*. New York: Wiley.

McMurray, R.N. (1973) The executive neurosis. In Nolan, R.L. (ed.), *The Failure of Success*. New York: AMACON.

Mettlin, C. and Woelfel, J. (1974) Interpersonal influence and symptoms of stress. *J. Health Soc. Behav.*, **15**: 311–319.

Minzberg, H. (1973) *The Nature of Managerial Work*, New York: Harper and Row.

Morris, J. (1975) Managerial stress and 'the cross of relationships'. In Gowler, D. and Legge, K. (eds), *Managerial Stress*. Epping: Gower Press.

38

Neff, W.S. (1968) *Work and Human Behaviour*. New York: Atherton Press.

Otway, H.J. and Misenta, R. (1980) The determinants of operator preparedness for emergency situations in nuclear powerplants. *Paper to Workshop*. International Institute for Applied Systems Analysis, Laxenberg, Austria, Jan.

Pahl, J.M. and Pahl, R.E. (1971) *Managers and their Wives*. London: Allen Lane.

Russeck, H.I. and Zohman, B.L. (1958) Relative significance of hereditary diet, and occupational stress in CHD of young adults. *Am. J. Med. Sci.*, **235**: 266–275.

Selyé, H. (1976) *Stress in Health and Disease*. London: Butterworth.

Shekelle, R.B., Ostfeld, A.M. and Paul, O. (1969) Social status and incidence of CHD. *J. Chron. Dis.*, **22**: 381–394.

Shepard, J.M. (1971) *Automation and Alienation*. Cambridge, Mass.: MIT Press.

Shirom, A., Eden, D., Silberwasser, S. and Kellerman, J.J. (1973) Job stresses and risk factors in CHD among occupational categories in kibbutzim. *Soc. Sci. Med.*, **7**: 875–892.

Sleeper, R.D. (1975) Labour mobility over the life cycle. *Bri. J. Ind. Rel.*, **13**.

Wan, T. (1971) Status stress and morbidity: a sociological investigation of selected categories of work-limiting chronic conditions. *J. Chron. Dis.*, **24**: 453–468.

Wardwell, W.I. and Bahnson, C.B. (1973) Behavioural variables and myocardial infarcation in the Southeastern Connecticut Heart Study. *J. Chron. Dis.*, **26**: 447–461.

Wright, H.B. (1975) Health hazards for executives. *J. Gen. Manage.*, **2**.

CHAPTER 3
Sources of stress in nursing

INTRODUCTION

As we became familiar with the work of the hospital, we were struck by the number of patients whose physical condition alone did not warrant hospitalization. In some cases, it was clear that they had been hospitalized because they and their relatives could not tolerate the stress of their being ill at home. (Menzies, 1970)

The nurse's role is therefore implicitly and chiefly one of handling stress. She is a focus for the stress of the patient, relatives, and doctor as well as her own. (Marshall, 1980)

We have seen in the preceding chapter that over the last 25 years there has been a determined effort on the part of social scientists working in a wide variety of disciplines to identify the sources of occupational stress. Cooper and Marshall's (1976) 'six element model' provides a comprehensive summary of the major findings and a useful framework within which to review the evidence of stress in the nursing profession.

Whether or not these potential stressors actually result in stress to the individual depends upon the characteristics of that person. Personality attributes such as motivation, tolerance of ambiguity, flexibility and the ability to cope with change are likely to be of particular importance. Although, as we will see later, it is the interaction of job and individual characteristics (the person–environment fit) which is all important, Cooper and Marshall's model helps focus on those elements of the nursing task that are inherently stress producing.

FACTORS INTRINSIC TO THE JOB—THE NATURE OF THE WORK

Professional sources of stress

A 'person centred' profession

Nurses as members of a caring profession have as their prime focus a responsibility for 'people' rather than 'things'. We have seen that occupational stress is likely to be substantially higher amongst those occupations whose task is 'person focused'. French and Caplan (1970) showed that staff who are responsible for people 'have more interactions, meetings, deadlines, smoke more and have a high diastolic blood pressure and serum cholesterol than those in jobs who are responsible for things,' and Cobb and Rose (1973) have noted that those with a close personal responsibility for the lives of others are more often victims of a range of stress-related diseases such as peptic ulcers, myocardial infarctions, hypertension and diabetes.

Workers in the 'caring professions' are faced with a number of additional stressors which are inherent to the nature of their job. A major potential source of stress is likely to be concerned with the client group itself. The majority of the caring professions finds itself dealing with those sections in our society who are seen to have problems. These may be social, psychological, or physical, but the day-to-day interaction is likely to focus upon matters that are seen to be 'abnormal' or 'dysfunctional', either to the individual or to society. In nursing, 'Nurses are confronted with the threat and the reality of suffering and death as few lay people are. Their work involves carrying out tasks which, by ordinary standards, are distasteful, disgusting, and frightening.' (Menzies 1970).

As a newly appointed ward sister commented, 'For the greater part of my waking hours I am surrounded by pain and suffering, by grief and death. Of course it has a long term effect upon me, but I am only just beginning to realise it . . . Surrounded by all this it is so very easy to lose sight of any wider reality—the fact that I am dealing with the exceptions, the darker side of life—and that most people in the world are happy and healthy and are not hospitalised. But that is "out there", and I am here, a part of all this. I just hope I am strong enough to cope, not so much with the suddenness of emergencies, but with the ongoing and relentless day to day strain of dealing with people in pain.'

Hadley (1977) makes a similar point and quotes a nurse's account of the effect that patients can have on staff: 'There is a lot of sadness around a hospital . . . If you come in tired or depressed even the smallest thing will bother you—just as in any other kind of work. But a hospital is different because you are working around so many depressed people . . . (a patient's) depression makes us all feel like failures. Situations like that we take home at night . . . and fret and fret about them.'

Professional competence

The importance of the individual's occupation in terms of status, self-esteem and economic security was discussed in the previous chapter. The personal significance of career choice, particularly of those entering the 'caring professions', is an interesting phenomenon, though largely ignored by researchers. Are certain types of individuals attracted to the work of caring for others, what are their expectations, needs, and rewards? As Cherniss (1980) remarks, 'human service work is expected to be more than just a job . . . it is a calling . . . identity and self-esteem thus will be tied to the outcomes of one's work much more than would be the case in other occupations.'

Certainly as far as nursing is concerned most nurses would identify 'the need to help others' as being a powerful reason why they entered the profession. Cherniss (1980), in his study of staff burnout in a variety of human services throughout the United States, suggests that many people are drawn towards this area of work because of their need for a high sense of efficacy, i.e. a personal feeling of effectiveness. 'For all individuals, competence seems to be a primary need . . . (but) . . . there is reason to believe that the quest for competence and efficacy is especially crucial for those engaged in human service work . . . The typical staff member strives to achieve a sense of efficacy in his or her own work. If this goal is blocked, the person's self-esteem is threatened and the stress response is strong. Thus, any factor that thwarts a worker's efforts to perform effectively or to feel effective will be a major source of job stress, strain, and burnout . . . empirical research suggests that achieving a sense of efficacy is perhaps the strongest job-related goal human service providers bring to their work.'

Sarata (1972) identified patient progress as the major source of job satisfaction, and Cherniss and Egntaois (1978) found that the staff of a community mental health programme saw sense of accomplishment as the single most important contribution to their level of job satisfaction.

The problem of feedback

The responsibility of the nurse for the lives of others can represent a major factor contributing to the special importance of efficacy in job satisfaction. Yet one of the inherent difficulties of all the caring professions revolves around the problem of judging personal efficacy and individual levels of professional competence. Yet competence can only be assessed against the criteria of effectiveness and success—notoriously difficult concepts to determine and measure. How does the Sister or Charge Nurse on the geriatric ward really know when she has done a good job? How can the District Nurse or Health Visitor assess objectively how effective her intervention has been? Where can Nursing Officers feel confident that their performance is better than just good enough?

Patient care involves both a process and a product. The patient is treated with a particular objective in mind; for example, he may have entered hospital to undergo specific surgery. This aspect of the nursing task will demand a high level of technical knowledge and competence—activities which lend themselves more easily to an objective assessment of standards. However, patient care also involves a process, the interaction of one individual with another. As one of the respondents put it, 'the *caring side* of patient-care plans'. However, it is much more difficult to determine criteria in this area.

A further problem arises because the patient/nurse contact is rigidly bounded by limitations of time. Judging personal competence is made more difficult or, indeed, impossible, since any measures of 'real' success are often lost to the nurse as the patient returns home or is transferred to another ward or unit. As one Charge Nurse remarked, 'It is only my failures that I get to hear about, and they come back to haunt me!'

Attempts to objectively assess the effectiveness of the total professional task have proved extremely difficult and have often been limited to those areas which were more easily measured, e.g. technical skills. In the final analysis feelings of competence and self-worth are more likely to be determined by subjective impressions determined and shaped by feedback for the immediate situation: feedback from the nurse's own perception of the situation, feedback from patients and colleagues and, perhaps most important of all, feedback from immediate superiors.

Dealing with death and dying

The threat of losing a patient can be seen to run counter to the generally held perception that nursing is about maintaining life (Menzies, 1970; Nurse, 1975). However, part of the task of nursing inevitably involves dealing with death and dying patients. How effectively the nurse copes with the process of dying and how she finally comes to terms with the inevitable feelings of loss will determine the degree of personal stress she experiences.

Much of the literature on stress in the profession centres around the high levels of anxiety which arise from nurses' continual exposure to death and dying (see Steffen, 1980). The degree of stress experienced is likely to be particularly high when the death is sudden (Jacobson, 1978), when it involves a certain category of patient, particularly children (Schowalter, 1975), or a 'special' patient with whom the nurse was closely involved (Glaser and Strauss, 1966).

Obviously exposure to death and dying is more common within certain specialisms, but it is part of all nurses' experience at some time. Of all the hospital staff it is the nurse who has the most ongoing contact with the individual patient and so the potential for closer involvement (and resultant anxiety) is that much greater. A growing aged population, the increasing hospitalization of terminally ill patients and rapid technical improvements in treatment and methods of care, means that there are likely to be an increasing number of patients who die in hospitals. Carr (1981) estimates that more than two people in every three of the total population will die in institutions of one form or another. In addition, recent changes in nursing practice, and in particular the use of the nursing process, has tended to increase the nurse/patient involvement, and so makes the alleviation of this source of stress of even greater concern.

The dying patient Glaser and Strauss (1966) have provided a well-known and useful perspective which throws light upon the 'negotiations' which surround the terminally ill patient. Patient/staff interaction, they suggest, can take a number of forms which they refer to as 'the four awareness contexts':

(1) *closed*, in which the patient does not know that he is dying and the nursing staff attempt to keep this from him;
(2) *suspicion*, where the patient has an idea that he is dying and tries to confirm it but the nurse pretends otherwise;
(3) *mutual pretence*, in which both the patient and the nurse know that death is inevitable, although each pretend otherwise;
(4) *open*, where both patient and nurse face up to the fact that death is inevitable and act on this awareness.

Each one of these 'awareness contexts' will have a different effect upon the relationship between the nurse and patient depending upon the negotiations that are necessary to sustain it. Each option presents its own problems and stressors.

(1) The difficulties arising from the 'closed' context are in its maintainance. If the patient is to be encouraged in the hope of recovery, there must be no indications which would reveal his true condition and cause him to lose motivation. This will depend upon a widely accepted 'conspiracy of silence' amongst all staff, and this is often only accomplished with a considerable amount of anxiety and stress.

(2) Stress levels are likely to become much greater if the patient does become suspicious of his true condition and tries to gain information from various members of staff. In this case, the 'conspiracy of silence' is likely to be challenged by the patient, and the individual nurse may find herself under a considerable degree of pressure and uncertainty.

(3) Mutual pretence is a 'negotiation', which avoids a confrontation with the reality of death. But this may be difficult to maintain on both sides, particularly when dependents are involved, or if the patient is rapidly deteriorating or unwilling to face death alone.

(4) 'Open awareness' involves the sharing of the situation, although when the death will occur is still unknown. Although a more realistic approach, this shared awareness can bring its own problems. As the nurse and patient are no longer obliged to maintain ignorance or pretence about the prognosis, both have now to move on to deal with the reality of death and the stresses that this will cause.

It can be seen that the tactics and subterfuges that the nurse must employ to maintain these 'negotiations' are likely to increase the stress and strain attached to her work.

An indication of the 'context' most frequently employed in practice is provided by the work of Carwright *et al.* (1973). They found that no more than 15 per cent of terminally ill cancer patients are told of their prognosis either by their general practitioner or by a hospital doctor. On the other hand, almost 90 per cent of the immediate relatives of terminally ill patients are aware of the situation and most of them learn this from the general practitioner or hospital doctor. There are a number of obvious implications. The first is that the patient and those nearest to him, including the nurse, have different sets of information. This pattern of response also suggests that doctors are often unwilling to tell patients that they are dying. Finally, and perhaps most important for the nurse, it means that she finds herself in the middle of a 'conspiracy of silence', which she can never be sure will not be broken by the relatives. If it is, then she is likely to bear the repercussions and her relationship with the patient is likely to be seriously affected. Grout (1980) highlights the importance of this final relationship for the nurse: 'The (final) interaction between patient and nurse is largely determined by the behaviour of the patient. The patient who, aware that he is dying, acts with composure and dignity and cooperates with the nurse is appreciated. This desire to have a poignant situation made less so also may be one reason why patient and nurse sometimes maintain the pretence of recovery or why the patient may not even want to know that he is dying.'

There will also be stress arising from the process of dying, and in particular with the various stages leading to death. A number of writers have suggested that it is possible to identify a number of phases, or patterns of coping, in the responses of the dying patient (Falek and Britton, 1974; Kasterbaum and Weisman, 1972). One of the foremost experts on death and dying, Kubler-Rose (1969), suggests that five discrete stages preceding death can be identified:

(1) In the first stage the patient is likely to deny that this is happening to him.
(2) This is likely to be followed by feelings of anger directed generally outwards, but often towards the caring staff and relatives.
(3) Next comes a period of unreality, the 'if only' stage, in which the patient attempts to find impossible solutions to his condition and often attempts to make a bargain that 'if only I could be allowed to live'.
(4) This is usually followed by a period of depression in which the reality of the situation begins to reassert itself.
(5) The final stage of the process is one of acceptance preceding death itself.

Kubler-Ross suggests that these stages are not only experienced by those who are facing death. They have also been observed in many other stressful situations that involve loss or uncontrollable harm, such as bereavement, amputation and imprisonment. Of course not all patients will work through this process in an orderly sequence; some will get so far and then regress to an earlier stage or may remain 'fixed' at one point in the process. However, it does give some indication of the range of emotional states that the nurse will be expected to deal with when treating the dying patient and of the demands that will be placed upon her. It is hardly surprising then that this aspect of nursing care is seen by most nurses as being particularly stressful.

When and how a patient is expected to die will also affect the behaviour of the caring staff. In this context, Glaser and Strauss (1968) point to the anxieties caused by the uncertainty of whether a patient is 'terminal', and if so the exact prognosis as to manner and time of death. They speak of a 'trajectory of death', and how important it is for staff to have some knowledge of this trajectory so that they can prepare both the patient and themselves for the inevitable end. Marshall (1980) comments that 'an unexpected death is particularly "uncomfortable" for staff, and there is the added threat that they may subsequently be charged with incompetence. Staff build up expectations about the progress of a patient's illness and it can be upsetting to them if he/she does not die as expected, but "lingers".'

Reactions to death A review of the literature suggests that two main themes can be distinguished concerning the reactions of nurses to patient death and that these seem to represent the two ends of a continuum. At one extreme the reaction is seen to be a complete distancing from the event itself, reflecting at times a degree of callousness. At the other there is evidence of a considerable emotional reaction to the death of the patient, often coupled with feelings of guilt and personal responsibility.

Sudnow (1967), in his study of the 'social organization' of dying, suggests that patient death does not always affect the individual nurse, and that a whole range of organizational strategies have been established to protect and detach the individual from a potentially stressful experience. In his discussion, he details established procedures for 'counting deaths', issuing the necessary forms and 'morgue bundles', the removal of the body, etc., all of which depersonalize the event and make it part of a wider organizational routine.

On the other hand, a number of authors point to the traumatic effect that patient death has on many nurses. Marshall (1980) highlights Schowalter's (1975) study of paediatric nurses as providing a particularly revealing account of some of these effects. The study is also of interest because of the methodology used by the researcher. His data are based largely on an examination of the dreams of the nurses and his observations of their weekly staff meetings. He found that nurses often felt guilty that they had not done enough for a troublesome or complaining child and this was likely to lead to heightened feelings of conflict and guilt when the child died: 'When you don't like a kid who's dying and you know you're working with him, it's really hard to get up to go to work in the morning. It's like it's more than just two separate things, but as if they climb on each other to make one gigantic problem. The scariest part is, what if you want them to die? Or, does even wondering if you wish it mean that you really do? You know in your mind that your wishes don't have any power anyway, but in your heart you're not so sure, and it makes you feel like a rotten person.'

In a different setting Price and Bergen's (1977) study of ICU (intensive care unit) nurses found similar internal conflicts expressed by many of the nurses, who felt in some way responsible for the patient's death. During a series of group meetings held to explore some of these problems, the researchers pointed to a fundamental conflict in the groups' reactions to patient death.

Nurses identified as problematic feelings of helplessness at not being able to do more for their patients, yet at the same time they were also troubled by the feeling that perhaps they were trying to do too much and had 'prevented nature taking its course'. Holding, and attempting to come to terms with, these opposing feelings was seen as particularly stressful by the group. In fact, the researchers found that much of their hostility and frustration was directed towards the doctors on the unit who, they felt, were playing 'both God and not God at the same time', a reaction which can be seen as a projection of their own internal conflicts.

Personal mortality

'In mourning the death of others people often lament for themselves as well'. (Grout, 1980)

Kubler-Ross (1975) makes the point that in order to be able to help another person to cope with death means that the person must have come to terms with his/her own mortality. Death is not discussed openly in our society; indeed, it is still very much a taboo subject. It is hardly surprising then that the death of a patient can trigger-off deep underlying anxieties in the nurse about her own mortality. A number of writers (Menzies, 1960a; Weissman, 1972) suggest that nurses may actively collude with their patient's denial in order to protect their own psychological equilibrium. Likewise, Price and Bergen (1977) suggest that the problems that the ICU nurses had in dealing with the death of their patients were due in part to their own needs to deny their own death.

Marshall (1980), reviewing the literature on death and dying, comments critically that the main tone of the majority of writers is one of directive rather than enquiry (i.e. what should be rather than what is) and that the orientation of many writers is still that of ideal conditions for patient care. 'In reviewing the literature on the care of the dying, it becomes evident that . . . although persons around the dying may be afraid of death themselves, this should not influence the care the dying receive.' (Geizhals, 1975). She goes on to comment that 'in terms of methodology this is a particularly mechanistic area. Authors seem more concerned with the structure, development, and internal consistency of death anxiety scales than with achieving an in-depth dynamic understanding of relationships with death.'

In one of the few relevant pieces of research carried out in this country, Whitfield (1979) studied the experience of student nurses of death on the wards. She emphasizes four categories of emotional response to the dying:

(1) the nurse's emotional involvement with the patient,
(2) the sense of real achievement when a patient died peacefully,
(3) mixed feelings of relief and depression centred around particular patients,
(4) the nurse's fear of her own death.

Whitfield suggests that most of the stress and anxiety experienced was due to The students inability to deal with their own feelings. She recommends that there should be 'more teaching on the care of the dying, more discussion in the wards about the needs of the terminally ill, and more support for nurses who are upset about a patient's death.' In particular, she highlights the need for 'a skilled counsellor or specially trained nurse clinician' who would be able to provide a support service for those nurses who experience stress in the care of the dying. Certainly it seems ironic that other 'caring professions' provide much better preparation for their students. Most social work training will contain a specific module on dealing with death and dying, and additional support is likely to be available for workers who experience difficulties in dealing with terminally ill clients.

In conclusion, it is relevant to highlight the lack of work in this area. In spite of the fact that it raises serious professional problems, affecting both the nurse's self-image and the quality of nursing care, the literature is disappointing. There seems very little of substance originating in this country, and the American literature seems focused largely upon the inherent problems of methodology and measurement. Perhaps this is yet another indication of the unease which appears to surround this subject?

Working conditions

Hospitals can be hazardous places in which to work. Lunn (1973), in a comprehensive review of the dangers present in the working environment of the hospital, lists them in some detail. He also highlights the long-term psychological effects upon the individual of poor working conditions, and discusses the particular problems faced by the nursing staff. 'It is well to remember, however, that nurses form by far the largest individual group of employees in a hospital (see Table 3.1) . . . What is constantly evident is the prominence of anxiety and depression, especially among trainee staff. The importance of this occupational problem in hospitals must not be under-estimated . . . Those planning new hospitals should understand that utter loneliness and boredom in off-duty hours can be contributory factors, and far more attention needs to be paid to the quality of working life and to the social and recreational facilities provided for staff.'

Table 3.1. Percentage distribution of staff in a typical district hospital.

Nursing	33
Domestic	18
Maintenance and porters	12
Paramedical	12
Catering	10
Administrative and secretarial	10
Doctors	5

Source: Lunn (1973).

The quality of the immediate working environment can ease or exacerbate the degree of strain experienced by the nurse. However, attention to the effect of working environment upon performance, whilst advanced in many other occupational fields, seems sadly neglected by hospital planners. Often existing plant, built to the needs of the previous century, has undergone a succession of modifications, each in effect a compromise between what is needed and what is possible.

Lack of privacy

Because the task of nursing is often open and public, nurses feel that they are always being subject to the critical scrutiny of patients, visitors and colleagues. An area away from the immediate pressures and demands of the job has been shown to be particularly beneficial in enabling those who work under constant pressure to regain motivation and retain a balanced perspective of the task. So, the provision of 'time-out accommodation in the form of rest rooms, re-creational facilities and dining areas, is of special importance to the nurse. A recurring complaint in the literature is the lack of privacy for the nurse and Marshall (1980) comments, 'Not only can this be stressful in itself if she is always "in public", but it means there is nowhere to get away for a few moments to cope with any stress she feels. Yet these are often the very areas that receive the lowest priority in planning and upgrading, and the first to suffer as a result of financial cut-backs.

Noxious stimuli

In her day-to-day duties, the nurse will be subject to a range of noxious stimuli, some with more obvious consequences than others. One of the most powerful stimuli in the working environment comes from the visual images that the individual perceives. Yet in the modern hospital the lighting is likely to be artificial and monotonous, the colours bright and garish. As Baj (1980) points out, in an article on humanizing the health care environment, light and colour will have physical and psychological effects on both the nurse and her patient. She concludes, 'Nurse managers must not only deepen their awareness relative to the impact of the environment on patients and health providers but, more importantly, they need to take action and facilitate change.' Hay and Oken (1972) in an examination of the problems experienced by nurses working in ICUs found that the oppressive visual environment was particularly stressful over a period of time. This, coupled with the incessant routine nature of many of the activities, led to feelings of being trapped, of claustrophobia and dehumanization; 'eventually the nurse begins to feel like a hamster on a treadmill.'

Smells—although often an acquired immunity soon builds up—are still identified by nurses as potential stressors. Unfortunately, adequate air conditioning/air replacement systems are not always available. High temperatures are also often problematic, particularly in some specialized areas. Lunn (1973) quotes a survey of the operating theatres in one hospital where temperatures of up to 95°F were recorded in the summer months, and where the air change was only two and a half times per hour. 'The present recommended standard temperature for operating theatres is a temperature of 70–72°F, 50–55 per cent humidity, and an air change 20 times in one hour. Only new hospitals have any hope of achieving these standards, but expert heating and ventilation engineers must be consulted more frequently when standards in old hospitals fall so far below optimum values. All too often in the past, this aspect of the hospital design has received insufficient attention. Not only is the comfort of the surgeons and nursing staff at issue, but also the efficiency of performance, since in industrial workers this is known to fall when temperatures are in excess of 80°F (26.70°C).'

Noise, although only having a detrimental effect on hearing if it consistently exceeds 75 decibels, does, at much lower levels, interfere with communication, impairs performance on complicated tasks, disturbs sleep or concentration, and can be a major source of annoyance. Over an extended period of time research suggests that high noise levels are associated with elevated blood pressure and a falling off of efficiency and performance (Weinstein, 1974; Sharrod et al., 1977). It is surprising how noisy a hospital can be. Again nurses can build up a tolerance for a high noise level threshold, but there is likely to be a cost in terms of efficiency and stress. Jacobson and McGrath (1983) report a recent study which found 'the minimum noise level of a university hospital's intensive care and coronary care unit to exceed 60 decibels. This low level was obtained around 4.00 a.m. The maximum levels occurred between 1.00 a.m. and 7.00 p.m., and approached 90 decibels. This is the intensity of the sound of an automobile horn.' (!)

Dobson (1982) gives a graphic description of the scene in an ICU in which the effect of the working environment is vividly illustrated. 'The emotionally charged unit is quite small but there are all kinds of sophisticated electronic equipment strategically placed in the cubicles according to requirements. The atmosphere is alarming for one who has not ventured into this unreal world of the critically ill and the dying. Repetitive sounds assail the ears from various pieces of frightening machinery. The respirator is striving valiantly to sustain the life of an old man in the end cubicle whose relatives are waiting outside in a state of expectancy. A suction pump makes a hideous sound in its attempts to help another patient in a second cubicle, and electrodes from an electroencephalogram are being attached to the scalp of a motor cycle accident victim who was admitted earlier to the Unit. In the distance outside can be heard the wailing siren of an ambulance as it speeds its way through a built-up area congested with traffic, and almost immediately the swing doors of the intensive care unit swing open to admit another desperately ill person. Meanwhile, a doctor and a nurse are bending over another patient in the first cubicle and a bleeping monitor at the side of the bed stops; soon the nurse will record that another life has been lost. On the positive side a patient on a trolley is being transferred to a medical ward. She is one of the successes whose life has been saved by the skill and efficiency of the staff in the intensive care unit. Yet even she will probably have many more weeks of anguish to face before an acceptable level of recovery is reached.'

Shift work

The NHS (National Health Service) is not only an exceptional employer of female labour, but also of night and shift workers and Gadbois (1981) has estimated that at any one time around one-sixth of the total nurse population would be involved in night work. The crux of the shift work problem is that this pattern of work is a major deviation from the normal cycle of day-time activity, followed by evening 'unwinding' and culminating in night-time rest. Shift work demands a degree of physical and psychological adjustment that not all individuals can achieve. Kemp (1984) provides a comprehensive review of the shift work literature as it pertains to nursing in general hospitals. In particular she highlights three main themes, the problems faced by night workers and shift workers, the maintenance of a round-the-clock service, and the activities on the ward during the night shift.

Problems of shift workers. Nurses working shifts will experience the general physical and psychological problems faced by all shift workers (see Chapter 2). Folkard (1981) examining the relationship between different patterns of shift work and the individual circadian rhythms of nurses has indicated that the quality of 'day sleep' is inferior to that of 'night sleep', and that permanent night workers are likely to suffer from chronic sleep deprivation and that task ability and performance during the night shift require a much greater effort for vigilance to be maintained. In addition, they are likely to experience difficulties peculiar to the profession. Kemp (1984) suggests that many of these revolve around the fact that nursing is predominantly a female profession and that the nurse may have additional problems related to her role as homemaker.

In a study of female night workers in French hospitals, Gadbois (1981) found that the different social and domestic responsibilities of male and female workers made 'the problem of interaction between the physiological and psycho-social aspects of adaptation to nightwork . . . more acute for women than for men'. In this country Mercer and Mold (1976) in their study of qualified staff turnover make a similar observation. They highlight the particular difficulties experienced by women, for whom 'unsocial' hours posed more of an acute problem than it did for their male counterparts.

Twenty-four-hour care. In most hospital settings patient care must be provided around the clock. This necessitates some nursing personnel working non-standard hours. Although little empirical research has been carried out in this country on the health consequences of shift work in nursing, the Stanford Research Institute has carried out a major study of American nurses which highlights a number of important points (Tasto *et al.*, 1978). Comparing staff on fixed and rotating shifts they found that those nurses on rotating shifts fared the worst, closely followed by night shift workers. Overall these two groups tended to have 'more frequent and more serious physical complaints, more digestive problems, more accidents, more clinical visits, worst sleeping problems and menstral difficulties. "Shift rotators" also reported a greater use of alcohol, a higher frequency of problems with their sex lives, and less satisfaction in their personal lives than other shift workers. Rotating shift nurses were significantly more confused, depressed, and anxious than those nurses on non-rotating shifts. The investigators concluded that rotation was a scheduling system that imposes excessive physical and psychological costs to the workers.' The study also found that, unlike fixed shift workers, there was little or no tendency for those on rotating shifts to adapt over a period of time.

However, there are positive aspects of shift work, particularly for those nurses who can adapt to the change in life-style. Watson (1982) points to the challenge and novelty of the increased level of responsibility that shift work can provide. Hockey (1976) in her Scottish study of women in nursing found that up to 50 per cent of the qualified staff working at night were part time. Typically they were married with dependent children and worked on average two nights per week. Hockey stresses the value of this pool of labour of part-time nurses who might eventually return to full-time employment as their children grow older. As Kemp (1984) observes, 'For many women, night duty was the best option within their profession, allowing them to continue nursing while tapping family resources for the night-care of their children.

However, Folkard *et al.* (1978) found that nurses working a full-time night shift showed markedly better long-term adjustments in their circadian rhythms than colleagues only working part-time. This they suggested was probably due to a greater commitment to a nocturnal work pattern and day-time sleeping. Nurses employed as part-time night staff were more likely to have dependent children at home and so remained 'day orientated' in their activities and were likely to have shorter periods of sleep. A similar pattern was observed in Gadbois' (1981) study, which found that domestic activities took precedence over day-time sleep for women who had dependent children.

Ward activities at night. Kemp (1984) points to the lack of research on night staff, 'Approximately 45 per cent of the time a patient spends in hospital is in the care of the night staff, yet research into the role and activity of nurses concentrates on the day shifts.' Goddard's (1953) original findings, that activity levels during the night rise and fall in an unpredictable way, and that up to 40 per cent of night duty could be inactive, have been borne out by later work by Grant (1979). A study of three medical wards identified *irregularity of demand* as a typical feature of night nursing and a distinction between 'planned' and 'unplanned' activities was made. The first consisted of work within the nurses' direct control, and included general clinical care and 'settling down and rousing activities'. This type of activity tended to take place at the beginning and end of each shift. The second activity was not nurse initiated and was composed in the main of general supervisory duties. This was likely to span the middle portion of the shift.

The supervisory role of the night nurse is one which seems to be treated with some ambivalence by the profession. While recognizing the essential role that night staff play they are often seen, and see themselves, as 'second class' in the professional hierarchy. It appears to be common for night-shift workers to feel undervalued and 'set apart' from their professional colleagues. Kemp (1984) recounting her own involvement with the problem, cites how the lack of research and the absence of comment from the profession disturbed her, 'What is the contribution of the night nurse? Is it so unremarkable to be unworthy of comment?' Contrasting groups of day and night sisters from the same hospital she comments, 'All worked in the same geriatric nursing division and had common knowledge of many of the patients but it quickly became apparent that the nurses did not perceive themselves as a company of equals . . . I found the impotence of the night nurses disturbing . . . It has always been difficult to staff British hospitals with full-time qualified nurses at night, so that the night shift tends to be regarded as a "problem area", with the consequent mistrust of those who work at night. The distinctive character of the night shift in a general hospital ward seems to be a product of its low levels of activity during long periods of the night. The nurse's contribution to patient care in her supervisory capacity is generally invisible and unreported and seems therefore to be undervalued.'

From the evidence it would seem that nurses who are engaged in shift work must cope with an additional range of potential stressors. Not only are they subject to the well-documented physical and psychosocial ill effects of this pattern of work but also they are likely to lose professional status and the respect of their immediate colleagues.

ROLE WITHIN THE ORGANIZATION

We have seen in the previous chapter how occupational stress can arise because of the role the individual plays within the work situation. Analyses of the worker's role focus in particular upon the stress produced by the problems of role conflict and role ambiguity. Indeed, these concepts are so central that one of the leading researchers in the field has equated occupational stress with problems of role definition, entitling his major work 'Organizational stress—studies in role conflict and ambiguity' (Kahn and Rosenthal, 1964).

At the general level Kahn and his colleagues found that the strain resulting from role problems was likely to lead to 'an increase in job tensions, a greater degree of job stress and an overall loss of self-confidence'. Similar patterns have been found within nursing. Corwin (1961), in a study of role conflict within the American nursing profession, concluded that if these conflicts remained unresolved, then the result was likely to be 'frustration, dissatisfaction and a lowered sense of worth'. Other American research has suggested that role conflict is often a major problem to the individual and one that many nurses find particularly difficult to deal with. Indeed, Kramer (1974) suggests that role conflict, together with unreal expectations of self, are the major causes of wastage within the profession. In a survey of over 500 registered staff nurses, Rosse and Rosse (1981) found that levels of role conflict and ambiguity were significantly related to job stress, organizational commitment, job satisfaction, and intentions to leave the profession.

The debate on the role and the function of the nurse is an on-going one pursued with some vigour in the UK nursing press. This in itself can be seen both as an indicator of the importance of the issue, and a reflection of the lack of general consensus on what a nurse does or should do. If these debates take place within the profession, it is not surprising that the individual nurse will experience conflict and ambiguity in carrying out her work, particularly as she is the focus of a wide range of expectations from her immediate 'role set'.

Role conflict

Role conflict occurs as the nurse attempts to satisfy a number of incompatible demands arising from other people's expectations of her role. One writer describes it as 'the experience of being pulled in several directions by people with different expectations of how you should behave as a nurse. These differences may concern what your priorities of patient care should be, how you dress, or how you should teach psychiatric nursing. Management may expect you to make their paperwork a priority, while your staff want you to help them with their busy clinical work. You may feel your priority is emotional patient care and yet have a number of patients to care for physically. In the first example the role conflict is triggered by direct external demands, in the latter the role conflict is internal.' (Lackman, 1983).

Benne and Bennis (1959), reviewing the role of the nurse, provide a useful and comprehensive model which locates the sources of stress within nursing. They suggest that four principle 'sets of expectations' can be identified in the nurse's role; three of these arise from external sources and the fourth is internal to the individual. In their view stress can arise from:

(1) official/institutional expectations,
(2) professional/peer expectations, i.e. from colleagues, peers and subordinates,
(3) communal/public expectations, i.e. from the nurse's reference group outside of the immediate work situation, and society at large, and
(4) personal/self-expectations, i.e. the individual's expectations of how she should perform within a particular role.

Benne and Bennis suggest that, when the expectations from these four sources are consistent and balanced, then the role is clearly defined, it is likely to be accepted by all involved and is unlikely to change. Lingren (1969), following this model, found that when two or more sets of expectations are incongruent, then 'role conflict and anxiety are likely to result'.

Sources of conflict in the nurse's role

(2) Official / institutional expectations

All members of the nursing profession work within a formal organization, whose values and structure are likely to be different from those of the profession (see Etzioni, 1964; Corwin, 1961) suggests that much of the role conflict in nursing can be accounted for by the differences between the bureaucratic and professional value systems. From a professional point of view nurses hold the value of individualized patient care as central to their role, yet the organizational structures demand a certain type of organized daily routine which in its extreme can take on a dehumanizing aspect. Activity often tends to become equated with effectiveness, and in their day-to-day work many nurses feel that they are likely to be criticized by superiors and peers if they are not continuously task orientated. Engagement in 'non-productive behaviour', such as chatting to patients or discussing patient care with colleagues, is often seen as wasting time (Kelly, 1982).

(2) Professional / peer expectations

The nursing task is essentially part of a group or team activity which involves members from a wide range of medical, paramedical and supportive professions. Within such a dynamic situation the nurse will find herself involved in an interdependent relationship with a bewildering variety of specialisms. During a normal working day she is likely to be in direct contact with physicians and doctors, other specialist nurses, a range of paramedical services such as occupational therapists, radiographers, physiotherapists, etc. She will also draw upon the supportive services of technicians, porters and auxillary staff. In addition she is likely to find herself in contact with social workers, trainee nurses, and medical students. Each of these relationships will involve a set of expectations concerning her role, how she should act, her professional responsibility and her position within the organizational hierarchy. Most of these expectations are likely to be accurate and realistic but, inevitably, others will be unreal or confused.

Everly and Falcione (1976), in a study of staff working in psychiatric units, found that relationships with co-workers and supervisors was one of the most important factors in determining the level of job satisfaction among the nursing staff, and that the quality of this relationship was determined in part by the absence of role conflict. In a study of 'head nurses' drawn from a variety of specialisms, Leatt and Schneck (1980) found that relationships with physicians was seen by all respondents as a major source of stress. The problem was particularly related to the differences in expectations that the two groups had of each other, and the resultant difficulties in relationships and communication which occurred when these differences remained unresolved.

Gray-Toft and Anderson (1981), in their study of nursing stress, found that of the seven factors identified, three related directly to expectations of the members of the nurses role set. They pointed to difficulties of role definition arising from (1) the immediate work group, (2) the physicians and doctors, and (3) other nurses, particularly supervisors. They concluded that, 'Role theory states that when the behaviour expected of the individual is inconsistent and there is ambiguity and conflict the individual will experience stress, become dissatisfied, and perform less effectively . . . (we found in our study that) . . . in the hospital, work overload results in part from multiple demands imposed upon the nursing personnel by the medical and administrative staffs . . . these dual lines of authority result in inter-role conflict and ambiguity in nurses.' (see also Claus and Bailey, 1980; Nichols *et al.*, 1981).

(3) Communal / public expectations

For any individual the work role is only one aspect of her total life activity. In addition, each person has a range of additional roles which will reflect her social and domestic commitments. So the nurse may also have a role of wife, sister, a member of a social or political group, etc. At times, the demands of work and non-work roles will come into direct conflict and the individual is faced with incompatible decisions regarding personal priorities. In the female-dominated profession of nursing, one of the most obvious problematic areas is likely to be that of balancing the demands of home and work. This home/work conflict causes a great deal of anxiety to many nurses and is explored in detail later in this chapter.

Another demand outside of the immediate work setting arises from the expectations of society itself. While the nurse may be struggling with the conception of her role within the hospital setting Kratz (1976) suggests that society and the general public are quite clear about their expectations, though how realistic these expectations are is another matter! As Shearer (1983) commented in the UK press, 'There should still, it seems, be something of an angel about a nurse. A job which draws its traditions from the middle classes ministering to the grateful poor, its hierarchy and ferociously differentiated uniforms from the armed services, its sense of self-sacrificing vocation from the church, and which is staffed mostly by women, doesn't fit easily with the notion that those who do it are prey to the usual human range of tragedies, depression and muddles, let alone the particular stresses of their work.'

In an interesting UK study, Murray (1983) explored the relationship between levels of role conflict and intentions to leave the profession. The research was based on a national sample of 246 nurses made up of a cross-section of all nursing grades, from first-year student to ward sister level. It was found that attempting to live up to unrealistic expectations could play a large part in engendering high levels of stress and anxiety: 'Certain characteristics of nursing itself may actually push nurses into leaving. While financial difficulties, shift work and the stress of patient care are probably the most important of these characteristics, other social psychological factors cannot be ignored. One such factor is the extent to which the nurse's own self-image conflicts with the public's role expectations for a nurse.'

The study focused upon the 'credibility gap' that existed between the nurse's self-perception of her role and what she believed to be the public's expectations. The latter were seen to be concerned with the traditional elements of the role, emphasizing in particular the 'expressive, caring' relationship of the nurse with the patient and, as such, were often at odds with the nurse's own role perception. It seems that nurses who feel that they are not living up to the public expectations of their profession are more likely to experience role conflict. Murray found that, the wider the 'credibility gap', the greater the likelihood of the nurse intending to leaving the profession.

These unrealistic demands on the profession can lead to anxiety and conflict as the nurse attempts and fails to live up to her stereotype. Even at the nurse/patient level there can be fundamental differences in the perception of the nurse's role. Kratz (1976) suggests that above all patients 'want the nurse to give loving care'. Yet there is a great deal of evidence which suggests that for their part nurses want to maintain a considerable distance between themselves and their patients (see Chapman, 1977; Murray, 1983).

(4) Personal / self-expectations

There is growing evidence that many of these unrealistic expectations are internalized by the profession itself, largely by an acceptance of society's stereotyping, but also through the process of professional socialization. A senior officer of the nurses' national UK counselling service has commented with feeling on the idealistic view of members of the profession. 'Nurses tend to see each other as a cross between Caesar's wife and the Virgin Mary—totally unblemished and beyond reproach! As soon as a nurse becomes ill or even has an accident, she ceases to be one of *Us* and becomes one of *Them*. She is immediately thrown out of the tribe. It seems we find it difficult if not impossible to relate to a fellow nurse as a colleague/patient.' (Crawley, 1984) in a similar vein, Hingley (1984) has remarked on the almost punitive responses aimed at those who do not live up to (often unreal) expectations of the profession. Shearer (1983), when visiting a nurse in prison, highlighted 'the frisson of dismay' this caused, and the ambivalent reactions of other professionals. It seems that 'Nurses do not commit crimes, any more than they fall prey to mental or physical sickness. Or if they do they can't expect much support from colleagues who, after coping with the pain of others all day, seem to have little energy left to cope with their own.'

Expectations from the profession

Even professional expectations may be contradictory and can often lead to feelings of anxiety and conflict as the nurse attempts to resolve an ambivalent situation. An example is the role conflict that occurs as the nurse attempts to meet the demands on her to operate effectively at both an expressive and a functional level. As Roch (1980) has pointed out, the individual nurse often finds herself in a 'no win situation'. On the one hand, she is expected to be able to relate at a personal level to her patients, a role demanding involvement and closeness. At the same time, and often with the same patient, there is an expectation of impartiality and 'professionalism', suggesting a degree of impersonality and distance. The nurse is expected to show equality to all, and yet at the same time be empathetic to individual patient's needs; a situation which can lead to a considerable degree of confusion, frustration and anxiety.

The process of professional training and socialization can also add to these unrealistic expectations. The whole process of professional socialization involves the nurse becoming indoctrinated into the values, assumptions and expectations of the profession. Professional socialization in many occupations, involves unrealistic and irrational expectations of its members, and certainly nursing is no exception. In a review of this socialization process Norris (1973) identifies three professional myths which are often accepted uncritically by the individual nurse: 'delusions that trap nurses and lead them into dead-end alleyways away from growth, relevance, and impact upon health care.' They are,

(1) that nurses significantly influence patients' lives,
(2) that increased knowledge will prevent disease and suffering,
(3) that nurses can really care and be concerned about all their patients.

The professional myth that nurses can fundamentally influence patients' lives is refuted by Norris, who points out that patients do not expect or receive real assistance in coping with their illness, establishing new health goals or in changing their life-style. She believes that it is completely unrealistic and irrational for the profession to think that any real change is likely to occur during a limited period of hospitalization. The only function of this myth, it seems, is to bolster the self-importance of the profession. However, it is likely to lead to frustration for a nurse who takes the myth seriously and who assesses her own professional worth in terms of the degree of behavioural change within her patients.

The second delusion fostered by the profession, concerning the prevention of disease through increased knowledge, reflects the profession's naive belief in the simplicity of change. 'Nurses act as if people will actually use health knowledge in determining their style of living and in the prevention of illness. Yet all the evidence concerning attempts to change habits of smoking, diet or general life-style suggest that increased knowledge does not automatically lead to the desired change.' (Norris, 1973). Again it is the individual nurse who is likely to suffer. A lack of response in her patients to use the newly imparted knowledge can lead to a sense of impotence and frustration, and a belief that she has failed in her professional task.

The final myth concerning the 'natural caring capacity' of the nurse is also challenged by Norris. She points out that these high ideals have an obvious value in terms of enhancing the status of the profession as a whole, but questions the reality of expecting the nurse to show empathy and concern for all her charges during what is often a comparatively short period of care. Yet the expectation and the delusion that this can happen is rarely questioned, because to do so would strike at the very heart of the professional value system. Again the cost of not living up to this myth will be felt at the individual level, and the nurse who fails to establish a special bond with each of her patients is in danger of seeing that as a reflection of her own inadequacies and as 'letting down the profession'.

As Gunderson *et al.* (1977) point out, 'Although myths serve a very useful function in promoting cohesiveness in a profession, they can translate into personal expectations that cause unnecessary frustration. The "super nurse" myth states that a nurse should be able to be all things to all people . . . When the nurse recognises that a multitude of needs are unmet, she tells herself that she is not a good nurse because she is unable to achieve her valued nursing goals.'

Role ambiguity

Role ambiguity is similar in many ways to role conflict in that the nurse experiences stress and anxiety because of conflict. But, in this case, the conflict is internal and results from feelings of uncertainty caused by unclear responsibilities. It is the uncertainty that arises because the nurse has insufficient information regarding the role itself. Inadequate or confused information about what work the nurse should cover, the limits of the role, and other people's expectations of how the nurse's role fits in with theirs produce role ambiguity. This is likely to express itself in concerns regarding the scope and responsibility of the professional task, the extent of professional power and authority and, in particular, the location of professional boundaries.

Often the newly appointed ward sister suffers from role ambiguity because no guidelines have been given to her for her new post: 'As I had worked in the unit for a number of years it was assumed that I knew "from experience" what would be needed. So I found myself in a double bind. I had been promoted because of my experience and expertise and I was faced on the first day with the risky situation of beginning my new job by admitting I did not know exactly what to do. I had to decide whether to expose my shortcomings and to admit to my uncertainties, or to put a bold face on it and bluff it out.

Unfortunately, and I suspect like many others, I chose the latter course of action. By doing so I lost the one natural opportunity to clarify several crucial areas which have since created a considerable degree of conflict. Once this opportunity had passed it could never be regained as it would have meant admitting that I had been operating since that time in some degree of confusion and lack of understanding. Hardly a professional attitude!' (Ward Sister)

Professional power and authority

This lack of role clarity is likely to become particularly problematic when the nurse interacts with other health care professionals and problems of demarcation and authority occur. A number of studies focus upon these problems of blurred boundaries (see Laube, 1973; Price and Bergen, 1977) and the demarcation of the limits of professional power and authority. Gunning (1983) suggests that nursing as a whole suffers from feelings of powerlessness because the scope and range of the nurse's professional authority is poorly defined and, indeed, often changes.

This ambiguity is particularly well illustrated in their relationships with doctors and physicians. In spite of the fact that nurses have greater contact with patients and are often in the best position to identify needs and recognize changes in an individual's condition, only the doctor is seen as having the formal authority to make independent decisions about patients (Aiken, 1981). This situation is often resolved by what Stein (1968) has described as the 'physician–nurse game'. 'The object of the game is as follows: The nurse is to be bold, have initiative and be responsible for making significant recommendations, while at the same time she must appear passive. This must be done in such a manner so as to make her recommendations appear to be initiated by the physician.'

Although this may allieviate the problem of conflicting professional boundaries, it does so in a devious way. The original problem still remains and the nurse's professional contribution to patient care is not only denied, but is credited to another professional. Yet another example of the ambiguity that surrounds the nurse's role and how professional authority can change, depending upon the circumstances, is provided by Gunning (1983) who points to the 'temporal dimension': 'To further complicate their function (vis-à-vis the medical staff), the nurse's authority is often related to time of day. During normal working hours, the physician assumes authority and makes all the decisions. During the night, authority for decision making is delegated to the nurse, but when daylight arrives, the authority again reverts to the physician.'

The effect of ambiguity and confusion surrounding professional authority can not only have a negative effect upon the individual's self-image but can lead to poor patient care. Dobson (1982) quotes an interesting experiment carried out by Hoffling and his colleagues (1966), which brings home forceably the potential cost of such confusion.

PROFESSIONAL AUTHORITY

Nurses from twenty-two wards of a private and a public hospital were selected to take part in the experiment. While she was engaged in her normal duties on the ward, a nurse received a telephone call from a 'doctor' whose name was known to her but whom she had never met. The 'doctor' announced that his name was Smith from the department of psychiatry. He explained that he had to see one of his patients, Mr Jones, that morning and again later in the evening. The 'doctor' wanted his patient to have been given some Astroten by the time he arrived on the ward to see him. The nurse was instructed to check the medicine cabinet to ascertain that there was some Astroten available.

When she looked in the cabinet, the nurse found a box labelled:

ASTROTEN
5 mg capsules
Usual dose: 5 mg
Maximum daily dose: 10 mg

The nurse informed the 'doctor' that the drug was available and he instructed her to give his patient a 20 mg dose of Astroten, promising that he would join the nurse in the ward and provide her with a signed authorization, by which time the drug would be taking effect on the patient. The nurse was left with three possible courses of action: (a) to administer the dose (which was actually a placebo), (b) to refuse to obey the order, or (c) to inform another member of staff. At this point in the experiment, when the nurse had made her decision, a genuine member of the medical staff who had unobtrusively witnessed the proceedings introduced himself and terminated the experiment.

The instruction which the 'doctor' had given was in contravention of several hospital rules:

(1) the prescribed dose was far in excess of the usual dose;
(2) doctors were forbidden to give instructions about a patient's treatment over the telephone;
(3) the drug was taken from a medicine cabinet and was not listed on the ward stock list;
(4) the person giving the instruction was unknown to the nurse;
(5) the nurse did not insist that the instruction was written and signed in advance of the medication being administered.

The results of this experiment indicated that 21 of the 22 nurses had been prepared to give medication in these circumstances. This is not only surprising but horrifying when one considers the potentially serious consequences for a patient. From the information given by the nurses during a post-experimental

Dobson (1984) *Stress: the Hidden Adversary*, pp. 301–302. We would like to thank the author and publishers (MTP Press, Lancaster) for permission to use this material.

interview, it appears that similar orders had actually been given by doctors in the past in real-life situations and they had become extremely angry with the nurses if their instructions were not carried out.

Situations such as the ones described above, where there is vagueness and confusion as concerning both the extent and content of the nurse's role, can create a great deal of distress to the individual nurse and can lead to disillusionment, self-doubt, and 'burnout' (Maslach, 1982).

Ambiguity and change

Of particular interest in the present climate of change within the NHS, is Kahn's and Rosenthal's (1964) observation that three conditions are likely to lead to increased role ambiguity among workers. These are:

(1) the degree of organizational complexity, i.e. the greater the complexity the greater the problem;
(2) the current managerial philosophy, in particular as it relates to the degree of staff involvement, i.e. the higher the level of staff involvement the less likelihood of role confusion;
(3) the presence of rapid organizational change, i.e. the more rapid and fundamental the change, the greater the potential for ambiguities to arise.

It would seem that all three of these elements are to be found within the NHS particularly during the current climate of rapid reorganization and change. Lysaught (1970), reviewing the American experience, points to a number of trends which will seem very familiar to nurses in this country. It was found that, as more hospital units were linked into one district, so the overall organization tended to become more complex; changes in management structures had a 'knock down' effect and led to a period of confusion and ambiguity; on-going advances in techniques of patient care continued at a rapid pace and so led to changes in the nurse's role. All of this led to a considerable degree of confusion and conflict. In the present situation in this country a similar pattern seems to be emerging. As Ogier (1984) comments, 'In the present system there is no one clearly defined line of professional authority within the hospital. Rather, in the ward, the nurse has the sister and nursing officers to be accountable to, the doctor prescribes the treatment for the patient, and the hospital administrator influences certain procedural and legal technicalities. With this formidable outlook how does the nurse . . . establish what her role is on the ward?'

Effect of reducing role conflict and ambiguity

Whatever the disagreements there are on the major sources of the problem most researchers suggest that a reduction of role conflict and ambiguity can have a marked positive effect upon nursing practice and a number of writers have proposed various strategies to alleviate the problem (see Lackman, 1983; Sarbin and Allen, 1968). Davis (1969) noted that increased clarity of role could lead directly to greater efficiency and an increase in the quality of patient care. Similarly, Revans (1976) has shown that when the roles inculcated during professional training are congruent and match those found in later clinical practice, then not only is staff morale likely to be higher but the period of patient hospitalization is likely to be shorter.

Kelly (1982) concludes that the solution lies with the profession itself, and that a greater clarification of roles and more open communication and discussion of potential problem areas would reduce the problem: 'By rating the roles in order of priority, a nurse can determine how much time and energy should be allocated to each role. If extra time is required for a role to be played more effectively, communication with the relevant significant others should help to improve the situation . . . Greater understanding of role relationships will lead to nurses being better equipped to cope with role conflict situations, and to adequately resolve the conflict personally.'

INTERPERSONAL RELATIONSHIPS AT WORK

We have already noted in Chapter 2 that the quality of working relationships has been found to be an important determinant of organizational and individual health. Cooper (1978) and others have noted that relationships with colleagues can have a decisive impact on performance and job satisfaction. At the interpersonal level nurses face problems arising from their immediate 'role set'. A review of the literature indicates that nurses identify two clearly differentiated sources of stress and anxiety:

(1) patient-related stressors,
(2) co-worker-related stressors.

The first revolves around problems of involvement and coping, with difficult patients, and dealing with the families of patients. The second concerns relationships with colleagues, subordinates, superiors, and specialists from other disciplines, especially physicians.

Bailey et al. (1980) in a comprehensive account of a large national study of American ICU nurses found that the problem of 'interpersonal conflict' was by far the most important source of identified stress in the work situation. They identify sources arising from the role set and report that, 'Responses of nearly 1800 ICU nurses relative to what they perceived to be stressful in their work environment indicated almost universal agreement among subjects. Although the nurses differed on variables such as age, experience, geographical location, and work setting, they were consistent in their agreement regarding the identification of work related stressors. Interpersonal conflict was identified, in the national survey, as the *major* source of stress . . . Conflicts included nurse–physician problems, nurse–nurse problems, and supervisor–nurse problems.'

The nurse–patient relationship

Traditionally, nursing has been seen to be based upon a close caring relationship between nurse and patient. It is the nurse who is responsible for the day-to-day care of the patient and as such the quality of this relationship is all important. It is a relationship based upon the care provided by the nurse, and on the physical and emotional trust assumed in the dependency of the patient–nurse interaction. It is the core element of care in the caring profession of nursing and as such is seen as central to the nursing task.

However, a review of the literature suggests that this trust and closeness cannot be assumed. There is growing evidence from several sources of the use of avoidance and distancing behaviour as an anxiety-avoidance technique by many nurses. In the late forties, Brown (1948) found that the assumed close and caring relationship was often absent and that the majority of nurses in his study were not closely involved with their patients at all. He advocated that nurse training should be revised and that psychological concepts should be incorporated alongside clinical skills in both nurse education and practice. Flaskerud et al. (1979), commenting upon this trend, cites Reiter and Kakosh (1954) as finding a similar lack of interpersonal awareness. Pointing to the need to incorporate psychosocial concepts into the practice of nursing they conclude, 'It can be inferred that leaders in nursing recognised a declining closeness between nurses and their patients, and felt an obligation to direct nurses back to a more intensive nurse–patient relationship.'

Closer to home the study carried out by Menzies (1960a) graphically illustrates the problem. Nursing, she suggests, develops its own 'defence mechanisms', one of the most important being the distancing and dehumanization of the patient. Such anxiety avoidance can simply take the form of a reduction of time spent with patients or, and potentially more serious, a reduction in the quality of the interaction. This lessening of the emotional bond between nurse and patient is seen by many writers as one of the classic indicators of the 'burnout syndrome' (see Cherniss 1980, Maslach 1982). More recently, Flaskerud et al. (1979) found that the situation does not seem to have changed: '. . . we realised that a common thread ran through all our observations. Nursing today seems to be characterised by a distancing and avoidance relationship with the patient . . . Apart from performing necessary tasks, interactions between nurses and patients are uninvolved and often dehumanizing. The nurse's relationship with the patient is likely to be characterised by avoidance of close and expressive concern, and by purposive distancing from involvement.'

Current nurse training still provides little in the way of interpersonal skill development. Rather it is based firmly on a medical model which emphasizes the clinical aspects of patient care. Evidence from the current study (see Chapter 4) suggests that, although nurses are secure in their clinical skills, they are less confident in the area of interpersonal relationships. Indeed some might argue it is not necessary. As one senior nurse remarked, 'No I do not want to get too close to my patients. I think it can lead to all sorts of problems. I am here to deal as effectively as I can with their illness, not to befriend them. I do not think that is part of the nurse's job. I am not trained to do it, and I do not want to do it. I think it would get in the way.'

This defensive reaction is particularly ironic as Chapman (1977) has found that 'patients frequently express a desire for more personal contact with the nurse whereas nurses obviously demonstrate a greater "task" than patient orientation.' Certainly it seems a long way from Valliot's ideal of the nurse who would use her 'self' as a central part of the nursing process, '. . . the therapeutic use of self is—or ought to be—part of (the nurse's) equipment. The therapeutic use of self is reference to a personal relationship between the nurse and her patient—one that is initiated by the nurse, controlled by her, and purposely directed towards improving the patients condition . . . However to be able to do this the individual nurse will need to be much more confident of her own abilities in this area, secure in her own self and have the support essential to play such a role as using one's self therapeutically will be extremely demanding of nurses' inner resources.' (Valliot, 1966)

The depersonalization of nurses It is interesting to observe that a similar 'depersonalization' can take place within the profession itself. Just as patients are often treated as categories rather than individuals, 'our manic-depressive', 'the young coronary', 'the stoma case in the side ward', etc., so too are nurses, who often become 'the night staff', 'second-years', 'my girls', etc. This point is borne out by Menzies (1960b) who observed that 'Duties, responsibilities and privileges are, on the whole, accorded to categories rather than individuals with their own capabilities and needs . . . all patients are the same, and all nurses are the same . . . The nursing service functions as though this were true although both patients and nurses know it is not. In the final analysis the nurse tends to be seen as an agglomeration of nursing skills at a certain level depending upon her phase of training, rather than a person doing a job according to her own capabilities and skills.'

Difficult patients

Most patients are cooperative, following the routine of the hospital and playing the 'good patient' role. However, a small minority are perceived by staff as troublesome and are seen as creating a considerable degree of stress for all concerned. It has been suggested that recent increases in public awareness and knowledge has led to a more demanding and questioning attitude on behalf of many patients and that this is likely to lead to more clashes with nursing and medical staff, particularly those who are jealous of their professional autonomy (Haugh and Sussman, 1969).

Most of the research on 'difficult' patients originates from the USA, though it is obvious that many of their findings can be applied to nursing in general. In this country Boorer (1970) gives a full account of a series of meetings held at the King's Fund in which nurses explored their attitudes to patients; and Stockwell (1972) has produced a research paper on the 'unpopular patient' for the Royal College of Nursing. A particularly useful and comprehensive review of the current literature has been provided by Kelly and May (1982).

Social and cultural differences

The nature of the nurse–patient interaction will be influenced because of fundamental differences in the 'construction of the social reality' of each group. Cultural and class differences will determine perception and understanding. What constitutes acceptable behaviour in the ward is often a matter of subjective opinion by both parties and can often lead to friction and conflict. Davitz et al. (1969) has pointed to the differences between nurse and patient in the understanding of pain and suffering. Schwap (1970) has highlighted the socio-demographic aspects at work in the nurse's perception of patient anxiety levels. Sudnow (1967) found that differences in in social class could lead to the negative stereotyping of patients by middle-class nurses (see also Altschul, 1972; Brand and Smith, 1974; Roth, 1972). Differences in age (Lamonica, 1979; Wells, 1980), sex (Altschul, 1972; Brand and Smith, 1974), and religion (Papper, 1970; Ujhely 1963) have been shown to influence the positive or negative evaluation of the patient by the nurse. Where patients are of a different racial grouping to the nursing or medical staff, there is evidence that this may encourage the formation of negative staff attitudes towards patients (Gillis and Biesheuvel, 1962; Ross, 1961; Roth, 1972; Stockwell, 1972.)

Clinical factors

A number of studies have suggested that certain illnesses or a cluster of symptoms are influential in how positively or negatively the nurse classifies and responds to the patient. Specific clinical conditions appear to be linked to negative attitudes in the nursing staff. These include incontinence (Ujhely, 1963), self-mutilation and attempted suicide (Simpson et al., 1979; Stockwell, 1972), and confused patients (Armitage, 1980; Rosenthal et al., 1980; Wells, 1980). Also eliciting negative reactions are a whole range of psychiatric conditions; it seems that those suffering from mental rather than physical conditions are likely to be seen as less attractive and so suffer from an increased 'social distancing' from the nursing staff (Katz, 1969; MacGregor, 1960; Stockwell, 1972; Wells, 1980). It is suggested by researchers that the terminally ill patient evokes particularly strong negative reactions from the caring staff

(Knight and Field, 1981; Papper, 1970; Simpson *et al.*, 1979; Strauss and Glover, 1977; Ujhely, 1963). There also appears to be a negative stereotyping of the alcoholic patient. Strong (1980), working with alcholics in Scotland, has noted that alcoholism tends to be categorized by staff more as a behavioural response than a real illness. The alcoholic patient is often considered to be responsible for his or her own condition rather than as a victim of a clinical illness. As such the alcoholic patient is likely to experience distancing and a lack of sympathy from the caring staff.

On the other hand, there are a number of clinical conditions which are seen by nurses in a more positive light. These are likely to be conditions which test specific nursing or clinical skills, e.g. specialized units such as ICUs, Accident and Emergency Units, etc. (see Jeffery, 1979; Ritvo, 1963; Stockwell, 1972). Kelly and May (1982) also comment that, 'It has also been noted that where patients make spectacular or dramatic recoveries, the staff rate them as positively good (Berkowitz and Berkowitz, 1960; Habenstein and Christ, 1963).

Patient attitudes

A whole range of patient attitudes have been identified as evoking positive or negative attitudes from hospital staff (see Kelly and May, 1982). In particular, the failure to conform and to play out the accepted patient role has been found by a number of researchers to result in staff perceiving those patients as 'difficult' or 'bad' (Basque and Merige, 1980; Brand and Smith, 1974; Jeffery, 1979; Rosenthal *et al.*, 1980). Gillis and Biesheuvel (1962) found that the stubborn patient was seen as problematic by many nurses, a finding supported by several other researchers (Jeffery, 1979; Sarosi, 1968). In this country Armitage (1980) has found a similar pattern. Patients who are seen as 'uncooperative', i.e. who refuse to accept all or part of the clinical regime, or refuse to accept the dependency that the sick role implies, are likely to be labelled as 'problem patients'. Indeed, the question of patient dependency has been extensively researched and the negative labelling resulting from the patient's refusal to accept this dependency has been noted in several studies (e.g. Basque and Merige, 1980; Brown, 1966; Highley and Norris, 1957; Lorber, 1975).

The central question of nurse control has been highlighted in a number of studies, which suggest that those patients who are seen as under the control of the nurse and who are least disruptive of the nurse's routine are evaluated more favourably (Stockwell, 1972; Spitzer and Sobel, 1962). Heyman and Shaw (1984) discuss the nurse's perception of the patient: 'Such findings suggest that nurses have a great need to control their relationships with patients unilaterally, and a fear of what might happen if such control broke down.' In their own research, they asked nurses to describe actual examples of *good* and *bad* relationships with patients, colleagues and friends. They found that 80 per cent of bad relationships with patients centred upon problems of non-compliance, compared with around 15 per cent in the non-patient group. They found that over half the poor relationships with non-patients were accounted for in terms of a two-way relationship which indicated a concern for the other's definition of the nurse as a person (e.g. disregarding her point of view, violating her autonomy, etc.). On the other hand, only 15 per cent of bad relationships with patients were described in this way. They conclude that, 'This finding of a relative lack of conscious concern with the patient's definition of her suggests again that nurses were viewing patients in terms of problems of control, rather than viewing them as persons whose definitions of the nurse mattered.'

In contrast, it has been shown that certain patient attitudes are positively evaluated by the nursing and medical staff, and tend to lead to favourable stereotyping. Kelly and May (1982) note that patients who are seen to be 'understanding', 'optimistic', and 'grateful' are those whom nurses see in a more positive light and whom they enjoy nursing (Ritvo, 1963; Stockwell, 1972; Spitzer and Sobel, 1962).

In conclusion, it can be seen that the perception and labelling of the patient as either 'good' or 'bad' revolves around issues of control and efficacy (the nurse's not the patient's!), and is determined largely in terms of the nurse's perception of her ideal role. Indeed, they are, in effect, the two sides of the same coin. The role of 'nurse' can only exist in terms of a relationship with a 'patient' role. Kelly and May (1982) in a sociological analysis of the nurse–patient interaction conclude, 'Roles, as we have argued, are not simply structured prescriptions for behaviour but exist and have meaning only in relation to other roles, real or imaginary, to which they are orientated (Turner, 1962). Thus the role of the caring nurse is only viable with reference to an appreciative patient. Nurses symbolically take the role of patient to make sense of their own role, and it is in so doing that the labelling of patients inevitably takes place. The good patient, is one who confirms the role of the nurse; the bad patient denies that legitimation.'

Relatives

Another potential area of stress in interpersonal relationships involves the relatives of patients. Relatives themselves are likely to be experiencing high levels of stress and anxiety when they visit the hopsital or unit. Unlike the patient they do not have such a clearly defined role or status within the hospital structure. They are likely to feel threatened and on uncertain ground in their relationships with the caring staff. A typical comment made by a relative to the researchers reflects this uncertainty and confusion: 'I feel I have to compete with other visitors, and of course the patients, to get the sister's attention. Even then I am not sure how much time she is willing or able to spend with me and I always get the feeling I am preventing her attending to the patients, but she is usually the only person available who can help me. Even when I get some time with her I am not sure what I can reasonably ask her or how much she is allowed to let me know. All this results in a lot of frustration and anxiety for me and I think the nursing staff also find relatives very threatening.'

As Marshall (1980) comments '. . . contacts with relatives are an additional source of pressure for the nurse. The nurse's responsibilities in these relationships are poorly defined, but many authors suggest that she has a key role to play in helping relatives to cope with their own stress and maintain a viable relationship with the patient . . . (yet) . . . It is even more difficult for the nurse to get to know relatives (than patients) and she will often be faced with imparting highly charged information to them with little idea of the effects it will have.'

Weeler and Miller (1977) suggest this closeness could enable the nurse to act as a 'link-pin' and to play a coordinating role in feeding back information on the relatives' relationship with the patient to other professionals involved in the patient's care. The same authors see this involvement with patients' relatives as an additional area of professional responsibility for the nurse. As such it adds a further complicating factor and an additional source of stress. Where previously there was only the nurse–patient interaction to consider, now there is the triad of nurse–patient–relative. Weeler and Miller (1977) highlight the negative repercussions if the timing or expectations of these three parties is out of phase, and suggest there is a need for both the care staff and the relatives to 'acknowledge their own feelings as reflective of, but separate from, the patients' needs'.

Doctors

Problems of interpersonal relationships between nurses and physicians can also be a source of stress and often seem to centre largely upon questions of professional power and status. 'The traditional role segregation between the responsible diagnosing and treating doctor and the caring nurse is not easily maintained even if both parties agree with all its underlying justice. As the nurse is in constant attendance, she may feel that she is more aware of the patient's condition than the doctor is, yet she has no official role as his advisor. The extent to which she tries to assume such a role, and the tactics she adopts, are delicate issues.' (Marshall, 1980)

Consequently, it is not surprising to find that many of the problems identified in the literature concern the demarcation of professional boundaries (Hadley, 1977). Steffen (1980) in an account of a major national study of ICU nurses highlights the difficult situation in which many nurses find themselves in their relationships with consultants: 'Some nurses spoke of the "double-edged sword", whereby they are blamed if they fail to inform the physician of pertinent facts, but when they do, it is often ignored or they are ridiculed for overstepping the boundaries of their role. The frustration of "being caught in the middle", relative to providing patients with adequate information about their diagnosis or prognosis, was another concern of ICU nurses. Other nurse–physician problems were also identified, such as the incongruity of orders when a number of physicians were attending the same patient or the unavailability of physicians, either because of apathy or poor coverage on the evening and night shifts.' Bilodeau (1973) also refers to the nursing staff feeling 'abandoned' by the doctor. Marshall (1980) echoes a similar theme: 'He is often not there when emergencies arise, according to many accounts he actively avoids more difficult or dying patients. The doctor may leave the nurse to deal with relatives. The latter are, any way, more likely to find her approachable and to persist in questioning with which they would not trouble the doctor. In addition, the doctor is not requred to tell the nurse his diagnosis and prognosis for the patient and she may find acting in ignorance difficult.'

CAREER: NURSING—A FEMALE PROFESSION

The status of nursing in all countries and at all times has depended, not entirely, but to a very large extent on the status of women. (Dock, 1920)

In Western society woman's traditional role has been that of wife, mother and home-maker. On the other hand, men are seen as the providers, bread-winners and decision-makers. The female stereotype often presents women as emotional and submissive, sensitive and non-intellectual, whilst men are seen as possessing the opposite traits, as being more powerful and rational, aggressive and intellectual. Women are stereotyped as dependent and controlled; men, on the other hand, are seen as independent and controlling. It has been suggested that recent changes in the role of women in Western society underlies many of the problems within the nursing profession (Jacobson and McGrath, 1983). Historically nursing has been identified as a female occupation, as a calling rather than a career, and particularly attractive to the more middle-class elements of society. Although the profession has recently attracted men in greater numbers the fact is that around 90 per cent of the workforce are female. Indeed, many writers point to the fact that the nursing task itself is a direct extension of the traditional female caring role. As Marshall (1980) comments, nursing literally means 'nurturing', and the nurturing role in our society is seen to be the responsibility of the female. Sanders (1980) holds the view that many nurses are experiencing stress symptoms mainly because they are women. 'Sexual discrimination and women's present complex role places extra stress on them. Besides a caring, giving and altruistic attitude towards clients, many (especially the middle-aged nurse) must also extend these same feelings to their husbands, children and perhaps aging parents and/or parents in law.' Sanders sees the main cause of burnout among health-care professionals to be 'working conditions combined with demanding home responsibilities . . . resulting in a distancing from patients, a lack of professional confidence, and in the more extreme cases complete physical or mental breakdown.' Cleland (1971) also sees sex discrimination as nursing's most pervasive problem and comments, 'There is no doubt in my mind that our most fundamental problem in nursing is that we are members of a woman's occupation in a male dominated culture.'

These male/female stereotypes are reflected within the health-care professions, both in relationships with other parallel disciplines and within the professional hierarchy. So the physician assumes the independent, intellectual, pro-active and controlling role of diagnosis and prescription; while the nurse's role is seen to be one of dependence, a reactive/passive role of nurturance and compassion.

Power

Gunning (1983) stresses that actual and perceived powerlessness is directly related to the female sex role. She argues that women have been socialized to see power as a male prerogative. These characteristics associated with the exercise of power, particularly independence and aggression, are generally viewed as unfeminine traits. 'Because women and nurses have generally acted as mediators, they have not learned to manage conflict constructively. This deficiency is a major obstacle to leadership.' McClure (1978) describes the profession as dogged by a 'psychological inertia that causes nurses to see themselves primarily as responders rather than initiators'. Jacobson and McGrath (1983), reviewing the American literature, points out that female employees are more likely than men to suffer from a lack of assertiveness and negotiating abilities, low self-confidence, and a marked inability to establish use of supportive networks in the job setting: 'These deficiencies dispose women to a kind of isolation and powerlessness in their work that men do not usually experience.'

Adkinson (1981), reviewing the research on women in school administration, comments in particular on a lack of ability to 'compete, cooperate, set goals and plan strategies to meet them, bend rules, and, if unsuccessful, to accept criticism and persist.' Grisson and Spengler (1976) propose that women have a basic lack of trust for each other because they have been socialized to compete for male partners and to view other women as a natural enemy! As one of our respondents commented, 'If you stand up for yourself in nursing you are likely to be "kneecapped" by your fellow professionals.'

Exacerbating this ambivalence to the exercise of power and conflict is a lack of group cohesiveness within the profession noted by many writers. It seems that nursing as a profession has not been able to establish common goals and plan the shared and initial action needed to accomplish them. Indeed, the history of nursing is a history of fragmentation, of specialist interest groups seemingly working in isolation and often in competition with each other. Only recently, with the formation of the English National Board, have these factions been forced by necessity to work more closely together. Whatever the causes, the nursing profession has seemed unable to act collectively and supportively and to assert the power that it should have as one of the largest bodies of employees in this country. As Gunning remarks, 'Nursing is a troubled profession . . . many stressful conditions for nurses cannot be remedied until the underlying issues are resolved by the profession as a whole.'

Career pathways

Traditionally women have not been expected to pursue their own career goals. Or, if they did, these were accommodated around their domestic responsibilities. Consequently, longer-term career commitment has not been expected in many female occupations, and the concept of the 'career woman' has met with misunderstanding and a considerable degree of resistance (Davidson and Cooper, 1983). Bhagat and Chassie (1981) found that satisfaction with career promotion and corresponding levels of salary was closely associated with increases in self-esteem and job commitment. However, as an occupational group, women are generally to be found clustered in the lower levels of the management hierarchy and are therefore more vulnerable to frustration and anxiety because of limited or blocked career prospects.

Structures for clear career pathways, advancement and training have not been provided for female employees in the same way they have for men. In nursing this is reflected in the almost total lack of support and guidance available to the nurse on career matters. Yet more and more nurses are attracted to the profession because of its career potential rather than as a 'calling', and this is generating pressures for change. As Jacobson and McGrath (1983) suggest, 'Young women increasingly plan to work most of their lives . . . and view that work as a career, rather than a mere job. The consequence of this change in aspirations is that women will no longer accept working conditions, or relationships with other professions that were tolerable when employment was temporary. This change in women underlies much of the current dissatisfaction among nurses'. A similar change is taking place in this country where Marshall (1980) notes an awakening militancy, and increased unionization, in a profession which has previously been content to remain politically inactive.

Under-representation of females in senior posts

Yet the opportunities for career advancement, even within a predominantly female profession, also reflect societal attitudes. The negative effects of female stereotyping upon career can be clearly seen within the nursing profession, where the relatively small proportion of males now account for an unrepresentative higher proportion of the more senior executive posts.

Choon and Skevington (1984) attribute this directly to the male/female socialization process at work in our society and, in particular, the stereotyping of the female nurse as a 'practitioner' rather than a 'manager'. They note that, 'In 1971, on average, there were seven women for every man in post. However, looking at the senior posts of chief and principal nursing officer and charge nurse, the proportion of women to men was only three to one. The proportion of women to men increases as the ranks are descended so that at the bottom of the hierarchy there were eleven women pupil nurses for each man in training. It is clear that men are over-represented at senior level and under-represented at junior level, when compared with the average number in this population . . . This indicates that there is a bias favouring the promotion of men in preference to women.'

Clinical/management career pathways

Finally, many nurses are promoted to managerial jobs on the basis of their technical nursing competence and not on administrative predispositions. Even when they are in the nurse manager role, they are often not adequately trained for the 'new role'. As a recent report indicates: 'Nurses have traditionally been promoted into administrative positions on the basis of their clinical capabilities. They have not been well prepared for the responsibility of managing a diverse working group nor for working with a team of professionals.' (King's Fund Project Paper, 1981)

ORGANIZATIONAL STRUCTURE AND CLIMATE

Another potential source of stress for the nurse arises from the organization itself—its climate and the structure of leadership. Wilson (1976) suggests that the key characteristics of health care organizations include comprehensiveness in time and space, an array of specialities, vulnerability to public scrutiny as an 'open' setting, groupings of highly autonomous departments, parallel administrative and technical/medical lines of authority, physician dominance, and an ambivalent status in the eyes of those it serves.

Differences in organizational setting

Within nursing most of the research in this area relates to the hospital setting. It is evident that hospitals cannot be seen as a homogeneous category. They are varied in structure, purpose, size and location. Similarly, within the hospital, wards and units will also differ and will provide a wide range of varied working environments. Miller (1976) explored the differences of three contrasting hospital types and found marked differences in organizational philosophy, structure, staff attitudes and morale, and in the types of patients. These differences he was able to relate to the specific 'stress profile' of each hospital. In a similar way Sudnow (1967) found significant differences between county and public hospitals.

Skevington (1984) has debated the usefulness of concepts such as organization climate, which may be too broad for use in predicting employee behaviour. She suggests that attention should focus on the individual's immediate job setting rather than the total organization. Within a single institution, Lawrence and Lorsch (1967) found that 'unit-specific' environments must be considered when accounting for individual behaviour. While Numerof and Abrams (1984) found that organizational factors were also differentially stressful for nurses as a function of their position in the hierarchy. On the other hand, Weeks (1978) in a review of the literature, suggests that, although there will be differences between institutions, these are likely to be a reflection of differences in emphasis and priorities rather than real variations in stress factors. The main stress factors, he holds, are likely to be shared by most hospitals. This view is borne out by Jacobson's (1978) comparative studies of ICUs. Her analysis indicated that there were no significant differences between the hospitals studied on the stress measures she used, and concluded that hospitals have more similarities than differences when it comes to potential stressors.

Control: autonomy versus authority

In the previous chapter the struggle for *control* emerged as a key concept in the discussion of autonomy versus authority and feelings of individual autonomy were linked to physical and mental well-being. Since its inception the National Health Service has struggled with the problems of trying to balance the demands of professional autonomy with the impositions of bureaucratic authority. As Jacobson and McGrath (1983) points out, the 'employment of professionals by bureaucratic organisations produces role conflict and reduces autonomy.' By comparison, doctors within the NHS achieved a high degree of professional autonomy from the very beginning, while the nursing profession continues to struggle for independence and self-regulation especially within the hospital setting.

The very characteristics of the hospital as a formal organization can in themselves be determinants of role conflict and stress. In particular, the classic professional/bureaucratic conflict will often lead to high levels of stress and anxiety. The professional's emphasis on autonomy, quality of individual service and the application of collegiate responsibility, clashes with bureaucratic requirements stressing supervision and control, routine and uniformity. The position of the nurse in this relationship is likely to be even more precarious as nursing is seen by many observers as lacking many of the attributes of the more established professions. As a 'semi-profession' it will not have the same degree of power and autonomy as its established counterparts, and so will be more vulnerable to bureaucratic demands (Etzioni, 1969). Bureaucratic structures are frequently seen as dysfunctional as they tend to separate the individual from the decision-making process. Workers in large formal organizations frequently complain that they have little influence on the policies under which they work. The system's employment practices, the way the nurse's performance is evaluated, current disciplinary and dismissal policies, leave and roster arrangements and other administrative procedures are frequent sources of frustration and tension. In these areas the organization can be seen to be a source of generalized and pervasive stress (Cooper, 1981).

The organization as a defence against stress

On the other hand a number of writers have pointed to the protective role that the organization can play. Marshall (1980) recognizes that the organization can be a particularly powerful element in the stress equation, and points to the potentially functional role it can play. 'There is, however, so much ambiguity surrounding the function of the highly hierarchic organization of nursing that this deserves a special qualifying role. This hierarchy is revealed as in part a reaction to stress—it reduces ambiguities about responsibility definitions—and as a source of support. Many factors have the potential to be sources of both stress and satisfaction, this is one of the most "ambiguous" elements in the profile of (stress).' Menzies (1970) also details how the organizational structure can protect the individual, though at some cost to autonomy and individual responsibility. Clinical methods, aimed at standardizing aspects of treatment and patient care, are set out in considerable written detail; procedures are checked and counter-checked; groups rather than individuals are made collectively responsible; and there is a marked degree of dependency upon superiors to approve actions and make decisions below their status. Marshall (1980) concludes, 'These defensive techniques help the individual avoid the experience of anxiety, guilt, doubt, and uncertainty . . . the organization of nursing, despite its apparent rigidities, appears to operate more towards protecting staff from, then causing, stress. Well defined hierarchies clarify the distribution of responsibility, for example. The lack of acknowledgement and discussion of nursing's more distasteful aspects suggests, however, that denial is the main coping strategy at organizational as well as individual levels.'

HOME/WORK CONFLICT

> Nurses working in the NHS who decide to have children are often forced to change jobs, give up work or are discriminated against in the promotion stakes according to a report published last week. (*Nursing Times*, 1985a)

Studies of mental health and the quality of life consistently find that most people believe that marriage and family life are more crucial than work to their overall well-being, and research is accumulating about which specific aspects are of most importance (Andrews and Withy, 1976; Bradburn, 1969; Campbell *et al.*, 1976). There is also growing evidence of the negative impact on the individual who is trying to meet all the demands arising from the roles of worker, spouse, and parent (Gove and Geerken, 1977). It is the nature of most professions that the boundary between work and non-work is often indistinct and blurred, and inevitably there will be some degree of 'overflow' in both directions. Work problems will find their way into the home, and domestic concerns are often taken into the work situation.

The 'caring' professions are female dominated. Particularly so in nursing, where approximately 85 per cent of the national labour force are women. In our survey, the majority were living with a partner and many had dependent children (see Chapter 4). Consequently, certain working conditions, such as the shift system and having to work unsocial hours, are likely to pose a particular problem to many nurses as they will directly affect family life. The demanding nature of the work itself, particularly the difficulties that can arise through over-emotional involvement with patients, can result in the nurse taking these problems into the home situation, often with negative consequences (e.g. see Hadley, 1977). The other side of this equation has been highlighted by Laube (1973), who points to the difficulties that can arise when the 'overspill' is in the other direction, and domestic pressures affect work performance.

The potential costs to the individual of trying to balance these competing demands can be serious. However, little research appears to have been done in this area and it is difficult to locate hard evidence. Attempts were made to obtain actuarial statistics, such as separation and divorce rates, from government and professional sources, but without success. It seems unfortunate that even the established professional bodies have not considered the collection of such data to be of high priority (compare this with the wealth of evidence available for other professions such as the police; Davidson and Veno, 1980), and there is an obvious need for further work in this area.

Ambivalence within the profession

In spite of marked changes in the status of women in Western society, attitudes towards working women are still ambivalent. This is especially true of attitudes towards married working women, even more so if they have dependent children. This ambivalence seems particularly strong within the profession itself. Even as this chapter is being written, a letter in the nursing press, responding to the article quoted at the beginning of this section, criticizes those nurses with dependent children who are also pursuing a career. The writer, a senior nurse concerned with the effects upon the child, vigorously attacks 'the sheer selfishness of females who want to have children but still think more of their career and their own self-satisfaction . . . wanting more nurseries, extending to unsocial hours, for them to dump their child in to be cared for by strangers for seven to eight hours a day, while they furthered their opportunities to rise up the NHS ladder . . . These so called "mothers" have the choice in their own hands—either the opportunity of climbing the ladder or having a family. I do not see why the NHS should have to provide for their selfishness and also why their children should suffer this way. They cannot be expected to have their cake and eat it.' (*Nursing Times*, 1985b). Even a recent Royal College of Nursing document warns that there will be no special recognition of the extra demands faced by married women entering the profession.

Both these responses indicate that the nurse with domestic commitment is likely not only to be disadvantaged in her professional career, but can expect to receive little understanding or support from sections of the profession itself. The cost is self-apparent. The nurse is likely to find herself in a particularly vulnerable and potentially stressful position, and the profession is not coming to terms with changes in the role of the growing majority of their members. As Marshall (1980) comments, 'The traditional role of the nurse as a single woman is fast disappearing and most now have family responsibilities which are important in the balance of their lives overall.' As yet there seems to be little recognition of these changes.

UK STUDIES OF STRESS IN NURSING

As our diagnostic work went on, our attention was repeatedly drawn to the high level of tension, distress and anxiety among the nurses. We found it hard to understand how nurses could tolerate so much anxiety and, indeed, we found much evidence that they could not. In one form or another withdrawal from duty was common. Almost one-third of student nurses did not complete their training . . . Senior staff changed their jobs appreciably more frequently than workers at similar levels in other professions . . . Sickness rates were high, especially for minor illnesses requiring only a few day's absence from duty. (Menzies, 1960a)

It is over a quarter of a century ago since Menzies drew attention to the inherent pressures of nursing and pointed out that the level of occupational stress is a significant factor in determining both job satisfaction and task performance. However, since that date little empirical research into the problem has been carried out in this country. Marshall (1980) reviewing the situation 20 years later comments, 'Having identified nursing as a potentially stressful occupation . . . I was unable to find anyone both willing and able to contribute a suitable chapter (to a book on occupational stress).' It seems particularly ironic that, largely as a result of Menzies' work, the study of stress in nursing in the USA has become a well-developed area in its own right, yet in this country it has been almost totally neglected.

A review of the UK literature reveals that evidence of stress in the nursing profession comes from a number of different sources. Each source reflects a different approach to the subject, and they can be roughly categorized as follows:

(1) 'Soft data'. This refers to the plethora of descriptive and anecdotal material in the British nursing literature which identifies stress as a problem but generally lacks supporting evidence. Perhaps the most valuable contribution of this material lies in its portrayal of the dominant attitudes and values held by members of the profession towards stress in nursing.

(2) 'Peripheral studies'. These include studies of problem areas within the UK nursing profession (e.g. absence, shift work, smoking) which have suggested that stress is a probable causal factor. However, a general criticism can be made that often these studies lack empirical evidence to support these conclusions.
(3) 'Case-study approaches'. In this approach the experiences and problems of a small number of nurses are examined in considerable depth. However, what these studies gain in depth they lose in breadth since it is difficult to generalize on the basis of the findings from a small sample.
(4) 'Stress surveys'. These are more ambitious in scale and tend to go for breadth rather than depth by examining the experiences of a large number of subjects. The obvious advantage of this approach is that it is possible to generalize from the results, provided that the sample is representative of the nursing population at large.

Soft data

Most of the relevant data in the popular nursing press is related to ways of coping with stress, and, despite a lack of empirical evidence, there is a marked tendency to emphasize personal rather than organizational or interactional methods of stress management (Marshall, 1980). Periodic 'campaigns' appear, often in the form of a series of articles aimed at heightening the individual nurse's awareness of stress, or at increasing her coping effectiveness (e.g. *Nursing Mirror*, 1980; Bond, 1982; *Nursing Times*, 1984). Another well-aired concern has been the debate surrounding the need for a comprehensive counselling service within the profession (Jones, 1978; Bailey, 1981; Annandale-Steiner, 1979). Again, the emphasis is on providing support at the personal level in order to increase individual coping ability.

A sample of articles from the popular nursing journals reveals that much less attention has been given to the nature of the 'stressful situations' in which nurses may find themselves. Intensive Care Units have received the most frequent attention in this respect (Melia, 1977; Boxall, 1982; *Nursing Times*, 1984). The Accident and Emergency Units have also been identified as highly stressful workplaces (Thompson, 1983; Brunt, 1984). However, there has been little attempt to demonstrate that the stresses in the ICU or in the A/E Units are quantitatively or qualitatively different than in any other area of nursing. Indeed in one of the few empirical investigations Nichols *et al.* (1980) found that the claims of 'high levels of discontent and distress in intensive therapy unit nurses do not stand up to empirical scrutiny.' Much the same pattern of stresses was recorded with medical and surgical nurses.

It is not sufficient simply to assume that if the situation is more stressful then the individual nurse will be more stressed. Nurses are not an homogeneous group. In fact, it is more likely that the ICUs and A/E departments, for example, attract and retain the nurse who does not feel overly threatened by this type of working environment.

'Peripheral' studies

Stress has frequently been cited as a contributory cause of absence and wastage. Lunn (1975) noted that rates of absence for nurse learners were at least double those for girls of a similar age in other occupations. He found that the learners did not appear to suffer an excess of any particular physical illness; in fact much of the illness associated with high absence appeared to be ill defined and of short duration. Lunn concludes that the 'very pronounced picture of stress reactions and anxiety' amongst nurse learners is a consequence of the unrestrained demands of nursing as an occupation. Similarly, in an earlier study, Menzies (1960b) attributed the high rates of sickness absence and voluntary withdrawal from training to the psychological distress associated with the nature of their work. In a comprehensive study of short-term absence among nurses, Clark (1975) concludes that absence behaviour cannot be adequately understood by reference to personal factors alone. Absence, it seems, is a product of the interactions between the employing institution and the organizational context. 'In addition, the reasons given by both high and low absence groups for absenteeism, could lend weight to the hypothesis that absence should be seen as a coping mechanism used by certain individuals in an effort to reduce anxiety or stress.'

As already noted shift work has frequently been associated with high levels of occupational stress. Within nursing, complaints that rotating shift work frequently disrupts family life, health, and effective job performance, are commonplace in the literature. The night nurse is often subject to the fluctuating demands of patient care, and we have seen that in her relationships with other staff she is commonly set apart and is often perceived as a professional inferior by day nurses of equal rank (Kemp, 1984). Similarly, individual smoking patterns have been linked with stress. Although the evidence suggests that nurses are no more likely to smoke than women in general, they do appear to have a higher incidence of smoking than other female professionals, and several studies suggest that these patterns may be stress induced, (Hawkins *et al.*, 1983; Davidson and Cooper, 1983).

Case-study approach

Runciman's (1982) in-depth study in a small group of nurses is a typical example of the 'case-study' approach. She focused on ward sisters as they have been frequently identified as the 'key middle managers' within the profession. Nine ward sisters participated in an in-depth study of their day-to-day practice over a period of a year. It was found that the sisters differed in 'professional and educational background, in their understanding of their role responsibilities, in their perception of and response to work difficulties, and in the context of their social and family commitments into which the work role had to fit.' The main areas of difficulty identified in this study included the problems of integrating their role as managers and clinicians, continual interruptions and the fragmentation of work, some aspects of relationships with nursing officers, and tasks of learning on the job and keeping up with professional developments. Introducing change and innovation were also seen as problematic. Some sisters felt that they were working in isolation and lacked peer group support. In conclusion the study identified the need for better training and preparation for the role, more effective on-going support for sisters and opportunities for continuing education.

The in-depth case-study approach is a valuable way of illustrating and highlighting the complexity and difficulties of the day-to-day work of the nurse. However, as we have noted before it also has its drawbacks. As Runciman points out in spite of the potential value of her study the findings must be treated with a certain degree of caution as, 'It would be unwise to generalise about the problems of sisters as a whole on the basis of such a small sample.'

Stress surveys

In this country there have been very few large-scale studies of stress in nursing. This may reflect the ambivalence of the profession towards recognizing the existence and implications of the problem, or it may be simply to do with the methodological difficulties of carrying out a large-scale survey of a complex phenomena. Of the studies carried out in recent years, two will be examined in detail (Birch, 1979; Parkes, 1980a,b). Both are directed at the student nurse population, each taking a different approach to the observation and measurement of stress.

Birch's (1979) research into anxiety levels in nurse learners was directly inspired by the Briggs Report, and focuses upon the pressures of the trainee nurse. A sample of 207 student and pupil nurses was taken from four schools of nursing in the north of England. Changes in the nurse learners' anxiety levels and sources of anxiety were measured during the first two years of hospital experience, using two instruments: Cattell's 16PF and a questionnaire, which Birch devised himself. Four measures on the 16PF scale were taken for each subject at eight-monthly intervals. The questionnaire (56 items) was administered first at eight months and again after two years training. Birch found that, contrary to expectations, anxiety levels had not reduced after two years of training. On the 16PF measures, during the introductory course, 43 per cent of the learners indicated 'borderline high anxiety levels', while 36 per cent were described as showing signs of 'definite psychological morbity, almost certain to have an adverse effect on work and social/emotional adjustment of the individual'. After a check at eight months anxiety levels returned to their initial high levels, and at the end of two years training the level of anxiety was shown to be significantly greater than patients about to undergo major surgery!

From the questionnaire, Birch identified 28 main stressors. Significantly all of these stressors were associated with the difficulty of understanding the psychological needs of patients and staff. Procedural items relating to routine patient care—a test of the nurse learners' clinical confidence—caused little or no stress. Most of the stressors showing increased levels of anxiety were related to dealing with 'death and dying' and including the problems of dealing with bereaved relatives. On the other hand, the learner's anxiety about her own death had tended to decrease over this two-year period. Difficulties in staff relationships were identified as stressful, and the extent of the problem seemed to depend upon the level of the nursing grade. By the end of the second year, dealing with ward sisters/charge nurses had ceased to be stressful. However, dealing with nursing officers was found to be more stressful than for any other person in the hierarchy, and remained twentieth in the overall ranking of stressors.

Table 3.2 shows the top ten stressors at eight months and their changing priority after 24 months training. It is evident that changing wards was still seen as a cause of anxiety even after 24 months of training, although to a lesser degree. These problems of adjustments were related to differences in management style and to the sisters' attitude towards their nursing personnel. About one-third of the respondents stated that their senior staff made no attempt to reduce the levels of stress occurring with each ward change. Perhaps not surprisingly, 'being disciplined in public' was seen as being particularly stressful and ranked second in the overall order of stressors. Birch remarks that, 'Learners continue to be under considerable strain because of public rebuke by senior nursing staff.'

Table 3.2. Rank order of stressors after eight months and 24 months of training.

Stressors	Rank order at	
	8 months	24 months
Nursing of patients in great pain	1	3
Being shown up on the wards in front of patient and other staff	2	2
Progress test in block study	3	6
Dealing with patients with cancer	4	5
Care of the terminally ill	5	4
Care of the dying	6	6
Dealing with bereaved relatives	7	7
Changing wards	8	13
Your feelings about your own death	9	12
Your feeling about growing old	9	11
Understaffing	10	1

Birch concludes that the majority of pupils and students believed that their training did not prepare them adequately for the care of dying patients, and less still for dealing with bereaved relatives. There is a need, he argues, to improve the psychological content of nurse training and education so that pupils and students are better able to cope with the interpersonal demands of the nursing task. He regrets that, unlike nurse training in other countries, 'in the UK there is no regulation or recommendation relating to the number of hours to be devoted to the psychological aspects of nursing care.'

Another major study of occupational stress in nursing within the UK was carried out by Parkes (1980a,b) and was aimed at exploring the effects of different working environments upon student nurses. As well as the actual findings of the study the methodology used is of particular interest. Parkes took advantage of the natural transitions of student nurses across different work environments during their training programme. The same individuals were repeatedly assessed on measures of psychological distress, work satisfaction and short-term sickness over the first six months of training. By collecting data before and after changes in the work environment, it was possible to distinguish individual differences from the effects of the work situation. Thus Parkes was able to separate out and report on the causal effects of the work setting in influencing mental health and well-being.

A total of 101 female students were assessed before the first ward placement, and again at the end of each ward allocation. At the initial assessment, they were found to be typical of the normal female population on all of the measures except two, i.e. they were significantly more extrovert and emotionally stable than females in the general population. This tends to suggest that nursing attracts and selects the more stable and extrovert type of person, 'types most likely to adapt well to the demands of nursing' (Parkes, 1980a).

Differences between medical and surgical wards

Data on 88 students were analysed for a systematic comparison of the effects of medical/surgical wards, and male/female ward allocation. Parkes found that differences in ward settings gave rise to significant differences on measures of well-being. Medical wards were associated with significantly higher levels of anxiety and depression and respondents also reported lower levels of job satisfaction. Although overall levels of involvement, staff support, autonomy, task orientation and innovation were not high in either type of setting, respondents reported higher levels in the surgical wards. Work pressure, on the other hand, was equally high in both the surgical and medical settings. In general, the study also found that the higher the level of work pressure, the lower the level of staff support, and Parkes suggests that the heavy work loads allowed senior nurses little time to teach, encourage or support the work of students on their ward.

Parkes discusses in some detail ways in which the medical and surgical wards may influence well-being amongst students.

(1) Inherent differences in the nature of the tasks between the two wards means that surgical nursing emphasizes the more cognitive 'instrumental' role (demanding rational, problem-solving and technical skills). On the other hand, the medical ward stresses the 'affective' role of the nurse (the compassionate, caring and protective aspects of nursing).

(2) The type of 'social climate' specific to the ward appears to be crucial, especially the influence of the variables of involvement, support, and task orientation.

(3) The physical location of the ward in relation to the central facilities of the hospital, such as staff dining rooms, administrative offices, etc., was also important. In her study it seemed significant that the surgical wards were usually much closer to these central facilities than were the medical wards.

Differences between male and female wards

The main differences between the male and female wards lay in the area of interpersonal relationships. Measures of the quality of peer relationships between students showed significantly higher levels on the male wards, as did other measures of involvement. At the same time these students were likely to experience significantly higher levels of anxiety, but levels of commitment and job satisfaction were also greater, especially in male surgical wards. In her study Parkes also suggests that the relationship between work satisfaction and measures of well-being is complicated by a number of interacting influences which are difficult to assess; for example, virtually all the students expressed a preference for working on the male wards. This could have a significant effect upon motivation and the levels of stress that were seen to be acceptable.

As we have noted in Chapter 2, there is a growing body of evidence linking short-term absence with stress-related illnesses and sickness, and absence rates are often used by researchers as an indicator of occupational stress. Parkes found that there were no significant differences in measures of short-term sickness/absence between the various wards and deduces that this form of absence is influenced primarily by individual attitudes, rather than by structural factors such as the nature of the ward. However, any generalization of this conclusion to the wider nurse population must be tentative. Student placements involve some degree of 'protection' for the individual student; they are also of relatively short duration. As such the student's position is fundamentally different from that of the qualified nurse, where stress is more likely to be experienced because the individual is under severe and sustained pressure.

Conclusion

Each of these four approaches to the collection of data on stress in nursing is very different; each is limited in its own way, yet each has something to add to the total picture. To return to where we started, and Menzies' original study of 25 years ago, in which she suggests that, 'the nature of the nursing task, in spite of its obvious difficulties, was not enough to account for their levels of anxiety and stress . . . the present organisation not only causes unnecessary stress but contributes to such phenomena as shortcomings in patient-care and wastage of good student nurses.' (Menzies, 1960a,b) It seems that an understanding of stress in nursing can only be understood by a comprehensive perspective, in which account is taken of the nursing task, the environment in which it takes place, the personality of the individual nurse and the way she perceives and interacts with her environment. From a theoretical point of view we return again to emphasize the importance of the person–environment fit, and our belief that an approach to stress based on only one part of this equation will be severely limited in both explanation and application.

Finally, the value of any research can best be measured in terms of the changes it helps to bring about. If this is true, then the achievements of researchers concerned with stress in nursing is minimal! Here we can only reiterate Menzie's astonishment at finding 'how little basic and dynamic change has taken place. Nurses have tended to receive reports and recommendations with a sense of outrage and to react to them by intensifying current attitudes and existing priorities' (Menzies, 1970). 'Efforts to initiate serious change were often met with acute anxiety and hostility, which conveyed the idea that the people concerned felt very threatened, threat being of nothing less than social chaos and individual breakdown. To give up ways of behaviour and embark on the unknown were felt to be intolerable.' (Menzies, 1960a) We can only hope that the future will give lie to Menzie's jaundiced view of the level of inertia within the nursing profession!

REFERENCES

Adkinson, J.A. (1981) Women in school administration: a review of the research. *Rev. Educ. Res.*, **51**: 311.

Aiken, L.H. (1981) Nursing priorities for the 1980's: hospitals and nursing homes. *Am. J. Nurs.*, **81**: 324.

Altschul, A.T. (1972) *Patient Nurse Interaction:A Study of Interaction Patterns in Acute Psychiatric Wards.* Edinburgh: Churchill Livingstone.

Andrews, F.M. and Withy, S.B. (1976) *Social Indicators of Well-being: Americans' Perceptions of Life Quality.* New York: Plenum.

Annandale-Steiner, D. (1979) Why nurses leave: Unhappiness is the nurse who expected more. *Nursing Mirror*, Nov. 29.

Armitage, S. (1980) Non-compliant recipients of health care. *Nursing Times*, **17**: 1–3.

Bailey, J.T., Steffen, S.M. and Grout, J.W. (1980) The stress audit: identifying the stressors of ICU nursing. *Jnl. of Nursing Education*, **9**: (June).

Bailey, R. (1981) Counselling services for nurses—a forgotten responsibility. *Apex J. Br. Inst. Ment. Hand.*, **9**: 45–47.

Baj, R.N. (1980) Management actions to humanize the health care environment. **19** (June).

Basque, L.O. and Merige, J. (1980) Nurses experiences with dangerous behaviour: implications for training. *J. Cont. Educ. Nurs.*, **11**: 47–51.

Benne, K.D. and Bennis, W. (1959) Role conflict and confusion in nursing: the role of the professional nurse. *Am. J. Nurs.* **59**: 196–198, 380–383.

Berkowitz, J.E. and Berkowitz, N.H. (1960) Nursing education and role conception. *Nurs. Res.* **9**: 18–219.

Bhagat, R.S. and Chassie, M.B. (1981) Determinants of organisational commitment in working women: some implications for organisational integration. *J. Occup. Behav.*, **2**: 17–30.

Bilodeau, C.B. (1973) The nurse and her reactions to critical care nursing *Heart Lung*, **2**: 358–363.

Birch, J. (1979) The anxious learners. *Nurs. Mirror*, Feb. 8.

Bond, M. (1982) Stress 1–4. *Nurs. Mirror*, Sept. 29 to Oct. 20.

Boorer, D. (1970) *A Question of Attitudes*. London: King's Fund Hospital Centre.

Boxall, J. (1982) Some thoughts on stress to staff in neonatal units. *Nurs. Times*, July 7.

Bradburn, N.M. (1969) *The Structure of Psychological Well-being*. Chicago: Aldine.

Brand, F.D. and Smith, R.T. (1974) Medical care and compliance among the elderly after hospitalization. *Int. J. Ageing Hum. Dev.* **5**: 331–346.

Brown, E.L. (1948) *Nursing for the Future*. New York: Russell Sage.

Brown, E.L. (1966) Nursing and patient care. In Davis, F. (ed.), *The Nursing Profession: Five Sociological Essays*. New York: Wiley.

Brunt, C. (1984) A very stressful place. *Nurs. Times*, Feb. 15.

Campbell, A., Converse, P.E. and Rodgers, W.L. (1976) *The Quality of American Life: Perceptions, Evaluations and Satisfactions*. New York: Russell Sage Foundation.

Carr, A.T. (1981) Dying and bereavement. In Herbert, M. (ed.), *Psychology for Social Workers*. London: Macmillan.

Carwright, A., Hockey, L. and Anderson, J.L. (1973), *Life Before Death*. London: Routledge and Kegan Paul.

Chapman, C.M. (1977) Sociology for Nurses. London: Bailliere Tindall.

Cherniss, C. (1980) *Staff Burnout: Job Stress in the Human Services*. London: Sage.

Cherniss, C. and Egntaios, E. (1978) Clinical supervision in community mental health. *Soc. Work*, **23**: 219–223.

Choon, G.L. and Skevington, S.M. (1984) How do women and men in nursing perceive each other? In Skevington, S.M. (ed.), *Understanding Nurses*. Chichester: Wiley.

Clark, J. (1975) *Time-out? A Study of Absenteeism among Nurses*. London: Royal College of Nursing.

Claus, K.E. and Bailey, J.T. (1980) *Living with Stress and Promoting Well-being*. St Louis: C.V. Mosby.

Cleland, V. (1971) Sex discrimination: nursing's most pervasive problem. *Am. J. Nurs.* **71**: 1,542.

Cobb, S. and Rose, R.M. (1973) Hypertension, peptic ulcer and diabetes in air traffic controllers. *J. Am. Med. Assoc.*, **224**: 489–492.

Cooper C.L. (1978) Work stress. In Warr, P.B. *Psychology at Work*. London: Penguin.

Cooper, C.L. (1981) *The Stress Check*. New Jersey: Prentice Hall.

Cooper, C.L. and Marshall, J. (1976) Occupational sources of stress. A review of the literature relating to coronary heart disease and mental ill health. *J. Occup. Psychol.*, **49**, 11–28.

Corwin, R.G. (1961) The professional employee: a study of conflict in nursing roles. *Am. J. Sociol.*, **66**: 604–615.

Crawley, P. (1984) King's Fund Conference, verbatim.

Davidson, M. and Cooper, C.L. (1983) *Stress and the Woman Manager*. Oxford: Martin Robertson.

Davidson, M. and Veno, A. (1980) Stress and the policeman. In Cooper, C.L. and Marshall, J. (eds.), *White Collar and Professional Stress*. Chichester: Wiley.

Davis, A.J. (1969) Self concept, occupational role expectations and occupational choice in nursing and social work. *Nurs. Res.*, **18**: 55–59.

Davitz, L.J. *et al.* (1969) Nurses' inferences of suffering. *Nurs. Res.*, **18**: 100–107.

Dobson, C.B. (1982) *Stress the Hidden Adversary*. Lancaster: MTP Press.

Dock, L.L. (1920) *A Short History of Nursing*. New York: Putnam.

Etzioni, A (1964) *Modern Organizations*. New Jersey: Prentice Hall.

Etzioni, A. (ed.) (1969) *The Semi-professions and their Organization*. New York: Free Press.

Everly, G.S. and Falcione, R.L. (1976) Perceived dimensions of job satisfaction on psychiatric units. *Nurs. Res.*, **23**: 482.

Falek, A. and Britton, S. (1974) Phases in coping: the hypothesis and its implications. *Soc. Bio.*, **21**: 1–7.

Flaskerud, J.H., Halloran, E.J., Janken, J., Lund, M. and Zetterlund, J. (1979) Avoidance and distancing: a descriptive view of nursing. *Nurs. Forum*, **8**: 158–174.

Folkard, S. (1981) Shiftwork and performance. In Johnson, L.C., Tepas, D.I., Colquhoun, W.P. and Colligan, M.J. (eds), *Billogical Rhythms, Sleep and Shiftwork*. Lancaster: MTP Press.

Folkard, S., Monk, T.H. and Lobban, M.C. (1978) Short and long-term adjustment of circadian rhythms in 'permanent' night nurses. *Ergonomics*, **21**: 785–799.

French, J.R.P. and Caplan, R.D. (1970) Psychosocial factors in coronary heart disease. *Ind. Med.*, **39**: 383–397.

Gadbois, C. (1981) Women on night shift: interdependence of sleep and off-the-job activities. In Reinberg, A., Vieux, N. and Andlauer, P. (eds), *Night and Shift Work*. Oxford: Pergamon.

Geizhals, J.S. (1975) Attitudes towards death and dying: a study of occupational therapists and nurses. *J. Thanatol.*, **3**: 243–269.

Gillis, L. and Biesheuvel, S. (1962) *Human Behaviour in Illness: Psychology and Interpersonal Relationships*. London: Faber and Faber.

Glaser, B.G. and Strauss, A.L. (1966) *Awareness of Dying*. London: Weidenfeld and Nicholson.

Goddard, H. (1953) *The Work of Nurses in Hospital Wards*. London: Nuffield Provincial Hospitals Trust.

Gove, W.R. and Geerken, M.R. (1977) The effect of children and employment on the mental health of married men and women. *Social Forces*, **56**, 66–76.

Grant, N. (1979) *Time to Care*. London: Royal College of Nursing.

Gray-Toft, P. and Anderson, J.G. (1981) Stress among hospital nursing staff: its causes and effects. *Soc. Sci. Med.*, **15a**: 639–647.

Grisson, M. and Spengler, C. (1976) *Women and Health Care*. Boston: Little, Brown.

Grout, J.W. (1980) Stress-reduction training modules for nurses. In Claus, K.E. and Bailey, J.T. (eds), *Living With Stress and Promoting Well-being*. St Louis: C.V. Mosby.

Gunderson, K., Percy, S., Canedy, B.H. and Pisani, S. (1977) How to control professional frustration. *Am. J. Nurs.*, **77**:7.

Gunning, C.S. (1983) The profession itself as a source of stress. In Jacobson, S.F. and McGrath, H.M. (eds), *Nurses Under Stress*. New York: Wiley.

Habenstein, R.W. and Christ, E.A. (1963) *Professionalizer, Traditionalizer and Utilizer*. Columbia: University of Missouri.

Hadley, R.D. (1977) Staff nurse cites challenge, satisfaction despite stress. *Am. Nurse*, **9**: 6–11.

Haugh, M.R. and Sussman, M.B. (1969) Professional autonomy and the revolt of the client. *Soc. Prob.*, **17**: 153.

Hawkins, L., White, M. and Morris, L. (1983) Smoking, stress and nurses. *Nurs. Mirror*, Oct. 13.

Hay, D. and Oken, D. (1972) The psychological stresses of intensive care nursing. *Psychosom. Med.*, **34**: 109–118.

Highley, B. and Norris, C. (1957) When a student dislikes a patient. *Am. J. Nurs.*, **57**: 1163–1166.

Hingley, P. (1984) The humane face of nursing. *Nurs. Mirror*, Dec.

Hockey, L. (1976) *Women in Nursing*. London: Hodder and Stoughton.

Hoffling, C.K., Brotzman, E., Dalrymple, S., Graves, N. and Pierce, C.M. (1966) An experimental study in nurse–physician relationships. *J. Nerv. Ment. Dis.*, **143**:171.

Jacobson, S.F. (1978) Stresses and coping strategies of neonatal care unit nurses. *Unpublished Doctoral Thesis*, University of Minnesota.

Jacobson, S.F. and McGrath, H.M. (1983) *Nurses Under Stress*. New York: Wiley.
Jeffery, R. (1979) Normal rubbish: deviant patients in casualty departments. *Soc. Health Illness*, **1**: 98–107.
Jones, D. (1978) The need for a comprehensive counselling service for nursing students. *J. Adv. Nurs.*, **3**: 359–368.
Kahn, R.L. and Rosenthal, R.A. (1964) *Organizational Stress: Studies in Role Conflict and Ambiguity*. New York: Wiley.
Kasterbaum, R. and Weisman, A.D. (1972) The psychological autopsy as a research procedure in gerontology. In Kent, D.P., Kastenbaum, R. and
Katz, F. (1969) Nurses. In Etzioni A. (ed.), *The Semi-professions and their Organization*. New York: Free Press.
Kelly, J. (1982) Role theory as a model for human interaction: its implications for nursing education. *Austr. Nurs.J.*, **12**: 42–43.
Kelly, M.P. and May, D. (1982) Good and bad patients: a review of the literature and a theoretical critique. *J. Adv. Nurs.*, **7**: 147–156.
Kemp, J. (1984) Nursing at night. *J. Adv. Nurs.*, **9**: 217–223.
King's Fund Report (1981) Project Paper No. 27: The preforation of senior nurse managers in the National Health Service. London: King's Fund Centre.
Knight, M. and Field, D. (1981) A silent conspiracy: coping with dying cancer patients in an acute surgical ward. *J. Adv. Nurs.*, **6**: 221–222.
Kramer, M. (1974) *Reality shock: why nurses leave nursing*. St Louis: C.V. Mosby.
Kratz, C. (1976) Roles and relatives. *Nurs. Times*, June 17, 923.
Kubler-Ross, E. (1969) *On Death and Dying*. New York. Macmillan.
Kubler-Ross, E. (1975) Death: how dare we face you? In Howells, J.G. (ed.), *Modern Perspectives in the Psychiatry of Old Age*. New York. Brunner, Mazel.
Lachman, V.D. (1983) *Stress Management: A Manual for Nurses*. New York: Grune and Stratton.
Lamonica, E. (1979) The nurse and the ageing client: positive attitude formation. *Nurs. Educ.*, **4**: 23–26.
Lawrence, P.R. and Lorsch, J.W. (1967) *Organization and Environment: Managing Differentiation and Integration*. Boston: Harvard University Press.
Laube, J. (1973) Death and dying workshop for nurses: its effect on their death anxiety level. *Int. J. Nurs. Stud.*, **14**: 111–120.
Leatt, P. and Schneck, R. (1980) Differences in stress perceived by headnurses across nursing specialities in hospitals. *J. Adv. Nurs.*, **5**: 31–46.
Lingren, H.C. (1969) *An Introduction to Social Psychology*. New York: Wiley.
Lorber, J. (1975) Good patients and problem patients: conformity and deviance in a general hospital. *J. Health Soc. Behav.*, **16**: 213–225.
Lunn, J.A. (1973) Hospital hazards. *The Practitioner*, **210** (April).
Lunn, J.A. (1975) Absenteeism—an occupational hazard. *Nurs. Mirror*, **140**, May 22/29, 65–66.
Lysaught, J.P. (1970) *An Abstract for Action. National Commission for the Study of Nursing and Nursing Education*. New York: McGraw-Hill.
MacGregor, F. (1960) *Social Science in Nursing: Applications for the Improvement of Patient Care*. New York: Russell Sage.
Marshall, J. (1980) Stress amongst nurses. In Cooper, C.L. and Marshall, J. (eds.), *White Collar and Professional Stress*. Chichester: Wiley.
Maslach, C. (1982) *Burnout: The Cost of Caring*. New Jersey: Prentice Hall.
McClure, M.L. (1978) The long road to accountability. *Nurs. Outlook*, **26**: 47.
Melia, K.M. (1977) The intensive care unit—a stress situation? *Nurs. Times*, Feb. 3.
Menzies, I.E.P. (1960a) A case study in the functioning of social systems as a defence against anxiety. *Hum. Rel.*, **13**: 95–121.
Menzies, I.E.P. (1960b) Nurses under stress: a social system functioning as a defence against anxiety. *Int. Nurs. Rev.*, **7**: 9–16.

Menzies, I.E.P. (1970) *The Functioning of Social Systems as a Defence against Anxiety.* London: Tavistock Institute.

Mercer, G. and Mold, C. (1976) *An Investigation into the Level and Character of Labour Turnover amongst Trained Nurses.* Leeds: University of Leeds.

Miller, G.A. (1974) Patient knowledge and nurse role strain in three hospital settings.

Murray, M. (1983) Role conflict and intention to leave nursing. *J. Adv. Nurs.*, **8**: 29–31.

Nichols, K., Springford, V. and Searle, J. (1981) An investigation of distress and discontent in various types of nursing. *J. Adv. Nurs.*, **6**: 311–318.

Norris, C.M. (1973) 'Delusions that trap nurses into dead end alleyways away from growth, relevance, and impact on health care. *Nurs. Outlook*, **21**: 18–21.

Nurse, G. (1975) *Counselling and the Nurse.* Aylesbury: HM and M.

Nursing Mirror (1980) Campaign—stress and relaxation. June 26 to July 10.

Nursing Times (1984) Nurses have needs too. Oct. 10 to Oct. 17.

Nursing Times (1985a) Nurses with children suffer in the NHS career stakes. July 10.

Nursing Times (1985b) Should nurses with children stay at home? Letters.

Numerof, R.E. and Abrams, M.N. (1984) Sources of stress among nurses: an empirical investigation. *J. Hum. Stress*, Summer, pp. 88–100.

Ogier, M. (1984) How do ward sisters influence learning by nurses in the wards? In Skevington, S. (ed.) *Understanding Nurses: The Social Psychology of Nursing.* Chichester: Wiley.

Papper, S. (1970) The undesirable patient. *J. Chron. Dis.*, **22**: 777–779.

Parkes, K.R. (1980a) Occupational stress among nurses. 1. A comparison of medical and surgical wards. *Nurs. Times*, Oct 30, 113–116.

Parkes, K.R. (1980b) Occupational stress among nurses. 2 A comparison of male and female wards. *Nurs. Times*, Nov. 6, 117–119.

Price, T.R. and Bergen, B.T. (1977) The relationship to death as a source of stress for nurses on a coronary care unit. *Omega. J. Death Dying*, **8**: 229–238.

Reiter, F. and Kakosh, M. (1954) Quality of nursing care: report of a field study to establish criteria. 1950–54. In Aydelotte, M. (ed.), *Nurse Staffing Methodology.* Washington, D.C.: DHEW.

Revans, R.W. (1976) *Action Learning in Hospitals: Diagnosis and Therapy.* London: McGraw-Hill.

Ritvo, M. (1963 Who are the good and bad patients? *Mod. Hosp.*, **100**: 79–81.

Roch, J. (1980) The uses and limitations of the concept of role for nurse education. *Nurs. Times*, **76**, 837–841.

Rosenthal, C.J., Marshall, V.W., Macpherson, A.S. and French, S. (1980) *Nurses, Patients and Families.* London: Croom Helm.

Ross, A. (1961) *Becoming a Nurse.* Toronto: Macmillan.

Rosse, J.G. and Rosse, P.H. (1981) Role conflict and ambiguity: an empirical investigation of nursing personnel. *Eval. Health Prof.*, **4**: 385–405.

Roth, J. (1972) Some contingencies of the moral evaluation and control of clientele: the case of the hospital emergency service. *Am. J. Sociol.*, **77**: 39–60.

Runciman, P. (1982) Ward sisters: their problems at work. 1 and 2. *Nurs. Times*, Occasional Papers, Vol. 78.

Sanders, M.M. (1980) Stressed? Or burnt-out. *Can. Nurs.*, Oct., 30–36.

Sarata, B.P.V. (1972) Job satisfaction of individuals working with the mentally retarded. Unpublished PhD thesis. Harem: Yale University.

Sarbin, T.R. and Allen, V.L. (1968) Role theory. In Lindzey, G. and Aronson, E. (eds), *The Handbook of Social Psychology.* Reading, Mass: Addison-Wesley.

Sarosi, G.M. (1968) A critical theory; the nurse as a fully human person. *Nurs. Forum*, **7**: 349–364.

Schowalter, J.E. (1975) Paediatric nurses dream of death. *J. Thanatol.*, **3**: 223–321.

Schwap, J.J. (1970) The differential perception of anxiety in medical patients: socio-demographic aspects. *Psychiatr. Med.*, **1**: 151–164.

Shearer, A. (1983) Angels in hell. *Guardian*, June 29, 11.

Sherrod *et al.* (1977) Effects of peroral causation and perceived control on responses to an aversive environment. *Jnl. Exp. Soc. Psychol.*, **13**: 14–27.

Simpson, I.H., Back, K., Ingles, T., Kerckhoff, A. and McKinney, J.C. (1979) Cambridge *From Student to Nurse: A Longitudinal Study of Socialization.* Cambridge: Cambridge University Press.

Skevington, S. (ed.) (1984) *Understanding Nurses: The Social Psychology of Nursing.* Chichester: Wiley.

Spitzer, S. and Sobel, R. (1962) Preferences for patients and patient behaviour. *Nurs. Res.*, **11**: 233–235.

Steffen, S.M. (1980) Perceptions of stress: 1800 nurses tell their stories. In Claus, K.E. and Bailey, J.T. (eds), *Living With Stress and Promoting Well-being.* St Louis: C.V. Mosby.

Stein, L.I. (1968) The doctor–nurse game. *Am. J. Nurs.*, **68**: 101.

Strauss, A. and Glaser, B. (1977) *Anguish: A Case History of a Dying Trajectory.* London: Martin Robertson.

Stockwell, F. (1972) *The Unpopular Patient.* London: Royal College of Nursing.

Strong, P. (1980) Doctors and dirty work: the case of alcoholism. *Sociol. Health Illlness*, **2**: 24–47.

Sudnow, D.I. (1967) *Passing On: The Social Organization of Dying.* New Jersey: Prentice Hall.

Tasto, D., Colligan, M.,Skjei, E. and Polly, S. (1978) *Health Consequences of Shift Work.* NIOSH. Washington, DC: US Government Printing Office.

Thompson, J. (1983) Call sister—stress in the A and E department. *Nurs. Times*, Aug. 3.

Turner, R.H. (1962) Role taking: process versus conformity. In Rose, A. (ed.), *Human Behaviour and the Social Process.* London: Routledge and Kegan Paul.

Ujhely, G.B. (1963) *The Nurse and her Problem Patient.* New York: Springer-Verlag.

Valliot, M.C. (1966) Existentialism: a philosophy of commitment. *Am. Jnl. Nurs.*, **66**: 500.

Watson, C. (1982) Sleepless night, peaceful night. *Nurs. Mirror*, **155**: 22.

Weeler, D.J. and Miller, P.M. (1977) Emotional reactions of patient, family, and staff in acute-care period of spinal cord injury: Part 2. *Soc. Work Health Care*, **3**: 7–17.

Weinstein, N.D. (1974) Effect of noise on intellectual performance. *J. Appl. Psychol.*, **59**: 548–554.

Weissman, A. (1972) *On Death and Denying.* New York: Behavioral Publications.

Wells, T.J. (1980) *Problems in Geriatric Nursing Care: A Study of Nurses' Problems in Care of Old people in Hospitals.* Edinburgh: Churchill Livingstone.

Whitfield, S. (1979) A descriptive study of student nurses' ward experiences with dying patients and their attitudes towards them. *Unpublished MSc Thesis*, Manchester University.

CHAPTER 4

Brief history of nurse management and introduction to study

As we have seen in a previous chapter, research into occupational stress has developed considerably over the past decade, and there is now a growing body of evidence relating both physical and mental well-being to work pressures (Cooper, 1982). The field is particularly well developed in the United States, which has long recognized the problem, and stress in the 'caring professions' has been the subject of considerable concern. This has led to a number of in-depth studies and a variety of responses aimed at alleviating the situation (e.g. Maslach, 1982).

Interest in the problems of occupational stress, particularly as it relates to managers, is increasing rapidly in this country, and there are a growing number of research studies focused upon specific occupations (Cooper and Payne, 1978, Cooper and Marshall, 1980). However, in spite of the concern expressed from a number of sources that occupational stress could be an important factor in determining morbidity and levels of absence and wastage amongst nurses, the amount of attention that has been paid to the nursing profession has been extremely limited (Menzies, 1960; Lunn, 1975; Clark, 1975), and those studies that do exist have focused almost exclusively upon the problems of the student nurse working within the hospital setting (Birch, 1979; Parkes, 1980). This is no doubt in part a reflection of the methodological difficulties that surround such an undertaking. But, from the authors' own observations, it is also likely to be accounted for by the attitudes of the profession itself, which seems intent on denying that nurses could suffer from such a problem.

NURSE MANAGEMENT

Just as every qualified nurse or midwife should be in some sense an educator, so every qualified nurse and midwife must be in some sense a manager. (Briggs Report, 1972)

89

As we have seen in Chapters 2 and 3, research evidence suggests that the task of management, and particularly middle management, is potentially highly stressful. Management, whatever the purpose of the institution in which it takes place, is about the achievement of organizational goals and making the best use of available resources to realize these goals.

Drucker (1977), one of the leading writers on the subject, refuses to supply a simple definition to what he sees as a complex task. In addition to the specific professional skills and abilities, which will reflect the nature of the organization, he identifies 'the five basic operations in the work of the manager . . . (which) . . . together result in the integration of resources into a viable growing organism (the organisation).' They are:

(1) *Setting objectives*—the management task will involve the individual in determining goals within his/her own sphere of responsibility and in planning the most effective way of achieving these goals within the resources that are available, i.e. involvement in the planning process. This will demand skills in planning, decision-making and communication.

(2) *Organization*—this involves the implementation in practice of the policies decided in (1) and overviewing and amending them in the light of day-to-day experience, i.e. the responsibility of running the ward, unit or department.

(3) *Motivation and communication*—the 'integrating' activity of management, i.e. the creation of a working team from a group of individuals. For this the nurse manager will need a wide range of interpersonal and leadership skills.

(4) *Assessment*—maintaining the accepted overall goals of the unit, i.e. general 'quality control'. For this operation the nurse manager will need a number of analytical and supervisory skills.

(5) *Staff development*—'finally a manager develops people, including himself or herself', i.e. encouraging and acting as a role model for on-going professional growth and development. To achieve this the nurse manager will need to be professionally aware and possess the interpersonal skills to encourage and assist the staff group in their own career development.

The role of management in the nursing profession

The National Health Service is one of the largest employers in Europe. It has over one million employees drawn from a bewildering array of professions and specialisms. Its organization is complex; it is sectionalized and it is hierarchical, the very attributes which lend themselves to ambiguity and conflict. Within this organization nursing is the largest single professional group. It constitutes over 50 per cent of the total labour force, and again within the profession one can see numerous specialisms and competing interests. Within such a complex organization the task of management, at both the general and the professional level, is of crucial importance in determining the quality of patient care, and the quality of individual managers is paramount.

Walton (1984), in an interesting analysis of the task of nurse management in the NHS, suggests that, as in all large organizations, it revolves around handling the five principle elements which effect health care delivery, i.e. (1) politics, (2) power, (3) anxiety, (4) uncertainty, and (5) change. Walton suggests that traditionally within the profession the meaning of management has often been restricted simply to ward activities and direct patient care. This is a very narrow and restricted view of, and undervalues, the need for the nurse to have a wider perspective; 'People tend not to talk about these features . . . (but) . . . the clearer you as a manager can become about how decisions are taken in your location, the more informed and appropriate your actions will be. An acute awareness of (a) the power forces at play, (b) the need to face uncertainty, and (c) the need to handle your own anxiety and that of junior staff, will help you to support your staff better than if you deny these factors.' The implications are obvious. If these are not managed efficiently and effectively, there will be a cost both at the individual level (stress and anxiety) and at the organizational level (a reduction in the quality and effectiveness of service delivery).

The changing role of the nurse manager

The history of the development of nurse management in the UK is not a particularly smooth or happy one. It is marked by a long period of stability (some would say stagnation), followed by a stage of rapid and fundamental change as frantic attempts were made to make up lost ground.

Traditionally nurse management in this country has taken place at the micro-level. The early days of health care provision reflected a pattern of small local hospital units, each acting independently, and enthusiastically maintaining their separateness and individual identity. The organizational and management structure introduced by Florence Nightingale, in which the matron led the nursing services within the hospital, remained the norm for almost a century. Contrasting the inherent conservatism of the profession with some of the recent rapid changes Smith (1977) remarks, 'No one can deny that we live in a period of rapid change and innovation. Indeed all of us who have received our basic nurse education during the last quarter of the century will have to admit that even in that short space of professional life the changes and innovations have been dramatic. Tuberculosis has been conquered, smallpox has been practically eradicated, cancer can be more speedily diagnosed by EMI scanners and therefore more easily arrested and cured, and people no longer have to die because their kidneys cease to function or indeed because other vital organs such as the heart cease to function. It is therefore inevitable that rapid changes and innovations should have occurred within the nursing profession. In fact, it is really amazing to think that the first system of nursing service organisation existed without change for almost 100 years or so in the UK.'

One can see the influence of this pattern continuing today. In spite of the degree of reorganization and change which has taken place within the NHS, this local perspective continues and permeates management philosophy and practice. As Walton (1984) suggests, 'This tradition of independence is still evident and influences management decision-making at a strategic level. The inception of the NHS threw into sharp relief differences and rivalries between different elements of the health services, and the reorganizations of 1974 and 1982 provided evidence of the continuing importance of the idea of separate local identities. It is important to remember how attached staff became to their own hospitals, authorities, regions, etc., and to take account of it in managerial actions and decision-making.

1948 onwards

With the creation of the NHS in 1948, the matron lost her individual power, and the management of nursing passed to an advisory committee composed largely of lay members. 'As a result the top nursing managers in the UK were in a state of professional limbo for a few years. Disenchantment, concern, frustration and debate were features of the nursing profession for the next decade.' (Smith, 1977)

The Salmon Report of 1966 was a turning point in nurse management as it marked the end of the 'vocational era of nursing' and established the importance of the management function in the professional role. Roles, responsibilities and accountability were perceived and defined in functional terms and delegated authority was to be the means by which to achieve the goals of the organization. The nurse's managerial duties were rationalized and marginal tasks removed in order that the senior nurse might concentrate upon the provision of 'total nursing care', i.e. from policy making to bedside care. The establishment of nursing policy was distinguished from the decisions concerning the programming of that policy, and was reflected in the new managerial structure. Policy makers were designated 'top managers' (Chief Nursing Officer; District Nursing Officer level), those who were concerned with programming this policy were designated 'middle managers' (Nursing Officer level), and those who were responsible for the execution of the programme, first-line managers (Sister and Charge Nurse level). 'Thus conceived, the role of senior nurses could be recognised as vital. Jobs would be reorganised and reassigned, delegation would be properly practised and the contribution of middle management to the common purpose would be seen to be more effective . . . by reason of the importance of the decisiosn taken.' (Webb, 1981). In this way Salmon, using established management theory, proposed a classic 'pyramid structure' in which specialized professional skills could be applied economically and which would, at the same time, offer an attractive career structure to employees.

In spite of Salmon's proposals that a number of pilot schemes should be set up in selected hospitals and the results carefully monitored, the recommendations of the report were used to completely restructure the service. The tripartite system of nurse management, with its accompanying grading system, was introduced nationally on the 1st January, 1969. This hasty and over-enthusiastic implementation carried out before the lessons of the pilot studies could be learned, was seen by Salmon himself as the source of many of the problems which eventually emerged. As an 'imposed' strategy, it was received by the profession with a certain degree of ambivalence, all the more so as it was introduced so quickly and in practice it raised a number of fundamental problems which remain, even today.

Career advancement was seen to lie away from direct patient care towards management and administration (although Salmon envisaged both a 'clinical' and 'management' career path). Consequently, many nurses moving up the career ladder suddenly found themselves faced with duties and responsibilities for which they had received little professional preparation. The provision of adequate training to meet these demands was often minimal. Management courses were provided for each level, but these were of short duration and their quality was often patchy or inappropriate. The profession itself is particularly critical of this lack of preparation. As a Health Authority report comments, 'Nurses attended middle management courses, these were largely theoretical and, by definition, concentrated upon the managerial side of the role. A man or woman is not transformed into an adequate manager by a course of this kind.' (SE Thames RHA, 1976)

Bolger (1985) points to the long-term effect of this lack of management training: 'Most of today's senior managers will have achieved their status in the post-Salmon era. For many, their management development will have been a two or three weeks' first line management course while at sister/charge nurse level, followed by a middle management course of about a month's duration at the nursing officer stage of their careers, finished off by a senior management course once they have reached the dizzy heights of power . . . the scrapping or mutation of many senior nurse posts at district level can be seen as judgement that the nursing profession has not got what it takes when it comes to senior management.'

Reorganization of the NHS

However, the new system was given little opportunity to become established before it was faced with further fundamental changes. In the same year as the introduction of the Salmon Report, the Government published its proposals on the first restructuring of the NHS, which took place in 1974. This was shortly followed by the 1982 reorganization which eliminated the Area tier in the service, and finally in 1983 by the Griffith's Report which led to further change in the overall management structure of the NHS in England.

The effect of change

Leaving the debate concerning the desirability of a restructured health service to one side, the effects of successive legislation following the radical change of nurse management has been to produce a high degree of anxiety and uncertainty at all levels of the profession. 'It seemed that hardly had the new management structure been accepted by the profession than the incumbents of these new roles, and I was one, were immediately faced with the problems of managing fundamental change on a scale rarely seen in this country. Many of us hardly had time to attend our training courses before we were in the thick of it!' (Nursing Officer).

In conclusion, it is suggested that the role of nurse manager can be seen to be particularly challenging because of five main factors:

(1) The potentially stressful nature of the management task itself,
(2) The fact that the majority of senior nurses are in 'middle management' positions, which can be particularly problematic,
(3) The ambivalence shown by the profession to the value of the management task in the delivery of health care,
(4) The paucity of appropriate training for the management role,
(5) The need to cope with rapid organizational change.

THE SURVEY

The present study focuses on the nurse manager for three reasons. First, little if any US or UK research has been carried out on this extremely pivotal group in the health service. Second, because many observers contend that they are the group of nurses most 'at risk'. And, finally, they have been at the 'hard end' of the enormous organizational and structural changes that have taken place in the National Health Service and the various health-providing organizations in North America and Europe.

The main aims of the study are:
(1) To determine the extent of the problem. As we have previously noted in Chapter 3, occupational stress has frequently been cited as a problem by the profession. However, little evidence has been advanced to back up this claim, and for this reason the existing evidence is reviewed to determine whether there is cause for concern.
(2) To locate the sources of occupational stress. The focus here is on determining the sources of stress in the day-to-day work of the 'nurse manager'. The term *nurse manager* is used to refer to nurses having a specific managerial responsibility. In practice, this included all nursing grades, from Sister/Charge Nurse level to Chief Nursing Officer, working in both community and hospital settings.

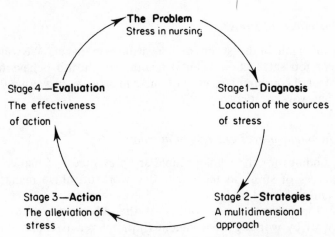

Figure 4.1 Four-stage problem-solving approach to stress management.

(3) To determine the differences in the patterns of stress experienced (1) in different settings, i.e. hospital versus community-based staff, (b) at different grades within the service, i.e. Sister/Charge Nurse level versus Nursing Officer level.
(4) To identify ways in which occupational stress might be allieviated.

A problem-solving approach

Before occupational stress can be successfully alleviated or managed it must be carefully located and identified. Consequently, we see our research as the first stage in a problem-solving process in which data collection and analysis provides the diagnostic evidence on which to base subsequent action. This problem-solving approach to stress management can be represented as the four stages shown in Figure 4.1. In essence this survey represents the first three stages and it addresses the following questions:

What is the extent of the problem?

Chapter 5 examines the existing evidence on the morbidity of nurses and the incidence of absence and wastage within the nursing profession, i.e. the cost of stress in nursing.

Stage 2: diagnosing the problem

Who are the nurse managers?

Chapter 6 provides a comprehensive description of the sample, and includes profiles of the personal, professional and current job details of nurse managers.

What are the effects of stress?

Chapter 7 will highlight the 'strains of being a nurse manager'. We will explore the levels of job satisfaction, mental health, and health behaviours (e.g. smoking, alcohol consumption, etc.) of nurse managers, answering the question, 'in what ways are they at risk'?

What are the main sources of stress in nursing?

The main findings for the whole sample are presented in Chapter 8 where general sources of stress in the day-to-day work of 'nurse managers' are identified and discussed in detail.

Chapter 9 presents 'stress profiles' of the sub-sampler and examines differences, a) by working environment (hospital versus community based nurses); b) by nursing grade (sister/charge nurse level versus senior nurses).

Stage 3: strategies for solving the problem

Where do we go from here?

Using the data from the study, a number of strategies for stress management are examined and discussed in Chapter 10.

REFERENCES

Birch, J. (1979) The anxious learners. *Nurs. Mirror*, Feb. 8.

Bolger, T. (1985) Do not underestimate yourself. *Nurs. Mirror*, May 1, 46.

Clark, J. (1975) *Time Out?—A Study of Absenteeism*. London: Royal College of Nursing.

Cooper, C.L. (1982) *Executive Families Under Stress*. New Jersey: Prentice Hall.

Cooper, C.L. and Marshall, J. (eds) (1980) *White Collar and Professional Stress* Chichester: Wiley.

Cooper, C.L. and Payne, R. (eds) (1978) *Stress at Work*. Chichester: Wiley.

Drucker, P.F. (1977) *Management*. New York: Harper's College Press.

Lunn, J.A. (1975) *The Health of Staff in Hospitals*. London: Heinemann.

Maslach, C. (1982) *Burnout: The Cost of Caring*. New Jersey: Prentice Hall.

Menzies, I.E.P. (1960). A case study in the functioning of social systems as a defence against anxiety. *Hum. Rel.*, **14**: 95–121.

Ministry of Health and Scottish Home and Health Department (1966) *Report on the Committee on Senior Nursing Staff Structure* (Salmon Report) Cmnd., London: HMSO.

Report on the Committee on Nursing (Briggs Report). Cmnd 5115, 972, London: HMSO.

NHS Management Inquiry (1983) *Letter of Report from Roy Griffiths to Norman Fowler*. London: DHSS.

Parkes, K.R. (1980a) Occupational stress among nurses. 1. A comparison of medical and surgical wards. *Nurs. Times*, Oct. 30, 113–116.

SE Thames RHA (1976) *Report of Committee of Enquiry*. Canterbury: St Augustine's Hospital.

Smith, J.P. (1977) A philosophy of change. In Raybold, E. (ed.), *A Guide for Nurse Managers*. Oxford: Blackwell.

Social Services Committee (1984) *Griffiths NHS Management Inquiry Report*. London: HMSO.

Walton, M. (1984) *Management and Managing: A Dynamic Approach*. London: Harper and Row.

Webb, C. (1981) Classification and framing: a sociological analysis of task centred nursing and the nursing process. Unpublished MSc thesis. University of London.

CHAPTER 5

The costs of stress in nursing

It is commonly believed that nursing is a stressful profession. Whilst 'not wishing to belittle the pressures involved, such a statement is open to criticism in that it makes assumptions about the meaning of the experience for nurses, which are seldom tested out by research.' (Marshall, 1980). This raises the question, 'What indications are there, if any, that nursing is a stressful profession?

Is there cause for concern?

Stress at work can be seen as having both positive and negative aspects: whereas a certain amount of pressure may boost our energy, too much pressure may have harmful effects. On this basis, information on the health of workers within particular occupations, especially mortality rates and the associated causes of death, are often taken as indicators of the harmful effects of the job. This occupational mortality rate can be seen as an index of the price paid by the individual for the work he or she does.

Absence and wastage, on the other hand, give some indication of the cost of these harmful effects to the service or industry. Absence and wastage rates are often associated with levels of job satisfaction. It is frequently believed that employees who are highly satisfied with their jobs are equally highly motivated to work. Conversely, low job satisfaction has been equated with high absence and wastage rates. The Office of Health Economics (OHE) found that job satisfaction varies according to an employee's status or position, the general working environment, and the quality of management (OHE, 1981).

This part of the report has two main purposes:

(1) To determine whether or not nurses have cause for concern about the potentially harmful effects of their jobs. This is attempted through a study of the available morbidity statistics for nurses.
(2) To evaluate the available evidence on the incidence and causes of absence and wastage in the nursing profession in the light of the costs of the NHS.

COSTS TO THE NURSE

For many of us work occupies much of our waking lives. It is an important source of satisfaction, self-esteem and status. Equally, a job may be an important contributor to 'life dissatisfaction' and may be detrimental to overall physical and mental well-being. This relationship between occupational stress and the quality of life is a particularly complex one. The researcher must take account of all available indices in order to more fully understand the dynamics at work.

Occupational mortality: an index of stress?

One index of the harmful effects associated with particular jobs is the occupational mortality rate. In the preface to the decennial report on 'occupational mortality' the Registrar General suggests that 'analyses of occupational mortality contribute to our understanding of the underlying causes of these chronic diseases and . . provide the basis for the further research necessary to achieve a safer and healthier environment.' (HMSO, 1970–72).

The changing focus of information associated with occupational mortality tends to reflect changes in environmental conditions. For example, industrialization has been linked with a rise in death rates from accidents and infectious diseases. On the other hand, improvements in sanitation, diet and working conditions have been shown to reduce the importance of these factors as causes of death.

More recently attention has been given to the psychosocial effects of stress and to occupation-related stressors. While the association between mortality and work under physically hazardous conditions is often immediately recognizable, psychosocial relationships are usually less obvious. However, increasingly there is evidence to suggest that stress can and does result in disease, sometimes of a chronic nature, and occasionally in death (Cooper, 1984).

Stress-related illnesses

Selyé identifies some common stress diseases: 'high blood pressure, heart accidents, mental breakdowns, migraines and insomnia' (Selyé, 1980). Bailey (1980) points to 'coronary thrombosis, rheumatoid arthritis, peripheral vascular disease, essential hypertension, and cancer' as representing only a few of the stress-related organic disturbances.

Cooper (1980) states that certain stress-related diseases, in particular coronary heart disease, have shown a steady increase in the UK over the last decade. He also notes that there has been an increase in other possible stress manifestations such as alcoholism, short-term illness and industrial accidents. Furthermore, it seems that the conventional wisdom that stress is a 'male executive' disease is a myth. In fact workers at all levels and of both sexes are vulnerable to the negative manifestations of stress arising from work pressure.

In the following section we will look at the statistical evidence which throws light on the price paid by nurses as compared with workers in other occupations. In addition, we will examine some of the causes which underlie their mortality rate. To do this, it is necessary first to explain briefly some of the terminology used in recording official occupational mortality statistics.

Occupational classification

The Registrar General's classification of occupations identifies 223 occupation units. These combine into 27 occupation orders. The classification 'Nurses' (occupation unit 183), includes 'persons providing or training to provide nursing or midwifery care. Ward orderlies and first aid workers are excluded.' Nurses are grouped with other 'Professional workers' and incorporated into 'occupation order xxv'. This order is a broad one including a wide range of professionals from 'Medical practitioners', 'Dental practitioners', 'Pharmacists', and 'Radiographers' to 'Electrical engineers' and 'Clergy, ministers, members of religious orders'.

Measures of mortality

The standardized mortality ratio (SMR) is a measure of mortality. It is calculated by comparing the observed number of deaths for a particular occupation with the number expected from standard death rates. The figure is expressed as

$$\text{SMR} = \frac{\text{Observed deaths}}{\text{Expected deaths}} \times 100$$

On this basis, an SMR greater than 100 suggests that the particular sub-population under scrutiny has a disproportionally high death rate when compared to the whole population. The reverse is true for an SMR of less than 100. The proportional mortality ratio (PMR) is derived in a similar way to the SMR. But in contrast to the SMR, the PMR only summarizes mortality by cause of death.

Do nurses have a high mortality rate?

A comparison of occupations

The information which follows has been extracted from the OPCS figures for the purpose of comparing the mortality ratio amongst nurses with ratios for workers in other occupations. Some limitations should be mentioned. Firstly, the figures for married women are based on their husband's occupation; this raises problems of interpretation. For this reason the ranking of occupations refs to the mortality ratios for men. Secondly, these figures are derived from the 1971 census information. Although this is the most recent information available, we look forward to the release of the 1981 figures, scheduled for the end of 1986.

However, in spite of these limitations a number of interesting patterns emerge. It is evident from Table 5.1 that the mortality ratio for 'professional workers', the occupation order to which nurses belong is one of the lowest of all occupation orders. As a general rule members of this group are likely to live longer than might be expected from the age-specific death rates for England and Wales. How then do nurses compare with other occupations within this order?

Table 5.1. SMRs by occupation order (highest–lowest).

Occupational order	SMR for men and women aged 15–64			
	Men	Married women	Single women	Rank
Armed forces	147	151	112	1 (highest)
Miners and quarrymen	144	159	–	2
Professional workers	75	81	83	26
Administrators and managers	73	79	59	27 (lowest)

From Table 5.2 it can be seen that nurses, like pharmacists, have a higher mortality ratio than might be expected within the 'professional workers' order. The figures for nurses are all the more striking if they are compared with those for other traditionally 'female' occupations such as 'school teachers', 'social welfare' workers, and 'typists'. As regards the teaching profession, Kyriacou (1980) concludes that overall there is little evidence to indicate that British teachers have a higher incidence of physical or mental ill health compared with

Table 5.2. Shows SMRs by occupation unit within the 'professional workers' order.

		SMR for men and women aged 15–64		
Unit	Occupation	Men	Married women	Single women
181	Medical practitioners	81	92	76
182	Dental practitioners	78	78	68
183	Nurses	112	114	96
184	Pharmacists	116	115	125
185	Radiographers	69	79	95
193	School teachers	66	80	69
215	Social welfare	69	84	76
141	Typists, secretaries, etc.	59	68	86

other occupational groups. Eaton (1980) presents a similar picture for English social workers and concludes that, on the whole, 'English social workers seem slightly healthier than teachers and medical practitioners, and *markedly more so than nurses.*'

The life expectancy figures shown in Table 5.3 appear to confirm this picture. It seems that nurses can expect to live shorter lives than teachers, social workers, and typists as well as doctors, hospital orderlies, and ambulance men.

Table 5.3. Shows life expectation by occupation unit.

Occupation unit	Life expectation at age 45	Number surviving at age 65*
221 Armed forces (UK)	22.0	42 524
007 Coal mine-workers underground	25.9	63 831
097 Bricklayers, etc.	21.3	41 228
155 Barmen, barmaids	26.0	64 148
181 Medical practitioners	27.9	74 109
183 Nurses	26.9	69 657
170 Hospital orderlies: ambulance men	27.3	69 399
193 School teachers	28.8	78 355
215 Social welfare	29.0	79 158
141 Typists, secretaries, etc.	29.3	83 442

* Numbers surviving out of 100 000.

How do nurses die?

Causes of death

The information about causes of death in the nursing profession is presented separately for men and women (Tables 5.4 and 5.5, respectively).

Table 5.4. Causes of death among nurses: men aged 15–64.

Cause of death	SMR	Number of deaths
Diseases of the musculoskeletal system	443	6
Suicide	297	34
Injury undetermined*	341	10

* Whether accidental or purposely inflicted.

Although it can be seen from Table 5.4 that the observed number of deaths from 'diseases of the muscloskeletal system' is comparatively small, the considerably raised SMR ($P<.01$) suggests that male nurses are much more likely to die in this way than members of the general public. Furthermore, the figures for men and women show that nurses rank sixth in the top 20 occupations most likely to suffer from diseases of the musculoskeletal system. At the present time, one can only guess at the physical hazards inherent in the nursing profession which have lead to this state of affairs.

Table 5.5. Causes of death among nurses: women aged 15–64 by own occupation.

Cause of death	PMR	Number of deaths
Fracture of skull, spine and trunk	152	61
Internal injury of chest abdomen and pelvis	160	40
Accidents	183	317
Accidental poisoning	231	24
Injury undertermined*	214	34
Suicide	262	133

* Whether accidental or purposely inflicted.

In another context, nurses rank seventeenth in the top 20 of occupation units with high mortality rates from mental disorders, although the actual number of deaths reported in this category is low. The suggestion that nursing is a mentally as well as physically stressful occupation tends to be sustained by an examination of the figures for suicide and suicide-related causes of death.

Death by suicide

Suicides are often difficult to identify. For a number of reasons such deaths are often recorded among accidental poisonings or among 'open verdicts'. Furthermore, occupations affording access to drugs are found to have high mortality rates from both causes: 'Access to an immediate, simple and painless means of ending life would appear to be one of the most important factors in suicide.' (OPCS, 1978) Amongst nurses, both men and women appear to suffer from abnormally high suicide rates (see Tables 5.4 and 5.5). In particular, the available information regarding the mortality of female workers strongly suggests that *women in the nursing profession are more likely to commit suicide than women in any other occupation!*

To recap, nurses as a group do seem to have a disproportionately high mortality rate compared with a number of other professions and occupations, and especially when compared with other female-dominated professions. By comparison, the number of suicides and suicide-related causes of death is alarmingly high.

COSTS TO THE SERVICE: ABSENCE AND WASTAGE

The costs of absence—a national problem?

In general, the indications are that absence is a widespread and accelerating problem in many occupations. In 1970, the CBI (1970) reported that absenteeism 'has risen alarmingly in recent years in spite of improvements in social and working conditions, income levels, and family health.' During 1978, 9.4 million working days were lost because of industrial disputes. In contrast, there were 371 million days of absence due to certified sickness in 1978/79 (approximately 6 per cent of the potential working days available). This represented an increase of 34 per cent over the figure recorded in 1954/55 (OHE, 1981).

When calculated in cash terms the costs of absence are considerable. In 1978/79 Britain's National Insurance Fund paid out £1479 million in the form of sickness and invalidity benefits. In terms of lost production, the costly figure of £5.5 billion has been estimated. This may be compared with Government expenditure in that year of £7.8 billion on the NHS and £5.4 billion on housing (OHE, 1981).

Absence in the nursing profession

We were surprised to find that no absence figures are available for the nursing profession at a national level. The DHSS (Department of Health and Social Security) calculates an absence rate of around 5 per cent when estimating its nursing budget. However a number of studies suggest that this figure underestimates the true rate of absence (Reader, 1981). Some local indications suggest that 'sickness absence' rates vary from as little as 4 per cent per annum in one hospital (Clarke and Hussey, 1979), to an average weekly rate of 11.84 per cent for a whole district (Reader, 1981). For a number of reasons (largely because of disparities in methods of data collection), it is not possible to generalize on the basis of these figures. However, it is possible to identify *trends* in the incidence of different types of absence.

Short-term versus long-term absence It is useful to distinguish between the effects of short-term and long-term absence. Short-term absence has been associated with more disruptive and costly effects to both industry and the national economy. From the individual's viewpoint, it is long-term rather than short-term absence that is likely to be linked with severest economic hardship. In the workplace, long-term absence can often be dealt with 'by making stable adjustments to the workforce, a strategy which is not realistic in the case of the recurrent but unpredictable nuisance of short-term absence' (Clark, 1975).

There appears to be a national trend towards more frequent but shorter spells of absence (OHE, 1971). This trend is also evident in the nursing profession (Clark, 1975). For example, in a study of sickness and absence amongst nursing staff in psychiatric/mental deficiency hospital group, Cormack (1973) found that over 70 per cent of sickness episodes were of less than eight days' duration. Thirty-six per cent of all sickness episodes were of one day's duration.

It is difficult to calculate the precise costs of absence in the nursing profession. But there is little doubt that 'sickness absence' causes acute difficulties within the NHS, which may ultimately reflect on patient care. Lunn (1975) points out that, 'It is not uncommon for hospitals to have to close some of their wards because of nurse shortages.' These shortages are often attributed directly to sickness absence.

The costs of wastage

Wastage in any occupation represents a loss, the cost of which may be examined at two levels. Too high a level of wastage is likely to 'be prohibitive in terms of recruitment, training, efficiency, quality of patient care, staff morale, etc., which may lead to more wastage. High wastage is disruptive to the work group, which may lack a cohesive and stable core of staff.' (Clark and Redfern, 1978) On the other hand, if wastage levels are too low there can also be a cost. There is a danger that this lack of staff movement 'may lead to stagnation, complacency, and lack of fresh ideas with which to improve the quality of patient care.' Clark and Redfern (1978) see that one of the most difficult but essential tasks of any organization is 'to strike the right balance between high and low levels of wastage.'

Comparisons of wastage figures from different sources are problematic because of the different definitions, measures and methods used. Due to this lack of uniformity, it is difficult, if not impossible, to generalize accurately about wastage rates within the nursing profession. However, a number of general patterns can be seen. One consistent finding has been a higher incidence of wastage amongst 'nurse learners' compared with the available figures for qualified and untrained nurses. Widespread concern with the high rates of drop out during training has stimulated a number of research projects focusing on this problem. Consequently, evidence for student nurse wastage is available over long periods of time. This evidence shows that the rates have actually fallen since 1950. The total training wastage is currently estimated to be some 35 per cent for registered nurses and some 30 per cent for enrolled nurses (although such estimates may vary considerably from one part of the UK to another). The wastage rates for higher education based training were often found to be significantly lower than these figures (Commission on Nursing Education, 1985).

Among trained nurses the information on wastage is less well documented. Again, there is no national source of data which records the numbers of nurses leaving the employment of the NHS. The Royal College of Nursing's recent report on nurse training suggests an overall wastage figure of 10 per cent as being the most reliable estimate for qualified nurses. There is some suggestion that this figure is much higher than certain other female-dominated professions, e.g. teaching and social work (CNE, 1985).

The causes of absence and wastage

Is stress a cause?

The available evidence suggests that sickness absence can only sometimes be seen primarily as a medical phenomenon susceptible to alleviation and control by specifically medical means (OHE, 1971). It is probable that short-term and uncertain absences have a much smaller sickness component than longer absences. Research suggests that, in general, the shorter the absence the less likely is its explanation in strictly medical terms. Similarly, only a small proportion of employees leave their jobs for reasons of ill health alone (OHE, 1971).

Much of the illness resulting in high absence rates is ill-defined and of short duration: 'It is generally agreed that the "medical component" of the spells of incapacity is relatively insignificant.' (OHE, 1981) There appears to have been a shift in the types of illness resulting in short-term absence in this country over the last 20 or 30 years. The incidence of minor psychological illness is on the increase whilst the rates of physical illnesses have remained relatively stable. This can be seen to reflect a growing incidence of stress-related causes of absence.

Stress-related illnesses

An examination of these changing patterns of sickness shows that there have been significant rises in the number of days lost due to stress-related illnesses for the general population. Table 5.6 gives some indication of this and shows substantial increases in relation to the incidence of 'nervousness, ill-defined symptoms, heart disease, hypertension, and mental disorders'.

Table 5.6. Comparisons between 1954/5 and 1978/9, showing the percentage increase in the number of days off due to stress-related illnesses (men only).

Diagnosis	Increase (%)
Nervousness, debility, headache	528
Ill-defined symptoms	101
Psychoneuroses and psychoses	49
Arteriosclerotic and degenerative disease	
Heart disease	134
Other forms of heart disease	38
Hypertensive disease	123

Within nursing, Cormack's (1973) study found that 'diseases of digestive system' and 'symptoms of ill-defined conditions', both conditions which have been found to be stress related, accounted for 52.6 per cent of the total sickness absence. There is growing evidence that clinical anxiety and depression are often a consequence of occupational strain. Both these conditions have been identified as significant factors in accounting for short-term absence among the nursing profession (Reader, 1981).

What other factors are associated with absence and wastage?

Absence patterns

A number of general patterns have been identified from absence statistics. These are evident in Clark's (1975) research into absenteeism among nurses. In this study, which was primarily concerned with identifying factors associated with short-term absence (defined as an absence of one, two, or three days), the distribution of absence was found to be non-random. It was found that:

(1) There was a particularly high incidence of absence on Monday.
(2) Over half of all short-term absence immediately preceded or followed an off-duty period.
(3) Two-thirds of all the short-term absence consisted of one-day absences.

Clark's results also showed that there were three main factors associated with short-term absence:

(1) *Nursing grade.* A tendency for absence to increase as rank decreases was identified. Pupil nurses take short spells of absence more frequently than all other grades of staff. This finding has been confirmed by others (Cormack, 1973; Lunn, 1975; Rushworth, 1975). Clark found that Sisters took significantly fewer short-term absence spells than all other groups.
(2) *Working environment.* Significant differences were found in the number of short-term absence spells observed in each of the five hospitals studied. These differences were not related to hospital size, but may be explained in terms of the quality of the constituent interpersonal relationships. There were also marked differences in terms of the short-term absence behaviour between wards. These differences did not appear to be affected by the speciality of the ward or the physical differences of the ward.
(3) *Job satisfaction.* Clark found that job satisfaction was not a significant predictor of absence behaviour either in isolation or in combination with other factors. However, findings in this area have often been contradictory: for example, Cormack (1973) states that 'Revans has firmly established the relationship between morale and sickness/absence levels in hospitals.'

Finally, Clark (1975) suggests that 'it may be more reasonable to view absence as a reflection of the quality of the relationship between the individual and employing institution.' However, she sees occupational stress as major cause of short-term absence and comments that 'The recognition of a relationship between stress and absence may be a crucial factor in the development of a deeper understanding of absence behaviour. Such an understanding may bring with it a change in conventional attitudes towards absenteeism.'

Wastage patterns

Wastage in the nursing profession has also been shown to vary considerably according to the same three factors:

(1) *Nursing grade.* There are several indications that wastage decreases with the seniority of trained nursing staff. This relationship is not a simple one and is likely to be complicated by family responsibilities and related factors (Lunn 1975). Moores (1983) found that the primary reason for leaving the profession, in a sample of inactive qualified female nurses, was the existence of a young child.

(2) *Working environment.* The research evidence suggests that wastage varies with the type of organization. Within the nursing profession there is some evidence that wastage varies according to hospital size. It seems that this may be a function of communication problems characteristic of large bureaucracies (Clark and Redfern, 1978).

(3) *Job satisfaction.* The relationship between job satisfaction and wastage is complex. In general low job satisfaction has not been consistently related to high levels of wastage. Low levels of job satisfaction have been strongly associated with employees' intention to leave, although in practice actual leaving might be prevented by other factors including family responsibilities and market forces.

CONCLUSIONS

It must be emphasized that because of the paucity of information concerning morbidity, absence, and wastage, conclusions made in this area can only be speculative and must be treated with some caution. However, an analysis of the available data suggests that nurses as an occupational group exhibit a number of patterns which must give rise for concern. Lower life expectancy and high suicide rates are difficult to explain, and several researchers suggest there may be a direct causal link with occupational stress. In addition there are indications that levels of short-term absence and wastage are higher within the nursing profession than in similar occupations. Again, there is growing evidence to suggest that stress, and stress related factors, may be important influences in determining levels of absence and wastage and that these factors may vary according to the type of working environment and the level of nursing grade.

It is obvious that these patterns of morbidity, absence and wastage can be extremely costly to both the individual and to the health service, and that there is an urgent need for more substantial research into this area. It has been stressed that the quality and reliability of the data have been identified as problematic and we reiterate the call made by a number of researchers for a standardized system of data collection to be developed throughout the National Health Service (Clarke and Redfern, 1978).

REFERENCES

Bailey, J.T. (1980) Stress and stress management: an overview. *J. Nurs. Educ.* **19**: 5–7.

Clark, J. (1975) *Time Out?—A Study of Absenteeism.* London: Royal College of Nursing.

Clark, J. and Redfern, S.J. (1978) Absence and wastage in nursing. *Nurs. Times*, April 20.

Clarke, S. and Hussey, D.G. (1979) Sickness absence amongst nursing staff at two hospitals. *J. Soc. Occup. Med.*, **19**: 126–130.

Commission on Nursing Education (The Judge Report) (1985) *The Education of Nurses: A New Dispensation.* London: Royal College of Nursing.

Confederation of British Industries (1970) *Absenteeism: An Analysis of the Problem.* London: Confederation of British Industry.

Cooper, C.L. (1980) Work stress in white- and blue-collar jobs. *Bull. Br. Psychol. Soc.*, **33**: 49–51.

Cooper, C.L. (1984) *Psychosocial Stress in Cancer.* Chichester: Wiley.

Cormack, D. (1973) *Sickness and Absence amongst Nursing Staffs in a Psychiatric / Mental Deficiency Hospital Group.* Dundee: Royal Dundee Liff Hospital.

Eaton, J.W. (1980) Stress in social work practice. In Cooper, C.L. and Marshall, J. (eds), *White Collar and Professional Stress.* Chichester: Wiley.

Kyriacou, C. (1980) Sources of stress amongst British teachers. In Cooper, C.L. and Marshall, J. (eds), *White Collar and Professional Stress.* London: Wiley.

Lunn, J.A. (1975) *The Health of Staff in Hospitals.* London: Heinemann.

Moores, B. (1983) An analysis of the factors which impinge on a nurse's decision to enter, stay in or leave the nursing profession. *J. Adv. Nurs.*, **8**: 227–235.

Office of Health Economics (1971) *Off Sick.* London: HMSO.

Office of Health Economics (1981) Sickness absence—a review. *Briefing*, No. 16. London: HMSO.

Office of Population Census and Surveys (1978) *Occupational Mortality: The Registrar General's Decennial Supplement for England and Wales, 1970–72.* London: HMSO.

Reader, A. (1981) One environment—different sickness rates. *Occup. Health*, Oct.

Rushworth, V. (1975) Not in today: absence survey. *Nurs. Times*, Dec. 11.

Selyé, H. (1980) *Selyé's Guide to Stress Research*, Vol. 1. New York: Van Nostrand.

CHAPTER 6
Investigating stress in nurse managers

METHODS

The main survey took place in a Health Authority in the south-west of England. The aims of the project were set out in a newsletter, which was sent out to all nursing personnel in the Authority. In addition, more than 15 open meetings were held throughout the area to provide further details and answer questions about the project.

Approximately 650 questionnaires were distributed to all staff, from Sister/ Charge Nurse level to District Nursing Officer. A total of 521 questionnaires were returned, an 80 per cent response rate. Six of these were incomplete and the remaining 515 questionnaires were analysed for this report. This was augmented by a number of meetings with groups, and interviews with individuals from Area Health Authorities across the country.

Data collection

The present report is largely based on information drawn from the first two sections of the questionnaire (see Appendix). Section I of the questionnaire explored demographic and job details, e.g. sex, age, marital status, working environment and nursing grade, etc. Section II was concerned with sources of pressure at work (potential stressors). The pool of items included in this section was generated from earlier studies of nursing staff in other Health Authorities. A variety of methods were used to obtain this information, viz. stress diaries, brain-storming sessions, taped interviews, direct observation, etc. This was supplemented by information from existing research findings. The resulting instrument—the Job Stress Questionnaire—was reviewed by a panel of 'experts' for clarity of wording and face validity, yielding the final format consisting of 71 items. Sections III and IV of the questionnaire were concerned with coping behaviour and individual differences.

Data analysis

This consisted of four stages:

(1) The data obtained from the completed questionnaires was translated into numerical form for computation.
(2) The biographical information, from Section I, was analysed in terms of the frequency of response for each category (e.g. *Sex*: females 475, males 40). Using this information it was possible to build up detailed profiles' of the groups under study.
(3) Using the statistical technique of factor analysis the information from Section II—the Job Stress Questionnaire—was reduced, to form a number of identifiable factors.
(4) Comparisons were made between respondents in different work settings (i.e. Hospital versus Community) and at different levels of nursing grade (i.e. Sister/Charge Nurse versus Nursing Officers).
Two-tailed *t*-tests were used to indicate significant differences between the groups. The probability of these differences being due to chance is indicated in parentheses for the relevant stressors. The results of these comparisons between subgroups are discussed in the following chapter.

WHO ARE THE NURSE MANAGERS?

Personal demographics

Sex

It can be seen from Table 6.1 that a total of 475 (92 per cent) females and 40 (8 per cent) males returned the questionnaire. Although it is not possible to make exact comparisons with national figures (as these are expressed in terms of 'whole-time equivalents'), these figures seem to roughly reflect the balance within the profession. In 1982, there were 40 129 male nurses and 416 205 female nurses in the United Kingdom (private communication with DHHS, 12.12.84); this represents a 9–91 per cent division nationally.

Table 6.1. Sex of respondents.

	%	n
Female	92.2	475
Male	7.8	40

Age

It can be seen from the age distribution (Table 6.2) that the overall profile of the sample is skewed towards the higher end of the continuum, with a peak in the 35–39-year age band, and then a gradual decline. As expected, a comparison with the national nurse population shows the group to be older, their more senior grade demanding a number of years of preparatory experience. It seems from the distribution that the careers of these senior nurses effectively commence in the 25–29-year age band. The mean for the whole group was 40, and the majority of respondents fell into the 35–45-year-old category. The pattern observed fits the typical career path of the nurse manager. Entering nurse training immediately after leaving school, she is likely to spend a number of years gaining wider experience as a staff nurse before gaining her post-professional qualifications and being promoted to ward sister in her late twenties.

Table 6.2. Age distribution.

Age range (years)	Sample (% & n)	Percentage of all registered nurses at Sept. 30th (1983)		(1982)
		Female	Male	Female/Male
21–24	1.6 (8)	19.3	4.8	16.7
25–29	9.8 (51)	19.8	17.2	19.3
30–34	16.5 (85)	13.0	22.8	14.7
35–39	20.9 (107)	12.8	18.7	13.9
40–44	18.4 (95)	11.4	11.2	11.4
45–49	13.5 (69)	10.4	9.1	10.2
50–54	12.0 (62)	7.8	7.3	7.7
55–59	7.1 (37)	4.7	5.7	4.9
+60	0.2 (1)	0.8	3.2	1.2

Source: private communication with DHSS 1985.

Country of origin and length of time in the UK

A specific item was included in the questionnaire on national origin, as it was considered that staff born and trained abroad were likely to experience different sources and levels of stress than British nationals trained in this country. In point of fact very few of our respondents, only 6 per cent of the total, fell into this category, and of the 37 who had been born abroad 33 had lived in this country for more than 10 years (Table 6.3). Because of these low numbers further investigation of this group was not pursued.

Marital status

From Table 6.4 we see that 66 per cent (*n* = 341) of our respondents were married, re-married or lived with a partner, and 33 per cent (*n* = 171) were

Table 6.3. Nationality/years in UK.

	%	n
Born in British Isles	93.2	480
Not born in British Isles	6.2	32
Nil response	0.6	3
Length of time resident in this country if born abroad:		
Under 1 year	0.2	1
1–5 years	0.4	2
5–10 years	0.2	1
Over 10 years	6.4	33

single, divorced/separated, a widow or a widower. Thus the majority of nurse managers had domestic commitments to balance against their professional role. Indeed, these figures are likely to be somewhat of an underestimation, as they do not include other forms of family responsibilities, e.g. caring for elderly parents, etc. Unfortunately, it is not possible to compare this distribution with the national pattern within the profession due to the lack of data in this area. However, the overall pattern is similar to that found in Davidson and Cooper's (1983) sample of female executives (see Table 6.4).

Table 6.4. Marital status.

Marital status	%	n	UK female executives* (n=696) %	n
Married	58.3	300	51.6	359
Re-married	5.0	26	4.9	34
Living with partner	2.9	15	8.2	57
Single	24.3	125	24.0	167
Divorced or separated	7.4	38	10.2	71
Widow or widower	1.6	8	1.1	8
Other	0.6	3	0.0	0

* Source: Davidson and Cooper, 1983.

It is interesting to note the general demographic changes in the role of women, and how this is reflected in the predominantly female profession of nursing. Twenty-five years ago only 25 per cent of working women were married, but by 1980 this had increased dramatically to 60 per cent (Cooper and Davidson, 1983). The 1984 DE/OPCS report 'Women and Employment' noted that in the UK 'There has been both an overall rise in levels of women's economic activity and the emergence of a bimodal or two phase work profile. These changes are related and are chiefly accounted for by the dramatic increase in the labour force participation of married women who have in growing numbers returned to the labour market after a period of domestic absence and who have done so after increasingly short absences from the labour market; a feature of most Western industrial societies over the last 30 years.' (Table 6.5) Indeed, Lockwood (1981) notes that the UK leads in this area, and that 'more women who leave the labour force before or during the early years of motherhood re-enter it in Great Britain, than in any other country in Western Europe.'

Table 6.5. Current economic activity of all women except full-time students.

	%
Working full time	35
Working part time	28
Total working	*63*
(Unemployed)	6
Total economically active	*69*

Source: 1980 DE/OPCS Survey.

Since the end of World War II there has been an increasing number of married nurses in practice. This increase has been viewed with a certain degree of ambivalence. It is still true to say that there exists a mythical stereotype of the nurse as someone who has sacrificed marriage and a family of her own in order to totally commit herself to a life of caring for others. A leading nursing academic noted, with some regret, that this change amongst members of the nursing profession was having 'far-reaching effects on both individual career structure and the composition of the profession as a whole. (Baly, 1980)

Dependent children

As well as domestic commitments, it can be seen from Table 6.6 that almost half the sample have dependent children living at home. Again these figures reflect general demographic trends. Data from the General Household Survey show that the number of working mothers increased from 45 per cent to 51 per cent between 1973 and 1980, and in the following year the DE/OPCS Women and Employment Survey found that 52 per cent of all working women had children under the age of 16 (i.e. roughly corresponding to our 'at home' category). It can be seen from Table 6.6 that our results indicate a slightly lower percentage of respondents with dependent children (44 per cent), although this is explained in part by the fact that 9 per cent of our respondents were male. Compared with female executives it seems that nurse managers tend to have a younger family than their peers in commerce and industry.

Table 6.6. Dependent children.

	%	n	UK female executives* (n=696) %	n
Number of children at home				
One child	19.4	100	13.0	90
Two children	18.3	94	15.0	104
Three children	6.2	32	5.0	35
Four or more children	1.2	6	3.2	22
Total	45.1	232	36.2	251
Age of children				
Pre-school age	4.5	23		
School age	21.6	111		
Post-school age	18.4	95		
Other	5.4	28		
Total	49.9	257		

* Source: Davidson and Cooper, 1983.

Level of education

Traditionally, nursing has been seen as a separate and self-contained career path, often attracting candidates in their mid teens. Almost half the sample (47 per cent) had 'O' levels as their highest educational qualification (see Table 6.7). Taking these together with the 21 per cent who had no educational qualifications, we see that the highest education level attained by 68 per cent of the sample was 'O' level. Only 20 per cent of the sample had 'A' levels or any higher educational qualifications. Over 1 in 5 of the sample, therefore, had no formal educational qualifications other than their nursing qualifications.

Table 6.7. Educational level.

Level	(n=696) %	n	UK female executives* %	n
'O' level/equivalent	47.4	244	21.5	149
'A' level/equivalent	13.6	70	14.0	97
Degree/equivalent	1.9	10	31.0	215
Post-graduate diploma	3.1	16	—	—
Higher degree	0.4	2	3.3	23
PhD	0	0	0.6	46
Other	12.4	64	6.6	46
NA	21.0	108	23.1	160

* Source: Davidson and Cooper, 1983.

Although it is true that nationally only 10 per cent of the general population obtain 5 or more 'O' levels, our sample was made up of the top strata of the nursing profession, and it is exceptional to find such a high proportion of middle and top managers without higher educational qualifications. Compared with a national sample of female managers drawn from a variety of occupations, it can be seen that the 'educational profile' falls well below their non-nursing peers, particularly in post-A level studies (see Table 6.7).

However, the majority of our sample (68 per cent) had obtained a post-professional qualification, and it is likely that many of those respondents without educational qualifications would be those who had entered the profession before it was necessary to have obtained a minimum educational level. The General Nursing Council was forced to introduce (as late as 1962) an entrance test for student nurse applications, so that there could be some screening of potential entrants before they started training, since there were no minimum educational requirements at this time. Until that date, the emphasis had been simply on recruitment rather than screening entrants (Baly, 1980).

Traditionally nursing tended to be thought of as a very 'practical' job, demanding little intellectual ability. Lack of formal educational qualifications did not prevent one from being professionally successful and, traditionally, the stereotype of the potential trainee was of a *practical* rather than a *thinking* candidate. Indeed, the Royal College of Nursing makes this very point in the recent proposals for a new form of nurse training. The report team was particularly critical of the message it felt the present system of nurse education relays to the public in general, and to school leavers in particular. 'That crude message is that a typical candidate should be drawn from that restricted band of school pupils clever enough to get give O levels, but not so clever as to do really well at A levels, who should not normally be boys or men . . . who should not be ambitious for a task of anything called higher education and who should be content often to be utilised as "a pair of hands".' (Judge Report, 1985)

Professional demographics

Professional qualifications

Table 6.8 shows the distribution of first and post-professional qualifications. The majority of respondents (74 per cent) had obtained their SRN (now RGN) as their first professional qualification. Two per cent of the sample had obtained an alternative first qualification, (e.g. Fever Nurse Certificate). These respondents and the 7 per cent who had first obtained their ONC are likely to have started their nursing career before they were of an age to start their SRN training.

The majority of our sample (68 per cent) had a post basic qualification making them clinically well trained and qualified. This contrasts strongly with attainments in general education and the level of higher educational qualifications.

Table 6.8. Professional qualifications.

	%	n
Initial		
SRN	74.0	381
ONC	7.0	36
RSCN	4.9	25
RMN	11.8	61
Others	2.3	12
Post		
With	68.5	353
Without	31.5	162

Years in nursing

It is interesting to note that, overall, these figures represent an 'inverted pyramid' (see Table 6.9). This raises an important question concerning career advancement: Is it a result of length of service or ability? In a recent survey of women managers in the UK, it was found that on average women managers had 15.5 years of previous employment (Cooper and Davidson, 1983). Our sample provided an average of about 19 years, which is considerably higher than Cooper and Davidson's national figure.

Table 6.9. Years in nursing.

	%	n
Less than 10	8.5	44
10–15	18.1	93
15–20	20.4	105
20–25	24.5	126
Over 25	28.3	146

Job demographics

Full-time/part-time

The majority of the sample (78 per cent) had full-time contracts with the Health District (see Table 6.10) and this proportion of full- and part-time staff closely reflects recent national figures for nursing staff.

Hours per week worked by part-time staff

Of the 22 per cent ($n=110$) of the total sample who had part-time contracts it was possible to obtain full details of the work patterns of 18 per cent ($n=95$). It

Table 6.10. Showing patterns of work.

	Full-time		Part-time	
	%	n	%	n
Day only	61.0	312	11.0	56
Shift	13.0	65	2.0	11
Nights only	5.0	23	8.0	41
Total	78.0	400	21.0	108

was evident that 20–25 hours per week was the most frequent pattern worked. This was considerably more than the national average. In 1980, the DE/OPCS 'Women and Employment Survey' found that the national average part-time working week was 18.5 hours. This gives some indication of the dependence of the NHS on their part-time staff, particularly within the hospital setting.

Patterns of work

This question confirmed that 78 per cent (n=400) of respondents worked full-time, and that 21 per cent (n=108) worked part-time. A much higher percentage of part-time staff worked night duty (38 per cent), compared with only 6 per cent of full-time staff. There was some indication that this pattern is particularly attractive to those with dependents, as working night duty fits in better with domestic commitments.

Length of service with current employer

Table 6.11 shows that about 70 per cent of respondents had been in their post for at least five years and about 40 per cent for over 10 years. It was further evident that 27 per cent (n=140) of the respondents had not moved from any other authority. Presumably this group were 'home-trained', i.e. they had completed their earlier training within the authority and remained until they took up their present post. This lack of movement can be seen either positively as an indicator of stability, or, more pessimistically, as stagnation. Unfortu-

Table 6.11. Length of service with current employer.

	%	n
< 1 year	6.6	34
1–3 years	12.4	64
3–5 years	10.3	53
5–10 years	30.1	155
> 10 years	38.8	200
Other	1.8	9

nately, it is not possible to obtain any reliable information regarding staff movement at the national level. However, it does raise fundamental questions regarding career advancement, professional development, and programmes of ongoing staff training within the Health Authority.

Reasons for moving to this area

From Table 6.12 we can see that 72 per cent of the whole sample ($n=372$) moved to the district from another area. Almost a quarter of those who had moved had done so as part of a 'positive' career step, to obtain promotion or to obtain better working conditions. However, 35 per cent of those who had moved (one-quarter of the whole sample) had done so because of their partner's work, i.e. mainly for domestic rather than career reasons. This suggests that many respondents who had moved had done so for reasons *other* than to improve their career or professional status. It seems that their career is secondary to that of their partner's. This raises interesting questions as to the level of motivation of this group and the cost to their own career of having to move for their partner's sake. Choosing between one's own career and one's partner's career is likely to become a growing source of conflict since, as already indicated, the number of married women within the profession is increasing.

Table 6.12. Staff moving from other areas.

Reason for moving	%	n
Promotion	11.1	57
Better working conditions	6.4	33
Better living conditions	5.4	28
Partner's work	25.0	129
Others	24.5	126
Total	72.4	373

Working environment

It can be seen from Table 6.13 that 52 per cent of the whole sample were hospital-based staff, and that 37 per cent were based in the community. Five per cent of the sample described themselves as working in central administration and planning (the remaining 6 per cent working in 'other' areas). Nationally, in 1982, there were 11 per cent ($n=48\ 000$) community-based nurses and 89 per cent ($n=407\ 894$) hospital-based nurses (private communication with DHSS. The difference between these figures and those obtained in our sample can be partly accounted for by the fact that the national figures include student nurses within the 'hospital-based' statistics, and our sample was of Sister/ Charge Nurse level and above.

Table 6.13. Working environment.

	%	n
Central administration	4.7	24
Nurse education	6.0	31
Accident/emergency department	3.1	16
Theatres	3.3	17
Out-patient/clinics	1.9	10
Wards/special units	38.4	198
Community-based	36.9	190
Others	5.6	29

Nursing grade

Table 6.14 shows the distribution of the total sample by career grade. Two sub-groups were identified. The first a group of 'first line managers' consisted of 394 staff at Sister/Charge Nurse level. It represents the largest single group in the sample, and includes both hospital and community based nurses. The second group was made up of 80 'Senior Nurses'. A number of levels were represented in this group vis. Clinical Nurse Managers (65), Directors of Nursing or Midwifery Services (10), and District Nursing Officers (5).

Forty-one of the respondents (8 per cent of the total) saw themselves as being on a different grade to those mentioned, and were not included in any subsequent analysis.

Table 6.14. Nursing grade.

	%	n
Sister/Charge Nurse level	76.5	394
'Senior nurses'	15.5	80
Others	8.0	41

Hospital-based staff details of working environment

Table 6.15 shows the distribution of all hospital-based staff by hospital size and specialist function. Because of the low response rate from people working in some specialist units, it was not considered viable to use individual specialist hospital types as a variable for data analysis.

Community-based staff: details of working environment

Table 6.16 gives some indication of the environmental setting of community-based staff. There was some confusion caused by this question; in particular,

Table 6.15. Hospital size and type.

	%	n
Hospital size		
< 100 beds	26.8	138
100–300 beds	7.2	37
> 300 beds	26.2	135
Hospital type		
General	27.6	142
Community (hospital)	7.0	36
Geriatric	10.9	56
Psychiatric	7.2	37
Rheumatoid diseases	1.9	10
Physically handicapped	0.2	1
Mentally handicapped	1.0	5
Other type of hospital	7.8	40
Not applicable	36.5	188

the definition of 'case-load size' proved problematic. For this reason the information on the average case-load of community-based staff is not reported.

Table 6.16. Community-based staff: details of working environment.

Setting	%	n
Rural	23.3	120
Urban	13.4	69

Personality demographics

Type A behaviour

Type A coronary-prone behaviour is made up of a cluster of traits, and is characterized by extremes of competitiveness, impatience, aggressiveness, and feelings of being continuously under pressure from time and from the challenge of responsibility (see Chapter 1).

To assess individual Type A tendency, the Bortner and Rosenman Scale (1967) was used. This is a 14-item scale yielding scores ranging from 14 to 154, the higher scores being indicative of Type A behaviour. With this inventory, one can crudely identify four approximate categories along the Type A continuum: Type A1 (score range 108–154), Type A2 (score range 93–107), Type B3 (score range 64–92), and Type B4 (score range 14–63). Davidson and Cooper (1983) have suggested that it is likely that a normal distribution of Type A scores within the general population is: A1, 10 per cent; A2, 40 per cent; B3,

40 per cent; B4, 10 per cent. Using an adapted version of the scale in a study of 135 UK female executives, it was found that 61.5 per cent of the sample could be classified as Type A: 'The sample contained over twice the proportion of the most extreme Type A1 individuals, who are most at risk in terms of stress-related illness.' (Davidson and Cooper, 1980a) In a later study of almost 700 women managers, Davidson found that they had a significantly higher mean score (81) than their male colleagues (79) (Davidson, 1983).

It can be seen in Table 6.17 that, like female executives, the distribution of Type A scores in the nurse manager sample is also positively skewed towards the higher end of the scale. Although appropriate comparative data are difficult to locate, as most of the research is American-based, by re-scaling the findings from the Davidson and Cooper study some general comparisons between the two patterns of distribution are possible. If these results are compared with Davidson's later findings, it can be seen that (once re-scaled) the mean scores of the two groups are very similar, namely female executives 94.5, nurses 94.4.

Table 6.17. Distribution of Type A scores.

	Female executives ($n=137$) %	Nurses ($n=515$) %
Type A1	21.5	21.2
Type A2	40.0	34.0
Type B3	38.5	41.4
Type B4	0.0	3.1

It is apparent from the data that nurse managers as a group exhibit more Type A traits than the normal population. No doubt this can be accounted for in part by the normal self-selection process noted by several researchers, i.e. that the Type A individual is more likely to be attracted to positions of power and responsibility (Rosenman, 1978). Waldron (1978) found that, like male Type As, high occupational status is related to Type A behaviour, particularly amongst working women in the 40–59 age range. In an earlier study, he suggests that there are indications of a 'filtering-out' process at work, whereby Type B females are more likely to abandon or interrupt their careers before the age of 30 in order to have a family. On the other hand the Type A female tends to persevere with an unbroken career pattern or, if she has children, to return to the workplace much earlier than her Type B colleague. With almost half of the sample with dependent children this filtering process could well apply to the current study and could account, in part, for the high proportion of Type A individuals.

It has been estimated that working women have one-third less free time than housewives (Davidson and Cooper, 1980b). Bearing this in mind it is not suprising that 'time pressures', 'work overload' and 'home/work conflict' are of particular concern to this group, nor that indicators of the cost of stress, in terms of excessive smoking and drinking patterns (not to mention patterns of morbidity), tend to be much higher than in the general population.

Locus of control

The concept of 'locus of control' was first outlined by Rotter (1966) who also developed the original scale of measurement (see Chapter 1). An amended version (17 items) of the Rotter scale was used in this study. The term locus of control literally refers to the 'place' of control. Exponents of the concept maintain that people can be classified along a bipolar continuum (Internal–External). At the Internal end there are people who perceive themselves as being in control of their own actions, i.e. they tend to believe that *they* act upon the world. At the other end of the continuum are the Externals, who perceive their behaviour as being influenced by events outside of their control, i.e. they tend to believe that the *world* acts upon them. Given the same situation, Internals are more confident that they can bring about changes in their environment and in their behaviour, whereas Externals feel comparatively powerless to produce change.

This concept has received a great deal of attention in recent years in a number of areas. Within the field of education, 'internality' has frequently been associated with academic success and greater motivation in achievement (Rotter, 1966). In studies of psychological adjustment and coping abilities Internals have commonly been found to be less anxious and more able to deal with frustration; conversely it seems 'the External is less "psychologically healthy".' (Peck and Whitlow, 1975). A number of studies specifically related to the control of stressful stimuli have suggested that perceived control over a situation (internality) is an advantage in managing environmental stressors (Glass *et al.*, 1969; Greer *et al.*, 1970). Finally within nursing, Parkes (1984) found that Internals reported patterns of coping which were potentially more adaptive than those of Externals.

The distribution of scores for the sample is shown in Figure 6.1; the pattern of scores is fairly normally distributed but with a slight skew in the direction of 'internality'. It seems that the typical Nurse Manager is more likely to have an Internal locus of control, although this tendency is not very marked. Using the full scale, Rotter (1966) has cited norms for a female student population (see Figure 6.2) with which the above findings may be cautiously compared. Allowing for differences in scale, the average scores strongly resemble those in the present study. More recently Parkes (1984) reported a mean locus of control of 12.5 (SD 3.8) for a sample of U.K. female student nurses.

Conclusion

Information from the total sample showed that the group was predominantly female (92 per cent), and had an average age of 40 years. They were more likely to be living with a partner (66 per cent) than living alone, and almost half

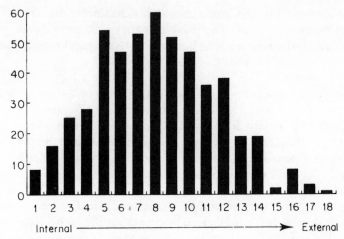

Figure 6.1 Distribution of locus of control scores for nurse managers. Mean = 7.0, SD = 3.6.

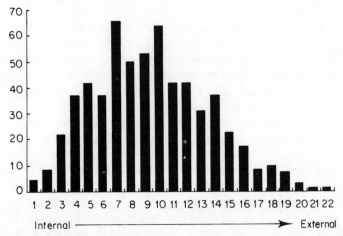

Figure 6.2 Distribution of locus of control scores for female students ($n = 605$). From Rotter (1966). Mean = 8.42, SD = 4.06.

of the group had dependent children (45 per cent). A majority of respondents (74 per cent) had obtained an SRN as their first professional qualification, and almost half of the sample had only GCE 'O' level/CSE as their highest general educational qualification.

The average length of time spent in nursing was between 15 and 20 years. Most of the group (78 per cent) were employed full time, and the majority were at sister/charge nurse level in the professional hierarchy (76.5 per cent). Over half of the respondents (52 per cent) carried out their work in a hospital setting, while 32 per cent described themselves as working in community-based services.

Data from the personality measures indicated that this group of nurse managers exhibited more Type A behaviour than would be expected from the normal population. No doubt this can be accounted for in part by the self-selection process noted by several researchers, i.e. that the Type A individual is more likely to be attracted to positions of power and responsibility (Rosenman, 1978). Measures of locus of control showed that Internal–External orientation was fairly evenly distributed across the sample. As might be expected from senior members of the profession there was a slight skew towards the Internal end of the continuum.

REFERENCES

Baly, M.E. (1980) *Nursing and Social Change.* London: Heinemann.

Bortner, R.W. and Rosenman, R.H. (1967) The measurement of Pattern A behaviour. *J. Chron. Dis.*, **20**: 525–533.

Davidson, M.J. and Cooper, C.L. (1983) *Stress and the Women Manager.* Oxford: Robertson.

Davidson, M.J. and Cooper, C.L. (1980a) The extra pressures on women executives. *Personnel Manager.*, **12**: 48–51.

Davidson, M.J. and Cooper, C.L. (1980b) Type A coronary-prone behaviour and stress in senior female managers and administrators. *J. Occup. Med.*, **22**: 801–805.

Davidson, M. (1983) *Stress in female managers. Unpublished PhD Thesis*, University of Manchester.

Department of Employment/Office of Population Census and Surveys (1984) *Women and Employment: A Lifetime Perspective.* London: HMSO.

Geer, J.H., Davison, G.C. and Gatchel, R.I. (1970) Reduction of stress in humans through nonveridical perceived control of aversive stimulation. *J. Personality Soc. Psychol.*, **16**: 731–738.

General Household Survey (1980) London: HMSO.

General Household Survey (1981) London: HMSO.

Glass, D., Singer, J.E. and Friedman, L.N. (1969) Psychic cost of adaptation to an environmental stressor. *J. Personality Soc. Psychol.*, **12**: 200–210.

Judge, H. (1985) *The Education of Nurses: A New Dispensation.* London: Royal College of Nursing.

Lockwood, B. (1981) Equal Opportunities for Women in Management. *Bus. Grad.*, **1**: 3–4.

Parkes, K.P. (1984) Smoking as a moderator of the relationship between affective state and absence from work. *J. Appl. Psychol.*, **68**: 698–708.

Peck, D. and Whitlow, D. (1975) *Approaches to Personality Theory.* London: Methuen.

Phares, E. (1976) *Locus of Control in Personality.* Morristown, NJ: General Learning Press.

Rosenman, R.H. (1978) The interview method of assessment of the coronary-prone behaviour pattern, in Dembroski *et al.*, (eds), *Coronary-prone Behaviour.* New York: Springer-Verlag.

Rotter, J.B. (1966) Generalized expectations for internal versus external control of reinforcement. *Psychol. Monogr.*, **80**.

Rotter, J.B. (1975) Some problems and misconceptions related to the construct of internal versus external control of reinforcement. *J. Consult. Clin. Psychol.*, **43**: 56–67.

Waldron, I. (1978) Type A behaviour pattern and coronary heart disease in men and women. *Soc. Sci. Med.*, **12b**: 167–170.

CHAPTER 7

Responses to the task of nurse management

Chapter 6 focused on an examination of the individual attributes of the nurse manager, and in particular upon her background and personality. The aim of this chapter is to supplement and complement this profile by the addition of another element in the model of stress which guided our research. Here we focus upon a further aspect of the person–environment fit by looking in some detail at the reactions of the individual nurse manager to pressure, how it affects her, how she responds, and how she attempts to cope with it. To achieve this, details of job satisfaction, absence patterns and mental health were obtained from the group. These were supplemented by information on personal 'reaction styles' to pressure, the extent of the support network available to the individual, and methods of coping and relaxation.

JOB SATISFACTION

Three aspects of individual job satisfaction were explored:

(1) the level of general job satisfaction,
(2) the degree of satisfaction with the present job, and
(3) the strength of commitment to nursing as a career.

A six-item inventory was used to assess job satisfaction. Each item was rated by means of a five-point scale. Scores on the inventory ranged from 6 to 30, the *lower* scores indicating *higher* job satisfaction. The mean score for the total sample on this measure was 13.94 (SD 4.1), which is well below the mid-point of 18 suggesting a relatively optimistic picture.

As can be seen from Table 7.1, overall there appears to be a high degree of job satisfaction. Over 68 per cent reported that they were satisfied or very satisfied with their work, although the majority also felt that their conditions could be improved. On the other hand, some 17 per cent were dissatisfied with their jobs and a further 15 per cent were undecided. It is also apparent from

Table 7.1. Job satisfaction.

Response	%	n
Satisfied	67.6	348
Dissatisfied	17.1	77
Conditions could be improved	86.6	446
Frequently thinking of changing		
(a) Job	20.8	107
(b) Profession	16.3	84

Table 7.1 that although most nurse managers were content in their job over one-fifth of the total sample were dissatisfied in their present post and were considering a change. The commitment by the majority of the sample to the profession was high, although around 16 per cent of the total sample appeared to be having serious thoughts about changing their profession. With nearly one in six of the more senior and experienced nurses thinking of leaving the profession, this must raise questions about the implications for morale.

ABSENCE

As suggested in Chapter 5, absence is often used as a general indicator of occupational stress. As it proved impractical to obtain absence records for the group over the previous year, an indication of absence levels was obtained by the inclusion of a self-report question. The overall results in Table 7.2 show that self-reported absence was low for the whole sample, with an individual average of only 6.5 days per annum. It can be seen that almost 88 per cent of the sample had 10 or less days absence per year, and only 7 per cent had absences which exceeded 21 days. This picture corresponds with the frequent finding that absence rates tend to be relatively low amongst more senior staff (see Chapter 5).

Table 7.2. Absence.

Number of days	n	%
0	219	42.52
<5	183	35.53
5–10	50	9.70
11–20	25	4.85
21–30	16	3.10
31–40	12	2.33
41–100	10	1.94
+ 100	4	0.77

MENTAL WELL-BEING

To obtain an overall measure of mental well-being, the Crown–Crisp Experiential Inventory was used. This is a 48-item questionnaire designed to give an overall measure of 'general emotionality or neuroticism'. It is made up of six subscales, each of which assess a specific area of behaviour:

1. Free floating anxiety (FFA).
2. Phobic anxiety (PHO).
3. Obsessionality (OBS).
4. Somatic concomitants of anxiety (SOM).
5. Depression (DEP).
6. Hysterical personality (HYS).

Using mean scores obtained from a sample of over 300 females (Crisp *et al.*, 1978b), a number of general observations concerning the profiles of the nurse manager group on each of the subscales can be made, although it is not possible to assume statistical significance (see Table 7.3). The nurse managers seem to differ from the general female population on three of the Crown–Crisp subscales; the general directions are indicated in Table 7.4.

Table 7.3. Scores on the Crown–Crisp experimental index (CCEI) showing mean (and standard deviation).

Subscale	General population*	Nurses
FFA	5.33	5.03
	(3.97)	(3.36)
PHO	4.76	3.52
	(3.15)	(2.54)
OBS	7.10	5.48
	(3.10)	(2.90)
SOM	4.86	3.43
	(3.28)	(2.61)
DEP	3.77	3.68
	(2.75)	(2.52)
HYS	3.36	4.77
	(3.00)	(3.21)
Total mean score	29.18	25.91
		(10.92)

* Crisp *et al.*, 1978b.

Obsessional

It might have been expected that a group of nurse managers would score more

Table 7.4. Differences from general female population.

Subscale	Direction
Obsessional	−
Somatic	−
Hysteria	+

highly than the general population on a subscale which meausures 'excessive meticulousness, adherence to routine, punctuality, dislike of sudden change, a tendency to overcheck', etc. (Crown and Crisp, 1979). However, this was not the case. Perhaps these professional 'characteristics' are a manifestation of organizational constraints rather than the product of personal obsessiveness.

Somatic

The somatic elements of neuroticism include 'breathlessness, headaches, other aches and pains'. The CCEI asks questions about dizziness, shortness of breath, digestive problems, physical sensations, appetite changes, tiredness and exhaustion, sweating and palpitations, and alteration of sexual interest. Overall it can be seen from Table 7.3 that nurse managers suffer less from somatic symptoms than the general female population. Perhaps the nature of their work, with its day-to-day exposure to serious levels of illness lead them to be more realistic about their own state of health.

Hysteria / extraversion

The definition of hysteria used by Crisp follows that used in the Glossary of Mental Disorders (1968): 'individuals with shallow, labile affectivity, and over-dependence on others. These individuals crave love and attention, though being unreliable and unsteady in their personal relationships. Under stress they may develop hysterical symptoms. They tend to over-dramatise situations.' It has been suggested (Crockett, 1979) that this subscale may be more a measure of extraversion than of hysteria. Indeed Eysenck and Eysenck (1963) suggest that extraversion has a dual nature and is composed of 'sociability' and 'impulsiveness'. The authors of the scale concede that 'certainly the items comprising the Hysteria sub-scale seem to be related to sociability . . . and . . . it seems reasonable to regard it as a measure of extraversion.' (Crown and Crisp, 1979) It can be seen from Table 7.3 that nurses score much higher on this dimension. Could this be a personality trait which explains why individuals are drawn in the first place towards a career in the 'caring professions'? As stated previously, nursing tends to attract the more stable, extravert type (Parkes, 1980a).

COPING BEHAVIOUR

We suggested in Chapter 1 that the ability to cope with the demands arising from the environment was a crucial factor in determining the levels of stress experienced by the individual. A number of measures were used to obtain data on how the group reacted and coped with the pressures of their task.

Responses to stress

Respondents were asked to recall a recent stressful situation at work and to indicate on a 12-item inventory how frequently they used particular strategies to help them cope (scores on each item ranged from 1—Never to 5—Always). By far the most popular coping mechanism was the logical process of 'taking one step at a time' when faced with a stressful situation. This was used by 63 per cent of the whole sample (see Table 7.5). Ranking second was talking to someone in the workplace. This could be either simply to ventilate feelings, or more specifically to enlist help in the solution of the problem. Of almost equal importance, though presumably used by a different section of the sample, was the seemingly opposite response of keeping feelings internalized. The next most popular response, continuing as if nothing had happened, was used by 28 per cent of the group.

Table 7.5. Responses to stress.

Often/always	%	n
Just concentrated on the next step	63.3	326
Talked to someone	46.8	241
Kept my feelings to myself	40.6	209
Talked to someone who could do something	36.9	190
Went on as if nothing had happened	28.0	144
Let my feelings out	26.8	138
Wished I could have changed what happened	24.2	125
Didn't let it get to me	18.4	95
Blamed myself	17.5	89
Got mad at people/things	15.0	77
Went over the problem in my mind	11.5	59
Avoided being with people	4.9	25

Patterns of response

The results shown in Table 7.5 suggest that there may be a number of 'coping strategies' employed by members of the sample. Consequently, this data was factor analysed in order to identify these underlying patterns. From this analysis a number of relatively independent factors were located made up of a cluster of elements. These were taken as representing four alternative coping styles.

(1) *Regretting*. This factor consisted of responses to a group of three questions in which the person,
    (i) 'Blamed myself',
    (ii) 'Wished I could have changed what happened'.
    (iii) 'Went over the problem in my mind'.

Individuals whose scores were high on the first two questions and low on the third were seen as employing a typical 'regret' response. In this response it seems that, although the problem is acknowledged, feelings about the situation and the inability to cope are kept within the person and there is an acceptance of some degree of individual responsibility or guilt.

(2) *Support seeking*. Two elements were identified within this area,
    (i) 'Talked to someone about how I was feeling'.
    (ii) 'Talked to someone who could do something about the situation'.

In this response the individual is more likely to externalize the problem and to take action by sharing the dilemma with a friend or colleague and/or seek help from another person.

(3) *Denying*. This style is composed of two related responses in which the individual,
    (i) 'Didn't let it get to me'.
    (ii) 'Went on as if nothing had happened'.

It can be seen that in this case the individual copes defensively by ignoring or denying that a problem exists.

(4) *Reacting*. Again this is a factor which is made up of two responses in which the individual typically reacts to pressure by,
    (i) 'Getting mad at people or things'.
    (ii) 'Letting my feelings out'.

In many ways this seems to be a completely opposite reaction to that used by the 'denyer'. Here the individual copes with stress by a reactive style in which emotions are often heightened and externalized.

Methods of coping and relaxation

An 11-item section of the questionnaire explored specific methods used by the group as aides to relaxation and coping. The most popular method of relaxing identified involved the support of other colleagues. Sessions during the working day in which they could 'let off steam or have a good moan with people I can talk to' seemed particularly important (see Table 7.6). The use of humour, often black and usually directed towards self though occasionally towards patients, was also seen as important by respondents. This was highlighted by individuals during the preliminary interview phase. Perhaps not unexpectedly nurses seemed more 'health aware' than the general population and were likely to use exercise as a form of relaxation. Indeed, for a small group of enthusiasts (5 per cent of the total) exercise provided their prime relaxation method. Its popularity may be explained to some degree by opportunity as it was noticed that a number of hospitals had well-publicized 'keep fit' programmes. It can be seen from Table 7.6 that the least popular methods appeared to be the use of formal relaxation methods, i.e. meditation, yoga, etc., and the use of medication such as tranquilizers, aspirin, etc.

Table 7.6. Methods of relaxation.

Often/always	%	n
Talk to others	52.4	270
Use humour	51.0	263
Drink coffee, tea or coke	31.1	160
Exercise	27.5	142
Smoke	17.6	91
Relaxation techniques (informal)	10.5	54
Drink	9.7	50
Leave the work area	9.5	49
Relaxation techniques (formal)	5.1	26
Use tranquillizers	1.8	9
Take aspirin	1.2	6

Table 7.7. Support.

	n	%
Partner	309	59.8
Friend at work	307	59.6
Friend	284	55.1
Mother	110	24.4
Relative	99	19.2
Daughter	71	13.8
Father	63	12.2
Son	43	8.3
Others	31	6.0

Support

A number of researchers have pointed to the importance of a 'support network' in enabling the individual to cope with stress (Winnubst *et al.*, 1982). Consequently it was seen as important to obtain an indication of where the nurse manager obtained her main support. From the responses to the relevant questionnaire items, it can be seen that almost all of the 66 per cent who were married or living with someone, saw their partner as providing their first line of support in a time of crisis (see Table 7.7). The second most important support group consisted of friends, both working colleagues and those outside of the work situation. Finally, a large proportion of the sample, almost 25 per cent, saw the support provided by their mother as being of particular importance. Interestingly it seemed that daughters, fathers and sons were used least by members of this group.

SMOKING AND DRINKING

The harmful effects of a psychological dependency upon smoking and drinking as a means of coping are well documented and it was decided to explore this aspect in a separate and more detailed analysis. High levels of smoking are not only associated with increased incidence of physical diseases such as bronchial complaints, lung cancer, hypertension, and coronary heart disease, but also with high levels of neurosis and anxiety (McCrea *et al.*, 1978). 'It has been calculated that the social cost to the nation due to alcohol misuse is in excess of £1500 million per year, and estimates for the proportion of people suffering from drinking problems vary from 1 per cent to 5 per cent of the population . . . The problems which have been associated with heavy drinking include the loss of jobs, cirrhosis of the liver, suicide, marriage breakdown, child abuse, and accidents at home or work.' (SAUS, 1985)

High levels of smoking and drinking are evidently more common in stressful occupations (Selyé, 1976; Margolis *et al.*, 1974). A major study of over 35 000 UK nurses found that smoking, together with alcohol and caffeine intake, were the most commonly identified ways of coping with stress (Hawkins *et al.*, 1983). Here we report on the smoking and drinking habits of our sample and compare them with the wider population.

Smoking habits

National trends

The decline in the popularity of smoking has been one of striking features of population trends over recent years. This decline is detailed in the 1982 General Household Survey which shows how smoking rates have decreased dramatically between 1972 and 1982, leaving smokers as a minority in all social groups. Overall the rate of cigarette smoking has fallen from 53 per cent to 38 per cent among men and from 41 per cent to 33 per cent among women.

Smoking in nurse managers

In Section III of the questionnaire we asked our sample four questions concerning their smoking habits: namely, the use of smoking as a means of relaxation (Q. 4); if they smoked or not (Q. 15); the number of cigarettes smoked per day (Q. 16); and the increase/decrease in consumption over the past year (Q. 17). The results are summarized in Tables 7.8–7.11.

Table 7.8. Smoking as a means of relaxation.

	%	n
Non-smokers	73.0	376
Smokers	27.0	139

Table 7.9. Numbers of cigarettes smoked.

	%	n
Quantity per day		
< 10	5.8	30
10–20	12.5	64
20–30	3.5	18
> 30	1.0	5
Total smokers	22.8	117
(Total non-smokers)	(77.3)	(398)

Table 7.10. Patterns of smoking.

Patterns of smoking over last year	%	n
Increased	4.7	24
Same	14.4	74
Decreased	4.1	21
Stopped	1.2	6
N/A	75.7	390

It seems that the nurses in our sample are less likely to smoke than are women in general, i.e. 27 per cent of nurses against 33 per cent of the general population. But comparative figures suggest that they smoke more than other female professionals (Davidson and Cooper, 1983). However, these figures may be an under-estimation as psychiatric nurses (who are more likely to smoke) are under-represented in our sample due to their low response rate. It is interesting to note that our figures varied to some degree, showing some internal inconsistencies. While 27 per cent of our sample stated that they smoked to help them relax (Table 7.8) only 22.8 per cent considered themselves as smokers (Table 7.9). It seems that some 'non-smokers' do occasionally smoke in order to relax! This suggests that a certain amount of denial about smoking may exist and that our figures may err on the conservative side. Perhaps this pattern of response is to be expected in a profession which is primarily concerned with health care.

These figures compare favourably with a recent nationwide survey into smoking and stress among nurses. Hawkins (1983) and his colleagues at the University of Surrey found that the incidence of smoking amongst nurses in his large national sample of nurses was 33.6 per cent. A comparison with similar social groups suggested that nurses do not smoke more than a matched sample from the general population.

Hospital versus community staff

Comparing the smoking habits of hospital-based nurses with those of community nurses revealed marked differences between the two groups. Table 7.11 shows that hospital staff were not only more likely to smoke ($P<0.002$), but that they were likely to smoke more heavily than their community-based colleagues $P<0.000$). This reflects the pattern of cigarette consumption found by Hawkins. He noted that 'community nurses in general, and health visitors in particular, show a very low incidence of smoking.' In this context, it is notable that the community staff in our sample were more likely to have decreased the quantity of cigarettes smoked over the past year ($P<0.006$). Again this is a pattern similar to that found by Hawkins in his national survey (Hawkins *et al.*, 1983).

Table 7.11. Smoking habits of hospital and community staff.

	Hospital n (%)	Community n (%)
Non-smokers	189 (70)	153 (80)
Smokers		
Rarely	6 (2)	9 (5)
Sometimes	13 (5)	9 (5)
Often	33 (12)	9 (5)
Always	31 (11)	10 (5)

Drinking habits

It is estimated that there are 40 000 alcoholic nurses in the United States. This represents 1 to 2 per cent of practicing nurses. The rate of narcotic addiction among nurses closely parallels that among physicians—their rate is 30 to 100 times greater than in the general population. The population equivalent of ten nursing schools and three medical schools is lost each year to narcotics addiction.' (Lachman, p. 69)

Although the problem of alcohol and drug abuse in this country has not reached the same proportions as in the USA there is growing apprehension that nurses are increasingly at risk. Recent evidence of increases in the use of hard drugs in the general population and the growing rate of alcoholism within the female population makes this a current cause for concern. Although the questionnaire format is limited in scope and is not the ideal method of enquiry for such a complex and emotive subject, the results that emerged indicated that there could well be a problem which deserves further and more specific investigation.

Comparisons with national trends

Three questions were included in Section III of the questionnaire regarding drinking habits:

1. whether alcohol was used as a means of relaxation,
2. the quantity of alcohol consumed, and
3. if there had been an increase or decrease in this pattern over the past year.

Table 7.12. Alcohol consumption in units*.

Amount	%	n
Teetotal	8.3	43
Occasional	52.6	271
Several units per week	30.5	157
Daily 1–2 units	6.4	33
Daily 3+ units	1.6	8
No response	0.6	3

* One unit is equivalent to one half pint of beer/single spirit/one glass of wine. In 1980, the OPCS gave 7.25 units of alcohols as the average weekly consumption for women between the ages of 35 and 54 years.

The findings are summarized in Tables 7.12–7.15. It can be seen that the large majority (92 per cent) of our sample used alcohol to some extent and only 8 per cent were teetotal. Reliable data concerning national patterns of alcohol consumption are difficult to locate and so comparisons must be made with some caution. However, use of available data on national drinking patterns amongst the female population reveals a number of interesting patterns.

In Table 7.13, data collected by the British Market Research Bureau (from 1973) (the Target Group Index, TGI) is presented alongside the results for the nurse manager group. Comparing the frequencies from both sources there is evidently a close correspondence between the categories 'teetotal', 'occasional' and 'several per week'. At the upper end of the continuum the difference is more marked. Whereas national figures indicate that only 4.8 per cent of the female population drink daily, our findings suggest that the incidence of daily drinking is much greater in the nurse manager sample; in fact, it is almost double at 8 per cent. Even when taking into account that our sample includes a small percentage of males (9 per cent), who often show a higher incidence of daily drinking, this still seems to be a substantial difference.

Table 7.13. Alcohol consumption: comparison with national trends.

	Nurse managers		All females (TGI)*
	%	n	%
Teetotal	8.3	43	9.0
Occasional	52.6	271	53.0
Several per week	30.5	157	33.6
Daily	8.0	41	4.8

* Source: British Market Research Bureau (1973)

Table 7.14 Trends in drinking.

	%	n
Increased	7.8	40
Remained same	71.1	366
Decreased	12.6	65
Stopped	0.4	2

Over 52 per cent of our sample identified alcohol consumption as a regular means of relaxation. It seems their drinking habits have remained relatively stable over the past year (Table 7.14). In the wider context it is relevant to note that alcoholism and alcohol abuse is becoming a particularly serious problem amongst women. The DHSS discussion document, 'Drinking Sensibly', highlighting this comments that, 'Alcoholism counselling agencies report an increasing number of women, especially young women, are asking for help. One in 2.4 of all the applicants at local councils for alcoholism in England and Wales in 1980/81 were women compared to one in 4 in 1974.' (p. 24) A recent national survey found that the two factors most commonly associated with women drinking heavily were 'being at work' and 'not having dependent children'. Social class, on the other hand, was not found to be related to the average consumption of women drinkers (OPCS, 1980).

Alcohol abuse has become cause of growing concern within the profession and it has been suggested that nurses are a 'high risk group'. A recent article in the nursing press drew attention to the fact that a growing number of nursing staff are frequently presenting themselves to treatment centres to seek help with their drinking problems (Booth, 1985). The same article suggests that vulnerability to alcohol misuse within the nursing profession appears to be related to a number of occupational influences. These have been identified by nurse managers as including, 'Too much or too little stress at work, shift work, peer group pressures on learners, the stress of staff shortages, the proximity of staff clubs and, interestingly, the number of functions attended by nurse managers where alcohol was available.' (Booth, 1985)

Safety limits

Although there is agreement that heavy users of alcohol run a high risk of health problems, the question frequently asked is how much can one habitually drink without provoking chronic malaise. A satisfactory answer is of particular importance to any campaign of alleviation or prevention which needs to be able to give realistic guidelines for healthy drinking habits. Anderson (1985) found that estimating the safe upper limits of drinking was as much 'a matter of intuition as of science'. Consequently, estimates vary, sometimes considerably. Anderson's own opinion is along the same lines as the limits recommended by the Health Education Council in their publication 'That's the Limit'. They make three points:

1. Drinking up to 20 units a week for men and 13 for women carries no long-term risk.
2. There is unlikely to be any long-term health damage between 21–36 units for men and 14–24 units for women.
3. Beyond 36 units a week for men and 24 for women, one is creeping up to levels where damage to health is likely.

In our sample, 66 of the nurses (6.4 per cent) regularly consumed 7–14 drinks per week, while 8 nurses (1.6 per cent) drank between 21–42 units per week. On the basis of these figures it seems safe to conclude that some nurses are putting their health at risk through their drinking habits. When one also considers that regular drinkers typically underestimate or under-report their actual consumption then this problem may be more serious than our figures indicate.

Nursing Officers versus Sisters / Charge Nurses

There was some indication that those at Nursing Officer level were likely to drink more heavily than the Sister/Charge Nurses (although this difference did not reach significance level, $P<0.064$). Table 7.15 shows that the differences were most marked in the frequent drinking categories, with some 18 per cent of Nursing Officers drinking daily compared with 5 per cent of Sister/Charges. US research suggests that nurses with a tendency towards heavy drinking patterns '. . . far from being "bad apples" of the profession are more likely to be outstanding, achievement oriented nurses.' (Green, 1984)

Table 7.15. Drinking habits of Nursing Officers and Sisters/Charge Nurses.

Amount	Nursing Officers n (%)	Sisters/ Charge Nurses n (%)
Teetotal	6 (7)	38 (10)
Occasional	41 (51)	211 (54)
Several units per week	19 (24)	124 (31)
1–2 units daily	12 (15)	16 (4)
+3 units daily	2 (3)	5 (1)

SUMMARY AND CONCLUSIONS

Job satisfaction and absence

Overall, these findings suggest a relatively optimistic picture with the large majority of our group of nurse managers indicating high levels of job satisfaction. Absence levels were low; a similar pattern has been found in other studies of the profession (Clark, 1975). The more pessimistic side of this picture is of a smaller, but significant, number of nurses (some 16 per cent), who represent a potential loss to the profession. This figure is considerably higher than the 10 per cent overall wastage figure for trained staff suggested in the Judge Report (1985), and represents a potentially serious threat both to nursing and to the NHS.

Mental health

The results of the Crown–Crisp Inventory suggests that our sample was in good mental health. It seems that the nurse manager has a lower level of general neuroticism than the normal female, and it can be seen from Table 7.4 that she is likely to score close to the norm on measures of anxiety, phobia and depression. She is likely to be less obsessional in her behaviour than the norm, and to suffer less anxiety from somatic sources. Finally, it seems that nurse managers are likely to be more extraverted than females in the general population.

Coping behaviour

Responses

The most common response to pressure was to concentrate on the immediate problem by taking one step at a time. This may have implications for long-term planning and reinforces the view that the typical nurse manager often spends her time 'fighting fires' rather than working to a plan (see Chapter 8).

Four coping styles were identified which suggests that individuals have characteristic patterns of responding to stressful situations. They were:
(1) Regretting
(2) Support-seeking
(3) Denying
(4) Reacting.

Relaxation

Typically the nurses in our sample relieved their tensions by ventilating their grievances in some way: Talking to others and the use of humour were popular means. Over a quarter of the sample exercised regularly. The use of relaxation techniques such as yoga and the use of medication were the least popular methods of relaxation.

Support

For the majority of our respondents, home appeared to be a very important source of support in dealing with the pressures arising from the work situation. There are two immediate implications. On the positive side, the potential value of this support should be recognized and utilized where appropriate. On the negative side, as we will see in the following chapter, stress can be engendered when home and work demands conflict.

Smoking and drinking

Although the nurses in our sample do not appear to be more likely to smoke than women in general, there is little cause for optimism. At least one-quarter of all the sample are smokers. Patterns of smoking (Table 7.2) appear to have remained relatively static, unlike the national trend which shows a rapidly decreasing level of consumption.

The pattern of drinking habits identified shows that alcohol is used by the large majority of nurses in our sample. There is some indication that a proportion of the sample shows a higher than average incidence of daily drinking and that for some individual nurses the level of alcohol consumed seems likely to endanger their health.

Overall, our findings suggest that a small percentage of nurses may be risking their health as a consequence of their smoking and drinking habits. We feel that this percentage is likely to be an under-estimate of the true figure and given their role as 'health educators' these patterns must give cause for concern. We see the need for a more careful and detailed examination of the extent of the problem so that a more comprehensive and reliable picture can be obtained of the national situation.

Conclusion

It seems that nurse managers are job satisfied, reasonably mentally healthy and report low levels of absence. Yet nurse managers themselves suggest they are under enormous pressures, which affect their daily well-being and health. Indeed, the data on mortality and longevity seem to indicate that nurses are a 'high risk' group. It is more than likely that the unremitting pressures take their toll on physical health by a slow process of attrition, eating away gradually at the physical resistance of the nurse. At the same time, commitment to the profession and high levels of job satisfaction may mask the more negative effects of occupational stress.

REFERENCES

Anderson, P. (1985) What's the limit. *Alcohol Concern*, **1**.

Booth, P. (1985) Back on the rails. *Nurs. Times*, Aug. 28, 16–17.

Clark, J. (1975) *Time Out?—A Study of Absenteeism*. London: Royal College of Nursing.

Cockett, R. (1969) A short diagnostic self-rating scale in the pre-adult remand setting. *Br. J. Psychiatr.*, **115**: 1141–1150.

Crown, S. and Crisp, A.H. (1979) *Manual of the Crown–Crisp Experiential Index*. London: Hodder and Stoughton.

Crisp, A.H., Ralph, P.C., McGuinness, B. and Harris, G. (1978) Psychoneurotic profiles in the adult population. *Br. J. Med. Psychol.*, **51**: 293–301.

Davidson, M.J. and Cooper, C.L. (1983). *Stress and the Woman Manager*. Oxford: Robertson.

DHSS (1981) Drinking Sensibly. London: HMSO.

Eysenck, S.B.G. and Eysenck, H.J. (1963) On the dual nature of extroversion. *Br. J. Soc. Clin. Psychol.*, **2**: 46–55.

General Household Survey (1982) London: HMSO.

Green, P. (1984) The impaired nurse: chemical dependency. *J. Emergency Nurs.*, **10**: Jan./Feb.

Hawkins, L., White, M. and Morris, L. (1983) Smoking, stress and nurses. *Nurs. Mirror*, Oct. 13.

Herzberg, F., Mausner, B. and Snyderman, B.B. (1959) *The Motivation to Work*, 2nd edition. New York: Wiley.

Judge, H. (1985) *The Education of Nurses: A New Dispensation*. London: Royal College of Nursing.

Lachman, V.D. (1983) *Stress Management: A Manual for Nurses.* New York: Grune and Stratton.

McCrae, R.R., Costa, P.T. and Bosse, R. (1978) Anxiety, extroversion and smoking. *Br. J. Soc. Clin. Psychol.*, **17**: 269–273.

Margolis, B.L. and Kroes, W.H. (1974) Work and health of man. In O'Toole, J. (ed.), *Work and the Quality of Life*, Cambridge, Mass. MIT Press.

OPCS Social Survey Division (1980) *Drinking in England and Wales.* London: HMSO.

Parkes, K.R. (1980a) Occupational stress among nurses. 1. A comparison of medical and surgical wards. *Nurs. Times*, Oct. 30, 113–116.

Parkes, K.R. (1980b) Occupational stress among nurses. 2. A comparison of male and female wards. *Nurs. Times*, Nov. 6, 117–119.

SAUS (School for Advanced Urban Studies) (1985) *Alcohol Education Programme: Regional Profile.* Bristol: University of Bristol.

Selyé, H. (1976) *Stress in Health and Disease.* London: Butterworth.

Target Group Index (Volumes from 1973) London: British Market Research Bureau.

Winnubst, J.A., Marcelissen, F.H.G. and Kleber, R.J. (1982) Effects of social support in the stressor–strain relationship: a Dutch sample. *Soc. Sci. Med.*, **16**: 475–482.

CHAPTER 8

The sources of stress among nurse managers

Nursing possesses a unique pattern of stress. The strains rooted in the conflicts of the changing role of women, the pressures for cost-effectiveness in health care, and disagreements on what the nurse does all result in a unique pattern of job stress. Nurses, while exerting their own expertise and independence, have to deal with others who expect them to do what they are told. They are expected to get more work done, more efficiently, and often with less staff in order to reduce the cost of health care. Finally, nurses must deal with the role conflicts engendered by others' expectations, since there is wide diversity of opinion within and without the nursing profession as to what the nurse should do.' (Johnson 1983)

In our study, computer analysis of the data identified eleven separate factors. These factors were grouped together to form nine areas or broad sources of stress, which overlapped with Cooper and Marshall's six-factor model (adding several nurse-specific stressors, e.g. death and dying). We found the following nine categories:

1. Workload,
2. Relationships with superiors,
3. The role,
4. Death and dying,
5. Home/work conflict,
6. Career,
7. Interpersonal relationships,
8. Physical resources,
9. Change.

In the tables accompanying the discussion below, responses to each of the stressors in the nine areas are indicated in two ways,

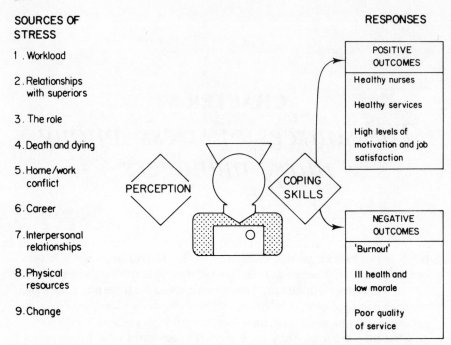

SOURCES OF
STRESS

1. Workload

2. Relationships
   with superiors

3. The role

4. Death and dying

5. Home/work
   conflict

6. Career

7. Interpersonal
   relationships

8. Physical
   resources

9. Change

PERCEPTION

COPING
SKILLS

RESPONSES

POSITIVE
OUTCOMES

Healthy nurses

Healthy services

High levels of
motivation and job
satisfaction

NEGATIVE
OUTCOMES

'Burnout'

Ill health and
low morale

Poor quality
of service

Figure 8.1 The nine broad sources of stress identified in our study, showing how the outcome is a direct response of an individual's perception of the sources of stress and her skill in coping with them.

1. The number of nurses who reported some degree of pressure from that stressor is indicated as a percentage (%) of the total sample.
2. The actual degree of pressure reported is given as an average (mean) using the following categories:
   2–3 = slight to moderate pressure
   3–4 = moderate to considerable pressure
   4–5 = considerable to extreme pressure.

For example, in *Area 1: Workload*, we see that 85 per cent of the total sample reported some pressure due to 'work overload'. The average pressure reported was 3.2, i.e. falling within the range Moderate to Considerable. So we can see that the stressor 'work overload' was identified as problematic by the large majority (85 per cent), causing them a moderate to considerable degree of stress (3.2).

AREA 1: WORKLOAD

Two aspects of work overload—quantitative and qualitative—have been identified in the field of occupational stress (French and Caplan, 1973).

Quantitative

The first aspect, quantitative work overload (having *too much* to do) has been strongly linked with a range of stress symptoms. Workers who perceive their task as being too demanding in this way tend to display significantly higher levels of stress symptoms than those experiencing lower levels of demands. Symptoms evident as a consequence of prolonged overload include: coronary attack (Russeck and Zohman, 1958); escapist drinking, absenteeism, low work motivation, and lowered self-esteem (Margolis *et al.*, 1974); and a general lack of feeling of control' often resulting in mental depression (Cooper *et al.*, 1982a).

Qualitative

The qualitative aspect of work overload, on the other hand, is concerned more with seeing the task as being *too difficult*. Again qualitative work overload has been shown to be linked with a number of physiological and psychological complaints. (French *et al.*, 1965; Dreyfuss and Czackes, 1959).

In the nursing profession

In the US, Gray-Toft and Anderson (1981) found that workload was cited as the most frequent cause of stress in a sample of 122 nurses in a general hospital. Our results also indicate that the workload is perceived as a major source of stress. It seems that our sample experienced stress in this area, regardless of their working environment or nursing grade, although the patterns of pressures reported do vary. From Table 8.1 it is evident that the quantitative aspect of work overload predominates. This was usually expressed in terms of demands upon time; a typical phrase describing this type of work overload would be, 'I simply need more time to get through all my tasks'. The problems of 'too little

Table 8.1. Workload stress.

Stressors	Reported pressure	
	%	Mean
Work overload	85	3.2
I have too little time in which to do what is expected of me	76	3.0
Others' demands for my time at work are in conflict	66	2.8
Management expects me to interrupt my work for new priorities	58	2.7
I spend my time 'fighting fires' rather than working to a plan	55	2.6
Time pressures and deadlines	83	2.9
Staff shortages	83	3.3

time' are likely to be exacerbated by conflicting demands and changing priorities in the workplace. There appears to be a general feeling that work schedules are determined by crises rather than by forward planning.

Staff shortages

In a review of the stress literature in nursing, Marshall (1980) notes that work overload 'figures prominently in many accounts, especially when coupled with staff shortages.' In the USA, Steffen (1980) has identified inadequate staffing as a major source of occupation stress. Quantitative problems—*inadequate* members of staff—as well as qualitative aspects—*incompetent* or poorly trained staff—were identified. Recently, in this country, the *Nursing Mirror*'s 'Stress Survey' (1985) reported understaffing as a major area of concern in the NHS (although it is unclear whether the respondents were simply 'concerned' nurses or a representative sample of the profession). For these reasons it is worth examining the information of staff shortages in more detail (Table 8.2).

Table 8.2. Staff shortages.

Category label	n	%
No pressure	83	16.1
Slight pressure	119	23.1
Moderate pressure	135	26.2
Considerable pressure	100	19.4
Extreme pressure	76	14.8
(No response)	2	0.4

It is evident that the number of nurses who perceived staff shortages as an *extreme* source of pressure was higher than for any other of the potential stressors considered. The average pressure (mean = 3.3) was also the highest recorded. These findings are echoed in the written comments of the nurses in the survey. When asked, 'What suggestions would you make to alleviate stress in nursing?', the most frequently cited suggestion made by over 40 per cent of the respondents indicated the need to attend to staffing levels. The comments were wide ranging and many reflected the quantitative aspects of the problem (i.e. not enough staff): 'It seems plain to everyone here that shortages of staff at ward level is the main cause of stress . . . I find it impossible to balance existing resources with demands. We desperately need more relief staff for holidays and to cover periods of sickness . . . We should never expect one person to do two people's work for any length of time.'

Qualitative aspects (i.e. not enough trained staff) were also of obvious concern: 'It's not so much the numbers of staff on the unit that is the problem. I'm more concerned about the quality of staff I am expected to work with . . . we need more trained staff in proportion to learners . . . at times some wards are almost completely run by learners.' 'Certainly within the hospital job stress would be best alleviated by more trained staff at working level. At the moment I feel there are far too many administrators and auxillary nurses.'

Levels of demand

Finally, a small percentage of nurses reported pressure due to 'work under-load' (17 per cent), although a larger number found 'fluctuations in workload' (66 per cent) a specific source of pressure. Undemanding work can lead to boredom and disinterest, and tends to reduce the worker's response to emergency situations. While sudden changes in the level of demand can have particularly detrimental effects on health (McCrae *et al.*, 1978; Davidson and Veno, 1980). These findings may be of special relevance to nurses in units such as accident and emergency departments, where the workload varies in an unpredictable way. Periods of reduced activity, largely occupied by repetitious and routine tasks (qualitative underload), are disrupted by emergency situations with high levels of demand (qualitative and quantitative overload).

AREA 2: RELATIONSHIPS WITH SUPERIORS

'It is sad that, on becoming ward sisters or charge nurses, many staff nurses appear to change their attitude to patients, relatives or subordinates, and lack an awareness of their psychological needs. As student nurses or staff nurses, they criticize the authoritarian attitude shown to them by some senior nurses, and then, when they reach that level, adopt the same attitude they had objected to earlier.' (Matthews, 1982)

> The stereotyped image of the qualified nurse is that she is committed totally to her patients, is skilled, fit and strong, and gives care as opposed to needing it. But of course like all stereotypes it just is not true. Nurses need help and support, albeit of a different type, just as much as our students and our patients. Unfortunately this does not seem to be recognized by the public, the organization, or indeed, the profession, itself. (Nursing Officer)

A second major source of occupational stress concerns the nature of relation-ships at work. Many studies have indicated that the quality of the working relationship is a crucial factor in determining individual and organizational health (Wardwell and Bahnson, 1973; Cooper and Melhuish, 1980).

A study of nursing personnel by Pearlin (1967), in the USA, found there was a tendency for feelings of alienation to increase as the distance between nursing grades increases. *Choice* and *control* emerged as important variables. Where the subordinate member is unable to exercise influence on her superiors feelings of powerlessness and alienation are exacerbated. In a study of 1800 ICU nurses, Bailey *et al.* (1980) identified 'Management of the Unit' as a major source of stress. In particular, 'unresponsive nursing leadership' and 'conflict with other health care providers' caused greatest levels of stress. They conclude that 'Nursing administrators need to recognize that stress, in a large measure, is a reflection of the impact of the organization, its leader, and the nature of the tasks on those who work there.' Similarly, Numerof and Abrams (1984) identified the organizational environment as a major area of perceived stress.

In this study the lack of feedback from supervisors regarding job performance and the problems of meeting the perceived demands of immediate supervisors were particular sources of anxiety. One respondent looked with some envy at the support provided in other professions.

My husband works locally as a social worker and it seems that he is part of a much more supportive system as far as his professional hierarchy is concerned. I feel jealous, and resentful, when he tells me about the supervision he expects and receives. It may only be an hour or so once a fortnight but it gives him the opportunity to meet with his senior, and it is *his* time which he can use to talk generally about alternative approaches to care or more specifically to review a particular case which may be causing him problems. It is not only a learning experience but it provides the opportunity for two professionals to share their knowledge and experience in a very positive way. I have never known of supervision of that nature in all my years of nursing. Nurses have "overlookers" not supervisors. It is not equal, it is not shared, and it is directed from the top down and all too often it is a very negative experience for all concerned. And you know that the real tragedy is that I have fitted into that system. I haven't demanded anything better and, to my shame, I don't think I have offered much more myself. As a profession we need to look at this aspect of our behaviour to our colleagues very carefully and we need to break out of this vicious circle.' (Ward Sister)

In the UK little attention appears to have been paid to the organizational structure of the nursing profession as a potential source of stress. In our study, 'Relationships with superiors' were clearly identified as problematic (Table 8.3). Pressures were associated with 'feelings of distance and isolation from those immediately above'. In particular, the lack of involvement in decision-making and the absence of positive feedback from immediate seniors were highlighted as specific problems. This reflected a 'credibility gap' that appeared to exist between levels of management, as one nurse manager put it,

'What is needed is much more support, cooperation and understanding from my seniors. If I am to operate more effectively there needs to be much more open discussion and a real opportunity to share in decision making.'

The lack of supportive feedback seemed to be of particular concern to many respondents.

'When I see my boss coming over to talk to me, or even if he calls me on the phone, then I know it will be to point out some shortcomings or fault. I really do not mind criticism—professional shortcomings have got to be faced if we are to improve practice—but it seems that as a profession nurses are locked into a style of negative criticism that is all their own. Perhaps it has a lot to do with our approach to training where everything is presented as very clear cut, either right or wrong, and "weaknesses cannot be tolerated". Whatever it is, the end result can be very very destructive and disheartening to the individual. I would dearly love to hear my boss say, "Brigid you really did a great job today in the unit." But if I did I think I would drop through the floor!' (Clinical Teacher)

Table 8.3. Relationships with superiors.

Stressors	Reported pressure	
	%	Mean
Decisions or changes which affect me are made 'above' without my knowledge or involvement	71	2.9
Lack of support from senior staff	67	3.1
I lack confidence in management	56	2.7
Relationships with superiors	55	2.6
I only get feedback when my performance is unsatisfactory	55	2.9
Avoiding conflict with superiors	52	2.7
Management misunderstand the real needs of my department	49	3.0
Relationships with administrators	44	2.5

'I absolutely dread reviews. In my experience it always degenerates into something which feels like the third-degree. Ideally it should be a balanced process. It should provide the safety and support in which we can identify our weaknesses and build upon our strengths. Often it just seems to be a check-list of faults and shortcomings. It feels a bit like going through an MOT test. The fear of "failure" is always there often not very far beneath the surface.' (Sister)

AREA 3: THE ROLE (FACTOR 3)

The nurse's role is therefore implicitly and chiefly one of handling stress. She is a focus for the stress of the patient, relatives, and doctors as well as her own. (Marshall, 1980).

Writers on role theory suggest that 'when the behaviour expected of an individual is inconsistent, and there is *ambiguity* and *conflict*, the individual will experience stress, become dissatisfied, and perform less effectively.' (Gray-Toft and Anderson, 1981). Problems of ambiguity and conflict revolving around the role of nurse managers may help to explain why workload and relationships with superiors are experienced as highly stressful.

A number of accounts of stress in nursing give a central place to the importance of role. In a Canadian study of 153 headnurses, Leatt and Schneck (1980) specifically identified role ambiguity as a potential source of stress. The headnurses suffered from the difficulties of handling their dual role as clinicians and managers. The researchers suggested that stress related primarily to the administrative role rather than the clinical area. From the results of their survey of 154 hospital-based nurses in the US, Numerof and Abrams (1984) argued that 'Organizations may unwittingly augment the supervisor's stress by failing to provide management training . . . These skills are quite different from the clinician's skills, requiring new knowledge, new tools and a new way

Table 8.4. The role.

Stressors	Reported pressure	
	%	Mean
Coping with new situations	69	2.6
Unrealistically high expectations by others of my role	56	2.7
Tasks outside of my competence	53	2.8
Uncertainty about the degree or area of my responsibility	49	2.5
Lack of specialized training for present task	39	2.5
I don't feel adequately trained for the job I have to do	34	2.5

of thinking.' In our study two interrelated elements were evident; both were concerned with problems of role ambiguity and conflicting expectations about the task (Table 8.4).

'My expectations of my job'

Uncertainty about the standard demanded by the role and expectations about the level of performance were reported as areas of concern by a considerable number of the sample. It seems that nurse managers consider they lack the specialized training that would enable them to feel more able and confident in their management role.

Another facet of role performance was an expressed fear of coping with new situations. This implies the need for clear expectations as to the content of the role. The importance of confidence and competence in role performance is summarized in the words of the respondent who commented, 'In my experience, above all else, the chosen leader of any team must be contented and confident in their role. Only then can they hope to gain the respect and cooperation of their staff.'

In addition, the literature suggests that nurses seem to suffer from the pursuit of very high and often unrealistic standards—the 'Angel Syndrome'—in which the nurse seems unable to come to terms with her own limitations (Hingley, 1984). In fact, Scully (1980) suggests that, 'Expecting too much from self can lead to burnout faster than any other single stressor.' As one senior nurse commented:

'All the time I was a student nurse I was told how important it was to maintain the standards of the School, and how we would be representatives of a famous and prestigious hospital. Continuously throughout our training the emphasis was on "maintaining the standards of the profession". But no-one ever spelt out to us what those standards were or what they meant in practice. They were a kind of unwritten law which guided our lives, but when we needed to measure ourselves up against them, then they just did not seem to exist. I suppose we assumed "being a professional" meant total dedication at all times, being always cool, clear-headed and in control. Able to cope with any emergency, able to cope with any type of patient in any solution. But of course the reality was nothing like that. I found that I wasn't always cool, calm and collected. Many times I felt confused and totally overwhelmed by the work—my first ward death was a completely shattering experience. I found I just could not relate to some of my patients as I felt I should and I found some aspects of their clinical care abhorrent. Consequently I was left feeling frightened, angry and sad. I was frightened in case it was found out that I was not reaching the standards I should be reaching. I was angry, mainly with myself, for my weaknesses and particularly those feelings which were not "professional". And I was sad because I believed I was letting everyone down. I was the "odd one out", the nurse who was not coping. Inside I knew I was a failure and a fake. After all everyone else seemed to be coping well and no-one else seemed to be feeling like I did. So for years I never talked to, or shared with anyone my problem and my failure. I just tried harder, raised my standards and kept failing to live up to them! Only much later in my professional life when I became a member of a peer-support group did I find that, far from being an exception, many nurses feel exactly the same. It seems it isn't only the Mafia that has a vow of silence!'

It is these in-built values, together with the problem shared by all 'caring professions' of seldom knowing how effective or successful one has been, that makes this an area of considerable concern.

'Expectations of my job by others'

Pressure was reported when there was a mismatch between one's own expectations and the expectations of others. This was particularly evident when the expectations of others were perceived as being unrealistically high. Feelings of ambiguity were often associated with (and exacerbated by) the lack of constructive feedback about work performance, thus emphasizing the individual's difficulty in assessing their professional worth. As one Nurse Manager put it,

'It is necessary to make sure that the right person is in the right job, with a clear understanding of what is expected of them and the knowledge that help and advice is always available. Unfortunately this doesn't happen as often as it should.'

AREA 4: DEATH AND DYING

I knew that my first experience of a death on the ward would literally be a make or break experience for me and I lived in fear and dread of it. Either I would be able to see it through and cope or I would leave nursing completely. My training had not prepared me at all for dealing with the feeling side of death and I just did not know what to expect of myself. As it turned out I was lucky as I had a very understanding and supportive ward sister. I was able to talk to her both before and after my patient died. It *was* luck, a different shift, a different sister and I wouldn't be talking to you now. (Nursing Officer)

Coping with death and dying emerged as a clearly identifiable area of stress. Not surprisingly, our respondents found that direct involvement in life and

152

death situations caused them a considerable degree of anxiety. On the other hand, simple 'exposure to death' was also perceived as stressful, although less frequently (Table 8.5).

Marshall (1980) suggests that caring for life in the face of death and dying, the primary task of nursing, is fundamentally threatening to the nurse in two ways: 'as a skilled worker whose competence (to heal) is on trial and, even more fundamentally, as a human being who is herself vulnerable to the illnesses and death she is nursing.' This is echoed by Gray-Toft and Anderson (1980) who argue that 'death is a universal problem for health professionals since it threatens their role perceptions.' In their study, death and dying also emerged as a discrete stress factor. Similarly, in a study of nurses working in an ICU, Steffen (1980) noted that 'the event of sudden death . . . was viewed as a direct affront to the nurses self-esteem, whereby she questioned her nursing role.' For some, the problem is more complex and revolves around the responsibility of sharing professional knowledge with the patient and relatives.

'The greatest source of stress for me is the guilt I feel when I know the patient's diagnosis and the patient and relatives are unaware of what is wrong. The continuous anxiety of being involved in this "web of deceit" eventually leads to complete emotional exhaustion and I have to take a couple of days off to recharge my batteries.' (Charge Nurse)

On the basis of a study of student nurses' experiences of death, Whitfield (1979) suggests that much of the stress and anxiety experienced stems from an inability to deal with their *own* feelings about death and dying (see Chapter 3). Bereavement counselling which requires the counsellor to have come to terms with her own feelings about death was also identified as a specific stressor by our sample. This raises fundamental questions about the scope and the effectiveness of training in this area.

Table 8.5. Death and dying.

Stressors	Reported pressure	
	%	Mean
Involvement in life and death situations	60	2.6
Bereavement counselling	55	2.6
Exposure to death	44	2.6

AREAS : HOME/WORK CONFLICT

The number of married working women has increased substantially in this country. Twenty-five years ago only 25 per cent of working women were married; by 1980 this had increased to 60 per cent (Cooper and Davidson,

1982). Involvement in both work and the family is likely to be stressful for the female nurse manager. Despite working full-time, women are often expected to continue to meet domestic commitments. Increasingly, there is evidence that conflicting demands from home and work can be very stressful. Cooper (1982b) found that more and more married women are either divorcing, limiting their family size, or coping with both worlds at the expense of their physical and psychological health. Generally it seems that married female managers who have young children find themselves less able to relax at the end of the day than male managers, and they are more susceptible to feelings of guilt, role conflict, work overload, tiredness and ill health (Larwood and Wood, 1979; Bhagat and Chassie, 1981).

Many of our respondents have two full-time jobs (nurse manager and home manager), so it is not surprising that a conflict of interests can and does occur. As one Nurse put it,

'When I get up in the morning I don't feel like going to work. But by 10 a.m. the feeling has worn off. The cause of this feeling is my two children whom I have to dress and feed before I can get off to work.'

Another commented:

'It is difficult for all nurses to completely separate their job and home life. The sort of work that nursing entails means that it is practically impossible to just forget about everything at the end of the shift. You often take your worries and problems home with you. This is fine if your partner understands and supports you. It can be a disaster if he doesn't . . . The problem of the working woman trying to balance the demands of a career and a home is that she is in double jeopardy. If too many of the difficulties of one area spill over into the other there is a very real danger of losing both career and home.' (Sister)

Two factors emerged in this area of home/work conflict: work 'overspill' and home 'overspill'.

Work 'overspill'

This is concerned with the effect of work on home. It is evident that some individuals have difficulty in *switching off* from work, especially when they feel that they are over-emotionally involved. Working unsocial hours may put an additional strain on social and family relationships (Table 8.6).

Table 8.6. Home/work conflict: work overspill.

Stressors	Reported pressure	
	%	Mean
Taking problems home	62	2.6
Over-emotional involvement	46	2.4

Home 'overspill' (Factor 7)

The second factor has to do with the effect of home on work. A minority of
nurses experienced a relatively high degree of pressure due to the feeling that
their domestic commitments inhibited their career prospects (Table 8.7).

Table 8.7. Home/work conflict: home overspill.

Stressors	Reported pressure	
	%	Mean
Job versus home demands	62	2.7
Domestic/family demands inhibit promotion	20	2.9
I need to absent myself from work to cope with domestic problems	11	2.6

AREA 6: CAREER

Career advancement is particularly important to many professionals. Promotion up the career ladder not only determines material rewards, but also
provides enhanced status and new challenges. Psychological disturbances and
frustrations resulting from an inability to achieve career aspirations have been
linked to stress and disease (Wan, 1971).

It seems that those in middle management levels are more likely to suffer
from dashed career hopes and aspirations, since it is at this stage that many
managers find their progress slowed and sometimes halted completely (Constandse, 1972). Cooper and Davidson (1982) found that career development
blockages were particularly evident among women managers. There is also
evidence to suggest that middle managers experience stress more frequently
than those in the top management. Mid-level managers found 'responsibility
without authority' particularly stressful, while persons at or near the top have
more control and power over the working environment. At this stage they are
also more likely to have fulfilled their career aspirations.

In this study we have loosely labelled this area 'career'. It consists of a
number of stressors highlighting the negative aspects of the professional role
(Table 8.8). About half our sample reported that they had experienced
pressure due to a 'lack of job satisfaction', although only 12 per cent of the
sample perceived this pressure as being considerable or extreme. This may
reflect the ambivalence felt when promoted away from a direct clinical role into
a more managerial position. 'I suspect I am like many nurses who are in this
position.

Because I was a good clinical practitioner I was promoted into my present post. But
my clinical skills and abilities, the very things which confirmed to me and to my
colleagues that I was professionally valuable, are now redundant. In fact they get in

the way of my present work! So I feel very threatened. I have lost what I knew I could do well and I am faced with a task in which people are expecting my old level of performance. What they do not realize is that the old me has been left on the wards. Even now I find it much easier to spend time with people from the clinical areas, or visiting wards or units' than here at my desk organizing paperwork and engaging in long-term planning.' (Senior Manager)

In addition, a number of respondents indicated their frustration with their low status and limited promotion prospects.

Table 8.8. Career.

Stressors	Reported pressure	
	%	Mean
Lack of job satisfaction	50	2.9
Low professional status	37	2.8
Lack of promotion prospects	31	2.8

AREA 7: INTERPERSONAL RELATIONSHIPS

'Like most of my colleagues I feel very competent in my clinical abilities. I think as nurses we have a first-class training in that area. But when it comes to interpersonal skills and the ability to relate well to patients, relatives and colleagues, then I think we are still in the Dark Ages. My own training has consisted of approximately three half days since I qualified. No wonder this is an area which is stressful to all levels of nurse.' (Sister, Accident and Emergency Unit).

Social relations are often a source of satisfaction and support at work, but, as we saw in the responses in Area 2 (Relationships with Superiors), they can also be a source of pressure. A number of studies have indicated the importance of positive relationships at work. Wardwell and Bahson (1973), for example, found a link between poor relationships at work, high blood pressure and increased smoking levels (see Chapter 2).

Two factors were identified within this area: patients and relatives, and staff.

Patients and relatives

In the first, problems with 'difficult patients' suggest that nurses felt that they lacked the skills needed to be assertive and manage in these situations. 'Dealing with relatives' was also a problem (Table 8.9). Marshall (1980) suggests that this is due in part to the fact that the nurses role is often poorly defined in this respect. The nurse's difficulty in dealing with distressed relatives may also be related to her own problems of coping with death and dying (see Area 4).

Table 8.9. Interpersonal relationships: patients/relatives.

Stressors	Reported pressure	
	%	Mean
Difficult patients	65	2.6
Dealing with relatives	47	2.4

Staff

Secondly, relationships with 'colleagues' and 'subordinates' were also identified as being potentially stressful (Table 8.10). This adds to the picture of a rigid hierarchical structure, in which pressures are perceived amongst staff as 'filtering down' from above. Our respondents saw their relations with subordinates as being less stressful than their relations with colleagues and considerably less stressful than relations with superiors.

Table 8.10. Interpersonal relationships: staff.

Stressors	Reported pressure	
	%	Mean
Relationship with colleagues	43	2.4
Relationship with subordinates	29	2.2

AREA 8: PHYSICAL RESOURCES

It often seems that hospitals are designed only with the needs of patients in mind, and that the people who have to work in them are given very little thought. In particular, nurses need to be able to get away from the pressures of the ward, even if it is only for a short break. In this hospital the nearest rest-room is in another block, a good five minutes walk away from here. No wonder that the toilets, sluice room, and even the telephone call boxes are used as refuges by my staff.' (Ward Sister)

A number of studies have commented on the need for sufficient resources within nursing (Steffen, 1980; Leatt and Schneck, 1980). In ours concern was evident both about the lack of essential resources and the poor quality of those which did exist (Table 8.11). In particular, there was widespread comment on the need for more 'suitable and adequate equipment'. There were also negative responses concerning the lack of privacy, as well as the poor quality of supporting staff.

Table 8.11. Physical resources.

Stressors	Reported pressure	
	%	Mean
Shortages of essential resources	72	2.8
Poor physical conditions	58	3.0

AREA 9: CHANGE

The information here suggests that change, particularly the problems of keeping abreast of professional developments and the frustrations of conflicting procedures, is perceived as stressful. This may be an indication of the strain engendered by the recent and continuing reorganization within the NHS (Table 8.12).

Table 8.12. Change.

Stressors	Reported pressure	
	%	Mean
Keeping up with professional developments	78	2.6
New technology	67	2.7
Frustration with conflicting procedures	66	2.6

At a different level, coping with new technology was seen as stressful and it seems that the vagaries of technology were also perceived as threatening.

'I am always on edge when they introduce the latest technology in to my unit. It is fine when it is working but when it goes wrong no one seems to want to know! Are we really technicians? Are we meant to be capable of fixing machines and discovering the causes of alarms due to malfunctions?' (ICU Sister)

Other studies within the profession have identified similar concerns. For example, Steffen (1980) found that 'the quality and variety of complex technical equipment posed tremendous demands on the knowledge base of the ICU nurses.'

Several respondents expressed a need for continuing education and training to keep abreast of new developments in the field. But often it seemed that the very people who needed this training the most found their way was obstructed, and in particular the difficulties of part-time, qualified staff returning to the profession after a number of years absence was highlighted. Recent advances in both technology and methods of care meant that many 'returnees' found themselves feeling de-skilled and out of touch. Although many authorities provide excellent in-service training and some 'return to nursing courses', part-time workers often find they are given low priority. In extreme cases this can lead to a rapid and negative downward spiral.

CONCLUSION

Nine areas, or broad sources, of stress have been identified and discussed. It is interesting to note that there are marked similarities between the results of this project and recent studies of the American nurse (see Steffen, 1980; Leatt and Schneck, 1980; Gray-Toft and Anderson, 1981; Numerof and Abrams 1984). In particular, this study has found that nurses are less likely to be stressed by factors intrinsic to the primary nursing task than by working relationships, formal structures within the organization, and factors external to their job. Indeed, only two areas of concern, 'Death and Dying', and 'Interpersonal Relationships' are directly related to patient care. The nurse is more likely to experience difficulties in coping with relationships with colleagues, conflicts and ambiguities in her role and in balancing the demands of home and work.

Finally, it should be remembered that these are general patterns of stress identified by the whole sample. This does not mean that all nurses have the same 'stress profile'. Individual differences in perception and response will influence the eventual outcome. Additionally, differences in the working environment will determine the source and intensity of potential stressors (see Chapter 9). In the last analysis stress must be seen as a product of a 'misfit' between the nurse and her work environment. From this perspective the individual is placed firmly in the centre of the stress equation, and as such can be seen as a potential source for change.

REFERENCES

Bailey, J.T., Steffen, S.M. and Grout, J.W. (1980) The stress audit: identifying the stressors of ICU nursing. *J. Nurs. Educ.*, **9**: 15–25.

Bhagat, R.S. and Chassie, M.B. (1981) Determinants of organisational commitment in working women: some implications for organisational integration. *J. Occup. Behav.*, **2**: 17–30.

Constandse, W.J. (1972) Mid-40's man: a neglected personnel problem. *Personnel J.*, **51**: 129–133.

Cooper, C.L. (1982a) *Stress Research*. Chichester: Wiley.

Cooper, C.L. (1982b) *Executive Families Under Stress*. New Jersey: Prentice Hall.

Cooper, C.L. and Davidson, M.J. (1982) *High Pressure: Working Lives of Women Managers*. London: Fontana.

Cooper, C.L. and Melhuish, A (1980) Occupational stress and managers. *J. Occup. Med.*, **22**: 588–592.

Cooper, C.L., Davidson, M.J. and Robinson, P. (1982) *Journal of Occupational Medicine*, **24**, 30–36.

Davidson, M.J. and Veno, A. (1980) Stress and the policeman. In Cooper, C.L. and Marshall, J. (eds), *White Collar and Professional Stress*. Chichester: Wiley.

Dreyfuss, F. and Czackes, J.W. (1959) Blood cholesterol and uric acid of healthy medical students under stress. *Arch. Intern. Med.*, **103**: 708.

French, J.R.P. and Caplan, R.D. (1973) Organizational stress and individual strain. In Marrow, A.J. (ed), *The Failure of Success*. New York: AMACOM.

French, J.R.P., Tupper, C.J. and Mueller, E.I. (1965) *Workload of univeristy professors. Unpublished Research Report*. Ann Arbor, Mich: University of Michigan.

Gray-Toft, P. and Anderson, J.G. (1981) Stress among hospital nursing staff: its causes and effects. *Soc. Sci. Med.*, **15A**: 639–647.

Hingley, P. (1984) The humane face of nursing. *Nurs. Mirror*, Dec.

Johnson, S.H. (1983) Foreward. In Lachman, V.D. (ed.), *Stress Management: A Manual for Nurses*. New York: Grune and Stratton.

Larwood, L. and Wood, M.M. (1979) *Women in Management*. London: Lexington Books.

Leatt, P. and Schneck, R. (1980) Differences in stress perceived by headnurses across nursing specialities in hospitals. *J. Adv. Nurs.*, **5**: 31–46.

Margolis, B.L., Kroes, W.H. and Quinn, R.P. (1974) Job stress: an unlisted occupational hazard. *J. Occup. Med.*, **16**: 654–661.

Marshall, J. (1980) Stress amongst nurses. In Cooper, C.L. and Marshall, J. (eds), *White Collar and Professional Stress*. Chichester: Wiley.

Matthews, A. (1982) *In Charge of the Ward*. London: Blackwell Scientific.

McCrae, R.R., Costa, P.T. and Bosse, R. (1978) Anxiety, extroversion and smoking. *Br. J. Soc. Clin. Psychol.*, **17**: 269–273.

Nursing Mirror (1985) Disturbing findings: stress survey. *Nurs. Mirror*, **160**: June 26.

Numerof, R.E. and Abrams, M.N. (1984) Sources of stress among nurses: an empirical investigation. *J. Hum. Stress*, Summer, 88–100.

Pearlin, L. (1967) Alienation from work: a study of nursing personnel. In Abrahamson, M. (ed.), *The Professional in the Organization*. Rand McNally.

Russeck, H.I. and Zohman, B.L. (1958) Relative significance of hereditary, diet, and occupational stress in CHD of young adults. *Am. J. Med. Sci.*, **235**: 266–275.

Scully, R. (1980) Stress in the nurse. *Am. J. Nurs.*, **80**: 911–915.

Steffen, S.M. (1980) Perceptions of stress: 1800 nurses tell their stories. In Claus, K.E. and Bailey, J.T. (eds), *Living with Stress and Promoting Well-being*. St Louis: C.V. Mosby.

Wan, T. (1971) Status, stress and morbidity: a sociological investigation of selected categories of work-limiting chronic conditions. *J. Chron. Dis*, **24**: 453–468.

Wardwell, W.I. and Bahnson, C.B. (1973) Behavioural variables and myocardial infarction in the South-eastern Connecticut Heart Study. *J Chron. Dis.*, **26**: 447–461.

Whitfield, S. (1979) A descriptive study of student nurses' ward experiences with dying patients and their attitudes towards them. *Unpublished MSc Thesis*, University of Manchester.

CHAPTER 9

Stress and strain differences between working environments and nursing grades

In order to obtain a more detailed picture of occupational stress, the total sample was examined in terms of working environment (i.e. hospital- and community-based nurses) and nursing grades (i.e. sister/charge nurse versus nursing officer level).

HOSPITAL- AND COMMUNITY-BASED STAFF: A COMPARISON BY WORKING ENVIRONMENT

Description of the groups

A breakdown of the whole sample by working environment resulted in the identification of three subgroups.

(1) Those nurse managers who worked in a *hospital* setting. This group was composed of staff from the following areas: nurse education (31), accident and emergency units (16), theatres (17), outpatients and clinics (10), wards and special units (198). In all, this group was made up of 272 respondents (52 per cent of the total sample).
(2) The second sub-group consisted of *community-based* staff. These totalled 190 (37 per cent of the whole sample), and included 70 health visitors and 80 community nurses.
(3) The final subgroup was made up of staff who described their working environment as *central administration and planning* and numbered 24 (5 per cent of the whole sample).

Twenty-nine respondents (6 per cent of the total sample) signified they worked in 'other' environments. The central administration and planning group (24) was judged to be too small to be analysed; consequently they were

160

omitted and the analysis was confined to a comparison of the responses between hospital-based (272) and community-based staff (190).

Comparison of the groups

Demographic details

A comparison of the background information of the two groups revealed many more similarities than differences. Indeed, there were only two differences which were statistically significant. Firstly, there were more males working in the hospital setting ($P<0.020$). In view of the low proportion of males working in the profession as a whole, this means that community based nursing is almost an exclusively female domain. Indeed, national figures indicate that from a total of over 19 000 health visitors and district nurses, only 500 (2.8 per cent) are males (private communication with the DHSS). This poses an interesting question: Why is hospital-based nursing (particularly psychiatric care) accepted as being open to males, yet this is not the case for community-based nursing?

Secondly, it was evident that the opportunity for part-time employment within the community was much less common than in the hospital setting ($P<0.001$). There are obvious organizational reasons for this: the need for 24-hour care and the larger size of the work unit provides the potential for more flexibility of work patterns. This raises questions concerning the qualified, but unemployed, pool of nurses which could be tapped in order to meet the demands brought about by recent moves towards increased community-based care.

The similarities between these two groups suggests that differences in the pressures experienced by hospital and community staff are more likely to be a reflection of problems associated with specific work settings (the person–environment fit) rather than simply personal differences between the two samples. Other studies of the profession have also found stress to be experienced differentially as a function of the work setting (Numerof and Adams, 1984).

Job satisfaction

There was no significant difference between the levels of job satisfaction reported by the hospital- and the community-based staff. Both groups experienced high levels of job satisfaction.

Sources of occupational stress

Eight areas were identified for the hospital-based and community-based staff. In the comparisons which follow, statistically significant differences are expressed in terms of 'levels of probability'. For example, compared with their community-based colleagues, nurse managers working within a hospital setting reported a higher incidence of pressure arising from their 'relationships with superiors. This difference was statistically significant at the probability level (P) of 0.001. This means that the probability of this difference being due to chance is less than one in a thousand (expressed as $P<0.001$). It is conventional to accept the level of $P<0.05$ as a minimal cut-off point.

Area 1: Workload

Hospital-based staff

In keeping with the findings for the main sample, this area was most frequently reported as a source of stress by both of the groups. Hospital staff, however, expressed a relatively greater concern about staff shortages and work overload than did community workers. The difficulty of ensuring adequate numbers of staff and balancing these against the often rapidly fluctuating levels of demand was evidently perceived as a greater source of pressure in this setting. As well as the problems of too much to do, time pressures of hospital-based staff are associated with the difficulties of conflicting demands. Nurse managers in this setting are bound by the organizational needs of hospital routine and suffer, accordingly, a more *qualitative* aspect of work overload.

Major stressor	Reported pressure		Significant
	%	Mean	differences
Work overload	87	3.3	($P<0.044$)
Staff shortages	87	3.5	($P<0.000$)
Time pressures and deadlines	82	2.9	
I have too little time in which to do what is expected of me	76	3.0	
Others' demands for my time at work are in conflict	67	2.9	($P<0.028$)

Community-based staff

The concerns of community staff within this area seem more confined to the *quantitative* aspects of work overload, i.e. having too much to do within the time available. Shortage of staff was also seen as a major source of pressure but to a lesser extent than in the hospital setting. The greater potential for flexibility and control over aspects of patient contact within the community may be an important mitigating factor in coping with the problem of work overload.

Major stressors	Reported pressure	
	%	Mean
Time pressures and deadlines	85	2.8
Work overload	84	3.1
Staff shortages	80	3.0
I have too little time in which to do what is expected of me	76	3.0

Area 2: Relationships with superiors

Hospital-based staff

The most striking finding in this area is that the nurse managers working within a hospital setting reported a much higher incidence of pressure arising from their relationships with their immediate superiors. Compared with community-based staff, there is evidence to suggest that nurses in this setting tended to see their relationships with senior staff as being particularly problematic. They reported that 'avoiding conflict with their superiors' was a particular source of pressure. Overall senior staff were seen by this group as being unsupportive and as misunderstanding the real needs of the unit or department. Problems of this kind appear to reflect a more rigid and hierarchical type of management style at work within the hospital setting.

Major stressors	Reported pressure		Significant
	%	Mean	differences
Lack support from senior staff	73	3.2	($P<0.052$)
Decisions or changes which affect me are made 'above' without my knowledge or involvement	73	2.9	
Relationships with superiors	63	2.6	($P<0.001$)
Lack of participation in planning/ decision making	62	2.7	
Management misunderstands the real needs of my department	60	3.0	($P<0.015$)
I only get feedback when my performance is unsatisfactory	60	2.9	
Avoiding conflict with superiors	57	2.7	($P<0.000$)
Relationships with administrators	44	2.5	

Community-based staff

Conflicting relationships with senior staff appear to be less marked among community staff; rather, a feeling of a lack of confidence in management is more in evidence. Again this seems to be a reflection of the relatively greater autonomy exercized by community workers over their own work situation.

In both work settings the need for involvement in decision making was strongly expressed. As one charge nurse commented, 'The lack of access to Senior Nurse Management causes a considerable amount of stress at my level. Charge nurses have policies given to them via nursing officers and have little opportunity to discuss these policies with the people responsible for issuing them.'

Major stressors	Reported pressure	
	%	Mean
Decisions or changes which affect me are made 'above' without my knowledge or involvement	73	2.8
Lack of support from senior staff	62	3.1
I lack confidence in management	59	2.8
Relationships with superiors	43	2.6
Relationships with administrators	43	2.5
Avoiding conflict with superiors	41	2.5

Area 3: The Role

Hospital-based staff

Three factors relating to role pressures have been included in this area: confidence and competence; training; and interdepartmental conflict.

Confidence and competence Here the underlying source of pressure seems to be associated with the nurse's confidence in her own professional competence. The pressure experienced as a consequence of 'work underload' may reflect the nurses sense of 'dis-ease' in managing relatively slack periods on the wards. This finding tends to illustrate the importance of having clearly defined expectations of the nurse's role in managing the workload.

Major stressors	Reported pressure	
	%	Mean
Coping with new situations	69	2.5
Tasks outside of my competence	54	2.7
Work underload (needing to look busy)	17	2.6

Training A feeling of being inadequately trained—another aspect of the role—was also reported as a source of pressure. A considerable number of nurses commented on the need for 'more in-service training and workshop days for *all* grades of nursing staff to enable them to keep abreast of continual professional changes'.

Major stressors	Reported pressure	
	%	Mean
Lack of special training for present task	41	2.5
I don't feel adequately trained for the job I have to do	37	2.4

Interdepartmental conflict and sex discrimination To a lesser degree the need for liaison with other departments was identified by some as a source of conflict. Finally although only few respondents reported pressure from sex discrimination, it appeared to be more of a male concern! Of the *total* sample 20 per cent of males and only 5.5 per cent of females identified this as a source of occupational stress.

Major stressors	Reported pressure	
	%	Mean
I must go to other departments to get my job done	28	2.5
Sex discrimination at work	8	2.4

Role conflict

In addition, two significant differences between hospital- and community-based staff were identified concerning their roles. Hospital-based nurses were more likely to feel pressure as a consequence of being 'promoted out of the caring role' ($P<0.009$) and as a result of their 'nursing and administrative roles being in conflict' ($P<0.000$). These differences suggest that nurse managers in the hospital setting experience greater difficulty in coping with their dual clinical—managerial role.

Community-based staff

For this group two factors relating to role were identified: confidence and training, and role conflict.

Confidence and training Feelings of confidence in their professional competence appeared to be more closely identified with the need for on-going training by staff in the community. A variety of training needs were mentioned including the need for 'More training in communication and team-work skills. More emphasis on the need for an improvement in interpersonal relationships in general.' 'We need more training in administration and management from *professional* administrators and not just from other nurses.'

Major stressors	Reported pressure	
	%	Mean
Coping with new situations	68	2.4
Tasks outside of my competence	48	2.7
Lack of specialized training for present task	34	2.4
I don't feel adequately trained for the job I have to do	31	2.5

Role conflict Conflicting procedures seem to form the core of role conflict problems for community staff. Many community nurses commented that they had purposely moved out of the hospital setting to escape 'the demands of bureaucratic constraints'. It seems that even community nursing is not completely free from the strictures of central control.

Major stressors	Reported pressure	
	%	Mean
Frustration with conflicting procedures	61	2.6
My professional expertise contradicts organizational practice	56	2.6
I find problems allocating resources	33	2.4

Finally, in this Area, nurses within the community were much more likely to report pressures due to others at work having unclear expectations about their job ($P<0.000$). This finding supports the view that the role of the community nurse is often perceived as being more ambiguous than that of the hospital nurse.

Area 4: Death and dying

This was identified as a specific area of concern for both the hospital and the community staff.

Hospital-based staff

In the hospital-based sample this factor seemed to centre around the awareness of death itself. This gave rise to greatest concern when actually dealing with life and death situations.

Community-based staff

Pressures here resembled those reported by hospital staff. However Community staff found the task of 'bereavement counselling' more problematic than their

Major stressors	Reported pressure	
	%	Mean
Involvement in life and death situations	61	2.7
Bereavement counselling	51	2.5
Exposure to death	43	2.6

hospital based colleagues. Again this reflects differences in the nature of the caring role between the two groups—community staff are more often expected to give on-going support to the bereaved after the death of a patient.

Major stressors	Reported pressure		Significant
	%	Mean	differences
Bereavement counselling	64	2.6	(P<0.019)
Involvement in life and death situations	60	2.6	
Exposure to death	47	2.7	

Area 5: Home/work conflict

Hospital-based staff

The effect of home pressures on work seems more problematic for hospital staff. This is probably a reflection of the demands of 'double jobbing' mentioned in the discussion on the total sample exacerbated by the more inflexible nature of the organization setting. Respondents indicated that the conflicts between home and work pressures were often not fully appreciated by their superiors and that this lack of understanding was in itself a source of stress. A few respondents reported that home demands actually impinged to the point of needing to absent themselves from work.

Major stressors	Reported pressure	
	%	Mean
Job versus home demands	61	2.7
My superiors do not appreciate my home pressures	21	2.6
Domestic/family demands inhibit promotion	20	2.9
I need to absent myself from work to cope with domestic problems	9	2.7

Unsocial hours It is appropriate to comment here on work patterns, since it would seem likely that working unsocial hours would be strongly associated with home/work conflicts. Our findings show that it is the hospital staff who are more likely to report more pressure as a consequence of working unsocial hours ($P<0.007$). This is not surprising since part-time and shift work is more common in this setting than in community nursing. Hospital-based shift workers (full- and part-time) and part-time night workers reported a significantly higher incidence of pressures due to working unsocial hours. Comparisons by work patterns, however, did not reveal any significant differences in the area of home/work conflict.

Community-based staff

For nurses based in the community this area is made up of two factors: work overspill and home overspill.

Work overspill Community staff differed significantly from the hospital staff on the two stressors within this factor. Nurses in the community expressed more pressure as a consequence of being over-emotionally involved with their patients. Perhaps, as a consequence of this, it was found that they were more likely to take their work problems home with them.

Major stressors	Reported pressure		Significant
differences	%	Mean	
Taking problems home	66	2.7	($P<0.041$)
Over-emotional involvement	55	2.5	($P<0.003$)

Home overspill Somewhat surprisingly, in view of the unsocial hours worked within hospitals, it was the community staff who were more likely to feel pressured as a consequence of the conflicting demands of home and work. In addition, there is some indication more community workers felt the need to absent themselves from work to cope with domestic problems, although this

Major stressors	Reported pressure		Significant
	%	Mean	differences
Job versus home demands	69	2.8	($P<0.034$)
Domestic/family demands inhibit promotion	20	3.0	
I need to absent myself from work to cope with domestic problems	15	2.8	

difference was not statistically significant. This is probably also a reflection of the more flexible nature of their work pattern.

Switching off It seems that community nurses have greater difficulty in switching off their work problems. Again this probably reflects the nature of their role. The hospital setting is more self-contained; in some ways this makes it easier to leave work problems behind when you leave the building, as one hospital nurse put it, 'When I switch on the ignition, I switch off work!'

Area 6: Career

Hospital-based staff

Concerns in this area tended to be associated with a lack of promotion prospects and low professional status. There were no significant differences between hospital and community staff in this respect. Nurses within the hospital setting, however, were evidently more concerned about their 'security of employment' ($P<0.036$). These fears may, in part, reflect the current shift in emphasis towards community care as well as government attempts to reduce costs within the NHS.

Major stressors	Reported pressure	
	%	Mean
Low professional status	36	2.6
Lack of promotion prospects	29	2.8

Community-based staff

For community-based staff this factor has two facets:

(1) The *subjective feelings* of job satisfaction—how worthwhile the practitioner considers her job to be, and
(2) Concern with the *external indicators* of professional status and promotion prospects—how the job is valued and rewarded by the wider organization.

Major stressors	Reported pressure	
	%	Mean
Lack of job satisfaction	49	2.8
Low professional status	35	2.7
Lack of promotion prospects	29	2.7
Work underload (needing to look busy)	19	2.5

Area 7: Interpersonal relationships

Hospital-based staff

This area was made up of two factors: working with staff, and dealing with patients and relatives. The first gives some impression of the pressures derived from working with colleagues within the profession, while the second indicates the difficulty of dealing with demanding patients and relatives.

Staff It was found that nurse managers based in the hospital setting were more likely to experience problems in their relationships with subordinates than were staff working within the community. Relationships between staff emerge in a clear hierarchical pattern. Frequencies of reported pressure increase as the level of interaction moves from subordinates to superiors. This pattern was not as marked for the community group (see Table 9.1).

Major stressors	Reported pressure		Significant
	%	Mean	differences
Relationships with colleagues	44	2.3	
Difficulty in dealing with passive people	45	2.4	
Relationships with subordinates	39	2.2	$(P<0.000)$

Table 9.1. Frequency of reported pressure in interpersonal relationships for hospital- and community-based staff.

	Reported pressure	
Relationships with:	Hospital staff (%)	Community staff (%)
Colleagues	44	43
Subordinates	39	18
Superiors	63	43

Patients and relatives This factor revolves around the problems of coping with difficult patients. Dealing with relatives and with aggressive people also emerged as stressors. There were no significant differences between community and hospital staff for this factor.

Major stressors	Reported pressure	
	%	Mean
Difficulty in dealing with aggressive people	74	2.7
Difficult patients	62	2.7
Dealing with relatives	45	2.3

Community-based staff

As for the hospital staff, two factors were included in this area: staff, and patients and relatives.

Staff This group also identified relationships between colleagues as a source of pressure. However, because of the differences in organizational structure (i.e. they are less likely to have the same degree of responsibility for subordinate staff) there were fewer reported problems with subordinates.

Major stressors	Reported pressure	
	%	Mean
Relationships with colleagues	43	2.5
Relationships with subordinates	28	2.2

Patients and relatives Dealing with difficult patients is frequently perceived as a source of pressure by hospital and community nurses alike. This may reflect the nurse's expectations about patients—a good patient is a passive patient. Understandably, difficult or uncooperative patients add to the strain of an already considerable workload. Such problems are an additional source of role conflict since the nurse is expected to be simultaneously assertive and caring towards the patient.

Major stressors	Reported pressure	
	%	Mean
Difficult patients	74	2.6
Dealing with relatives	52	2.4

Area 8: Resources

Community-based staff

A specific 'physical resources' factor emerged from the responses of the

Major stressors	Reported pressure	
	%	Mean
Poor physical working conditions	48	2.9
Lack of privacy	36	2.8

community staff revolving around the quality of working conditions. However, it was evident that the *hospital* group reported a significantly higher degree of pressure in relation to their 'poor physical working conditions' ($P<0.000$).

Transport Transport problems were identified as a specific source of stress by community-based staff. 'My biggest source of stress is not the demands of my patients, or even the uncertainty of my workload. It is the worry caused by the need to keep my car in good condition for community work. My constant fear is what shall I do if my car breaks down?'

Summary and conclusions

Overall, it was evident that the hospital staff tended to report pressure more frequently and with greater intensity, particularly in the areas of 'Workload' and 'Relationships with Superiors. Although both groups reported that their level of occupational stress had increased over the past few years' hospital staff reported a significantly higher level of increase than community staff. Both hospital and community-based staff reported high levels of job satisfaction, and there was no significant difference between the levels reported by the two groups.

Hospital-based staff

In general, nurses in the hospital-based sample seem to have more difficulty in coping with their dual work roles of clinician and manager. The higher incidence of pressure reported between staff at different levels of the hierarchy, and especially in relationships with superiors, appears to stem from the more autocratic nature of management within the hospital setting. Nurses, especially those at lower levels of management, tend to feel that they lack control over their work situation.

These pressures, as well as those within the area of 'Workload', may reflect the continuing process of structural reorganization within the NHS. In the current financial climate it has usually been the hospitals that have been the prime target for government economies and cut-backs. At the same time there has been a growing commitment to a move towards more community-based care—a trend which may pose an additional threat to hospital personnel.

Community nurses

Although hospital-based staff tended to report higher levels of stress, this does not mean that the task of the community nurse is any less demanding. Rather they experience stress from different sources. Unlike hospital-based nurses working within a large bureaucratic structure, they are not pressured to the same extent by organizational constraints on their professional practice. They have a relatively greater degree of individual autonomy over their work situation and are more likely to feel in control of their work situation.

There are also indications that the community nurse requires a different professional orientation from the hospital nurse. They need to be more flexible in their approach as patients are likely to expect something more than just clinical expertise. This can give rise to quite different sorts of pressures. The boundary between being on and off duty is not as clear-cut. The role sometimes overlaps with that of the social worker, at least in the eyes of the patient, and patients are more likely to contact the community-based nurse in her own home. Consequently, over-emotional involvement and 'switching off' from the job become greater problems for this group.

Although we have been concerned with highlighting the differences between the two working environments, it is important to remember that there are common concerns in most of the areas identified. These considerations have implications for any programme which attempts to allieviate the negative effects of stress within the profession. 'General stressors' are more appropriately dealt with by organization-wide programmes, while other more specific programmes would be necessary when focusing upon the problems of particular work settings.

NURSING OFFICER AND SISTER/CHARGE NURSE LEVELS: A COMPARISON BY NURSING GRADE

The picture of occupational stress was further developed by subdividing the total sample according to different levels of nursing grade (i.e. Nursing Officer and Sister/Charge Nurse). The two groups were compared and their differences and similarities are discussed in this section.

Description of the groups

Two subgroups were identified

(1) The first group of 'first-line managers' consisted of 394 staff at *Sister/Charge Nurse* level, and accounted for 76.5 per cent of the total sample. It represented the largest single group and included both hospital- and community-based nurses.
(2) The second group was made up of 80 *Nursing Officers* (15.5 per cent of the whole sample). A number of levels were represented in this group: Clinical Nurse Managers (65), Directors of Nursing or Midwifery Services (10), and District Nursing Officers (5).

Forty-one of the respondents (8 per cent of the total) saw themselves as being on a different grade to those mentioned, and were not included in this analysis.

Comparison of the groups

Demographic details

An examination of the data from Section I of the questionnaire revealed that the two groups had much in common. However, there were a number of interesting differences which were statistically significant. Individuals in the Nursing Officer group were likely to be younger than their Sister/Charge Nurse colleagues ($P<0.006$). At the same time, they had, on average, considerably longer serving experience within the profession ($P<0.000$), and were more likely to have gained a post-professional qualification ($P<0.037$). This would seem to indicate that they are more commited to a long-term career in nursing. Certainly there is some evidence from their responses to the Type A questionnaire they are more ambitious than the Sister/Charge Nurse group.

At the Sister/Charge Nurse level it seems that length of service is likely to be affected by a break in order to have a family, many then re-enter at a later date, often at a lower grade of seniority.

These differences between Nursing Officers and Sister/Charge Nurses seem to reflect a separation within the profession of two distinct lines of career development. The first, a 'clinical career', is more restricted in setting and advancement, but has the possibility of merging professional and domestic commitments. The second, a 'management career', often involves rapid progression through the clinical area to management status; however, there seems to be less likelihood of pursuing both professional and domestic ambitions.

Job satisfaction

Overall, both Nursing Officers and Sister/Charge Nurses indicated that they experienced high levels of job satisfaction. There was no significant difference between the levels reported by the two groups in this area. However, it is interesting to note that Nursing Officers believed that more of the total stress in their lives resulted directly from their job whereas Sister/Charge Nurses located more of their life stress in sources unrelated to their occupation ($P<0.012$).

Sources of occupational stress

The responses from the two groups on the Job Stress Questionnaire were factor analysed. Eight areas were identified for each of the grades.

Area 1: Workload

Sister/Charge Nurse

As for all the subgroups we examined 'Workload' was consistently reported as a major source of pressure. For Sister/Charge Nurses the quantitative and qualitative aspects of the area emerged as two discrete factors.

Quantitative aspects These three stressors demonstrate the quantitative pressures of the workload at Sister/Charge Nurse level. It is interesting to note that staff shortages were seen as a considerable source of pressure by the majority of nurses in the total sample, irrespective of their nursing grade. This is a further indication of the strength of feelings within the profession regarding the inadequacy of the present number of nurses within the NHS.

Major stressors	Reported pressure	
	%	Mean
Work overload	85	3.2
Staff shortages	85	3.3
Time pressures and deadlines	81	2.8

Qualitative aspects This factor tends to illustrate the more qualitative aspects of the workload. Conflicting demands, too little time to do the task properly, and the feeling that work time is not properly planned were all reported as sources of pressure.

Major stressors	Reported pressure	
	%	Mean
I have too little time in which to do what is expected of me	74	3.0
Others' demands for my time at work are in conflict	64	2.7
I spend my time 'fighting fires' rather than working to a plan	52	2.5

Nursing Officer

The Nursing Officers, however, were more likely to perceive their task as being too demanding. They reported significantly more pressure on both the quantitative and qualitative aspects of time-related demands. Time pressure and deadlines were seen as a greater source of pressure. In particular, this group was more likely to feel that their time was subject to the conflicting demands of others. Generally, the stressors in this area seem to reflect problems associated with the wider managerial role of the Nursing Officer.

Major stressors	Reported pressure		Significant
	%	Mean	differences
Work overload	87	3.3	
Time pressures and deadlines	82	3.0	($P<0.000$)
I have too little time in which to do what is expected of me	82	3.0	
Staff shortages	79	3.4	
Others' demands for my time at work are in conflict	76	3.0	($P<0.007$)
I expect too much of myself	75	3.1	
I spend my time 'fighting fires' rather than working to a plan	64	2.8	
Management expects me to interrupt my work for new priorities	62	2.7	

Area 2: Relationships with superiors

Sister/Charge Nurse

The pattern of stressors and pressures reported in this area strongly resemble those identified in Chapter 8. It seems that the results from the total sample are dominated by the experiences of this group. They were particularly concerned about their lack of involvement in decision making and the lack of support from senior staff.

Major stressors	Reported pressure	
	%	Mean
Decisions or changes which affect me are made 'above', without my knowledge or involvement	73	2.8
Lack of support from senior staff	69	3.1
Management misunderstands the real needs of my department	58	3.0
I lack confidence in management	57	2.7
Relationships with superiors	54	2.6
I only get feedback when my performance is unsatisfactory	54	2.9
Avoiding conflict with superiors	49	2.6
Relationships with administrators	44	2.5

Nursing Officer

The Nursing Officers appear to share a number of concerns with the Sister/ Charge Nurse group. These common stressors represent a discrete factor, which appears to be a source of pressure independent of the level of nursing grade. Surprisingly, there were no significant differences between the frequency and levels of pressure reported by the two subgroups in this area. It seems that even the senior staff find their 'relationships with superiors' a considerable source of pressure!

Major stressors	Reported pressure	
	%	Mean
Decisions or changes which affect me are made 'above' without my knowledge or involvement	64	3.2
Lack of support from senior staff	60	3.2
I only get feedback when my performance is unsatisfactory	56	3.1
Avoiding conflict with superiors	55	2.7
Management misunderstands the real needs of my department	54	3.0
Relationships with superiors	52	2.8
I lack confidence in management	51	2.8

Area 3: The role

Sister/Charge Nurse

Three aspects of the Sister/Charge Nurse role emerged as sources of pressure: confidence and competence, professional developments, conflicting demands.

Confidence and competence The first was concerned with the nurse's feeling of competence in her clinical role. In general, nurses at this level in the hierarchy appear to have more confidence in their role. Perhaps this is not surprising, since their training prepares them for clinical practice rather than managerial tasks. A main plea in this area was for a reduction in non-nursing duties, particularly paperwork, which some ward sisters and health visitors believed was excessive. Other nurses suggested that more clerical workers be employed 'in order to allow trained staff to spend more time with their patients.'

Major stressors	Reported pressure	
	%	Mean
Coping with new situations	69	2.4
Tasks outside of my competence	50	2.7
Uncertainty about the degree or area of my responsibility	46	2.4

Professional developments The second aspect of role-related problems concerned the difficulty of keeping abreast of recent professional developments. This was seen largely as part of the general problem of finding the time needed in the light of the existing excessive demands of the daily workload.

Major stressors	Reported pressure	
	%	Mean
Keeping up with professional developments	76	2.6

Conflicting demands The final aspect of role-related pressures was concerned with liaison and sexual discrimination and reflects the concerns expressed by hospital-based staff.

Major stressors	Reported pressure	
	%	Mean
I must go to other departments to get my job done	46	2.5
Sexual discrimination at work	7	2.5

Nursing Officer

The principal differences between Nursing Officers and the Sister/Charge Nurse group were evident in this area. It seems that role conflict and role ambiguity were experienced more often and to a higher degree by Nursing Officers. Compared with their Sister/Charge Nurse colleagues, Nursing Officers were much more likely to be concerned about their ability to cope with their present role and their overall professional competence appeared to be lower. Their difficulties seem to be related directly to their managerial role and they felt the need for more specialized training to deal with these managerial tasks. As one Nursing Officer commented, 'There is a need for greater preparation for managerial roles before appointments. At the moment we are expected to become managers overnight.'

Major stressors	Reported pressure		Significant
	%	Mean	differences
Deciding priorities	67	2.4	
Tasks outside of my competence	56	3.0	
Lack of specialized training for present task	50	2.7	($P<0.004$)
I don't feel adequately trained for the job I have to do	46	2.6	($P<0.010$)

A number of other significant differences were apparent between Nursing Officers and Sister/Charge Nurses in the area of role and differences relating to 'change' and managerial responsibilities were identified. Nursing Officers were more likely to be concerned about their responsibilities for 'organizational change' ($P<0.038$) and 'bringing about changes in staff' ($P<0.002$). The liaison aspect of the management role, such as 'having to attend meetings' ($P<0.017$) and 'having to go to other departments' ($P<0.041$) to get the job done were also more of a problem for the Nursing Officers.

Finally, this group demonstrated more concern about 'being promoted out of the caring role' ($P<0.021$). They felt more 'uncertain about the degree or area of their responsibility' ($P<0.011$) than their Sister/Charge Nurse colleagues, and were more likely to feel that others at work were 'unclear about what their job is' (*P*<0.000).

Area 4: Death and dying

Sister/Charge Nurse

This factor emerged as a discrete source of stress for Sisters/Charge Nurses, reflecting the difficulties of continual face-to-face contact with death and dying. This group reported significantly greater pressure on all the stressors in this area.

Major stressors	Reported pressure		Significant
	%	Mean	differences
Involvement with life and death situations	63	2.6	(*P*<0.054)
Bereavement counselling	59	2.6	(*P*<0.005)
Exposure to death	47	2.6	(*P*<0.006)

Area 4: Emotional situations

Nursing Officers

The problem of dealing with death and dying did not emerge as a separate factor for Nursing Officers, but as part of a more general concern about dealing with emotionally difficult situations. Generally, the level of reported pressure in these areas was lower than at Sister/Charge Nurse level, no doubt reflecting differences in the degree of face-to-face contact that this group has with patients and relatives.

In the US, Leatt and Schneck (1980) found that the occurrence of patient-based stress amongst 'headnurses' varied according to the type of nursing unit. It was highest in intensive care units, medical units and auxiliary units where the headnurses were more frequently exposed to stress from patients with poor prognoses, upset families and providing painful nursing care.

Major stressors	Reported pressure	
	%	Mean
Difficult patients	49	2.4
Involvement with life and death situations	45	2.7
Bereavement counselling	41	2.5
Over-emotional involvement	37	2.5
Dealing with relatives	36	2.2
Exposure to death	27	2.6

Area 5: Home/work conflict

Sister/Charge Nurse

As for the whole sample, two aspects of home/work conflict were identified home overspill and work overspill.

Home overspill The findings of the effects of home pressures upon the work situation were similar to those for the main sample. One additional element was present i.e. 'Superiors do not appreciate my home pressures'. This again suggests that problems of relationships with superiors was more strongly felt at the lower echelons of management.

Major stressors	Reported pressure	
	%	Mean
Job versus home demands	62	2.7
Domestic/family demands inhibit promotion	20	2.8
My superiors do not appreciate my home pressures	19	2.8
I need to absent myself from work to cope with domestic problems	10	2.6

Work overspill Here problems with 'switching-off' from work were evidently the major cause of concern to this group.

Major stressors	Reported pressure	
	%	Mean
Taking problems home	61	2.6
Over-emotional involvement	46	2.4

Nursing Officers

Here, only the effect of home on work emerged as a discrete factor. This may reflect the professional ambitions of the Nursing Officer group, for whom work takes up a more central part of their lives. There were no significant differences in the findings between the two groups in this area.

Major stressors	Reported pressure	
	%	Mean
Job versus home demands	57	2.9
Domestic/family demands inhibit promotion	21	3.4
I need to absent myself from work to cope with domestic problems	11	2.3

Area 6: Career

Sister/Charge Nurse

Less than one-third of the group reported feeling pressure due to a lack of career prospects. A slightly larger number reported 'low professional status' as a particular source of pressure.

Major stressors	Reported pressure	
	%	Mean
Low professional status	35	2.6
Lack of promotion prospects	27	2.7

Nursing Officers

There is evidence that Nursing Officers are more conscious of a need to advance their career. They were found to be significantly more concerned about the lack of promotion prospects within the profession. This is further support for the idea that the job is more likely to be of central importance in the life of many Nursing Officers.

Major stressors	Reported pressure		Significant
	%	Mean	differences
Lack of participation in planning/ decision making	59	2.9	
Lack of job satisfaction	50	3.1	
Low professional status	36	2.9	
Lack of promotion prospects	26	2.9	(P<0.056)

Area 7: Interpersonal relationships

Sister/Charge Nurse

Patients and relatives Dealing with relatives and difficult patients was found to be a significantly greater source of pressure for first-line managers. Again this reflects their different role orientation.

Major stressors	Reported pressure		Significant
	%	Mean	differences
Difficult patients	71	2.6	(P<0.000)
Dealing with relatives	50	2.4	(P>0.002)

Staff The second factor in this area suggests that interpersonal relationships with colleagues are also an important source of pressure.

Major stressors	Reported pressure	
	%	Mean
Relationships with colleages	42	2.4

Nursing Officers

Similar percentages of Nursing Officers indicated that they found dealing with colleagues potentially stressful. In addition, relationships with subordinates were reported as a source of pressure.

Major stressors	Reported pressure	
	%	Mean
Relationships with colleagues	41	2.3
Relationship with subordinates	39	2.3

Area 8: Resources

Sister/Charge Nurse

A large number of the group were concerned about shortages of essential resources and poor physical working conditions. These concerns seemed to be focused particularly on the physical resources necessary for the day-to-day completion of the professional task.

Major stressors	Reported pressure	
	%	Mean
Shortages of essential resources	70	2.8
Poor physical working conditions	59	3.0

Nursing Officers

Concerns about the quantity and quality of essential resources were also evident here. Nursing Officers reported a significantly higher incidence of pressure regarding the shortages of essential resources. Concerns about the poor quality of supporting staff and the lack of privacy are also evident in this

group. Again, these issues can be seen as reflecting the managerial orientation
of the Nursing Officer's task.

Major stressors	Reported pressure		Significant
	%	Mean	differences
Shortages of essential resources	82	2.9	(P<0.014)
Poor quality of supporting staff	64	3.0	
Poor physical working conditions	51	2.9	
Lack of privacy	42	2.9	

Summary and conclusions

There was no significant difference between the two groups regarding levels of
occupation stress. However, the Nursing Officer group believed that more of
the total stress in their lives resulted from their job. Both groups reported that
levels of stress had increased over the past few years, and both reported
equally high levels of job satisfaction. The comparison between Sister/Charge
Nurses and Nursing Officers revealed some interesting differences in their
sources of stress. These are probably best explained in terms of differing
roles. Essentially, Sister/Charge Nurses experienced greater pressures due to
their 'caring role'. For example, they expressed relatively greater difficulties in
coping with death and dying situations and in dealing with relatives and difficult
patients. Nursing Officers, on the other hand, appeared to be more anxious
about coping with their managerial tasks. They seemed to experience a higher
degree of role conflict as a consequence of being promoted out of the 'caring
role'. They were particularly concerned about their lack of training and
preparation for a managerial position.

These differences in role parallel two distinct lines of career development
associated with nursing grade. Sisters/Charge Nurses appear to follow a
clinically based career often leaving the service to have a family and re-entering
the profession at a later date, while Nursing Officers are evidently more career
orientated, and more likely to pursue a full-time career in nurse management
with less time for domestic commitments. Here, again, there are implications
for stress-alleviating programmes, some stressors are role specific, while others
are of a more general nature, acting as a source of pressure regardless of the
nurse's position in the organizational hierarchy.

REFERENCES

Leatt, P. and Schneck, R. (1980) Differences in stress perceived by headnurses across
nursing specialities in hospitals. *J. Adv. Nurs.*, **5** 31–46
Numerof, R.E., and Abrams, M.N. (1984) Sources of stress among nurses: on empirical
investigation. *J. Hum. stress*, Summer, pp 88–100

CHAPTER 10

Managing stress

In the final chapter we conclude our study of stress in nurse managers by returning to the questions asked at the beginning. This is followed by a discussion of the possible courses of action for alleviating stress in nursing.

Is nursing a stressful occupation?

There is little doubt that occupational stress is a problem within the profession. Rates of occupational mortality, wastage and absenteeism all indicate that the cost, both to the individual nurse and to the service, can be considerable.

Smoking, drinking and stress

Research findings suggest that increased smoking and excessive drinking are often behavioural manifestations of stress. Analyses of the smoking and drinking habits of our sample indicated that nurses were less likely to smoke than women in general, but more likely than other female professionals. At least 27 per cent of our sample smoked and their smoking patterns had remained relatively stable over the last year. It was found that nurses in the hospital setting were more likely to smoke, and smoked more heavily than their community-based colleagues.

As far as drinking patterns were concerned 92 per cent consumed alcohol, with some 8 per cent (41) drinking daily. This percentage of daily drinkers was higher amongst nurses than women in the general population. There were differences in patterns of drinking within the sample. The Nursing Officer group seemed more likely to drink than their Sister/Charge Nurse colleagues (although the difference was not statistically significant).

To be able to identify and alleviate stressful aspects of the job will help to reduce the pressures which lead to smoking and drinking as stress-relieving activities. To date the profession has done little to tackle this problem.

Is it possible to identify the sources of stress in nursing?

Through our analysis we were able to identify a number of potentially stressful areas in nursing. There was general agreement about the nature of these areas, and most of our respondents perceived the demands of the 'Workload', 'Relationships with Superiors', and the conflicts and ambiguities of 'The Role' as being particularly stressful. Not all nurses responded in the same way. A number of differences between groups of nurses were found to be related to the type of setting in which they worked and their level of nursing grade.

Does this mean that nurses are dissatisfied with their job?

The relationship between occupational stress and job satisfaction is complex. Stress at work does not necessarily lead to low job satisfaction. However, each individual appears to have an optimum level of stress—a 'stress threshold'. Exceeding this threshold is likely to result in fatigue, disillusionment and 'burnout'.

In our sample most of the nurses were satisfied with their job and had every intention of remaining within the profession. However, some 17 per cent (88 respondents) were very dissatisfied with their job, and a similar number (16 per cent) were thinking of changing to an occupation other than nursing. It was possible to identify this group of 'potential leavers' by their significantly higher stress profiles on the Job Stress Questionnaire. It seems that they had reached or exceeded their 'stress threshold' and the demands of the job outweighed the rewards.

WHAT CAN BE DONE?

Action without research is blind, but research without action is sterile. (Anon)

The main purpose of this research was to identify sources of stress in nursing. However, it would be incomplete not to comment on possible courses of action to alleviate these problems.

Stress alleviation

The low level of stress awareness

It seems that nursing is generally recognized as being a very demanding occupation, yet the level of stress awareness within the profession is low. Rather than seeing stress as something which can be successfully dealt with, thus reducing its costs, the prevailing attitude seems to be that 'nurses should either put up with the difficulties or get out of the profession.' To alleviate the effects of stress in nursing the profession must first acknowledge that there is a problem.

A multidimensional approach

The individual nurse will suffer stress like all other nurses, like some other nurses and like no other nurse.

Taking responsibility for those in our soceity who are ill and in pain means that nursing will always be a potentially high stress occupation and, for these reasons, it is all the more important to locate and to minimize the pressures. The evidence suggests that sources of stress are located at both the individual and the organizational levels, and that action must be taken at both these levels if the problem is to be alleviated. Unfortunately, it seems that the nursing profession tends to see stress primarily as an individual problem and alleviation as a personal responsibility. Attempts at stress management have aimed almost exclusively at increasing individual coping mechanisms with the in-built, but unexpressed assumption, that it is the individual who must change. Consequently, very little attention has been given to organizational strategies for decreasing the effect of potentially stressful situations. Yet, it is apparent from our study that many of the sources of stress identified lie within the organization. Therefore, any attempt to ameliorate the negative effects of stress must be addressed to both individual and organizational levels.

At the individual level

A number of courses on coping with stress aimed at a general audience are offered throughout the country. Often these are based on a problem-solving approach to stress management and cover methods of diagnosis, skills training and action planning. Many of the techniques focus upon dealing with the symptoms of stress and employ a variety of methods and approaches, often borrowed from behaviour therapy. Much attention is paid to self-diagnosis of the causes, with a review of the individual's existing 'coping skills'. Training in a range of specific work-related skills is usually provided so that the individual can strengthen areas of identified weakness which are identified as potentially stressful (see Bond, 1986).

Other techniques, aimed to promote more general personal growth, and often with an emphasis on increasing interpersonal skills, are likely to be used (e.g. transactional analysis, T-groups, assertiveness training, etc.). These can play a considerable (if somewhat unquantifiable) part in helping the individual to cope with both the pressures of the job and life events in general.

At the organizational level

Again a problem-solving approach can be successfully utilized to reduce stress levels. Two main stages can be identified:

Stage one: diagnosis This involves identifying areas of stress in the working environment, so that subsequent intervention can be planned and directed as effectively as possible. A valid and reliable instrument for locating and measuring sources of stress in nursing has yet to be developed. It is the intention of the researchers to develop a version of the Job Stress Question-naire used in this study, so that an easily administered instrument is available for use at individual, unit, or hospital level.

Stage two: intervention Having identified sources of stress, the second stage involves planned intervention. Given the complexity of the problem it would be foolish to provide simple prescriptions for stress alleviation. However, in the light of our findings we can indicate three areas which merit close attention:

1. Resources
2. Training
3. Support.

RESOURCES

A good nursing staff will perform their duties more or less satisfactorily under every disadvantage. But while doing so, their head will always try to improve their surroundings in such a way as to liberate them from subsidiary work, and to enable them to devote their time more exclus-ively to the care of the sick. This is, after all, the real purpose of their being there at all, not to act as lifts, water-carriers, beasts of burden, or steam engines—articles whose labour can be had at vastly less cost than that of educated human beings. (Florence Nightingale, 1867, quoted in Byrnes, 1982)

Our findings clearly indicate that there are problems concerning the provision of resources. The need for both quantitative and qualitative improvements were identified. Nurses told us 'we need more resources, and we need *better* resources.' The possibility of attracting additional resources in these times of financial stringency is often slight. When funds are being curtailed or even eliminated completely, the problem becomes one of how to bring about improvements with fixed or shrinking resources. While we do not condone this state of affairs, it is nevertheless a situation faced by most Health Authorities. Under these circumstances, attention must be given not only to means of increasing the resources available, but also to the ways in which existing resources can be used to greatest effect.

Staffing

The problems of staff shortages were identified as a serious source of stress. There was also concern about the quality of staff; a need for better trained nurses was expressed. Both of these issues are related to the quality of patient care. Research suggests that simply increasing staffing levels does not necessarily lead to better patient care (Aydelotle and Tener, 1960; Harris 1970). Rather, staffing requirements need to be based on patients' nursing needs. McFarlane (1980) points out that the problems identified by the Briggs Committee with respect to nurse man-power still remain. 'No satisfactory measure of general staffing needs has yet been devised. What attempts have been made to measure the need for nursing staff have concentrated on acute hospitals. Little effort has been made to extend the study of staffing difficulties into community nursing or in those areas and sectors in hospital where there seems to be the worst problems, particularly psychiatric, geriatric and long stay hospitals.'

While there were undoubtedly a number of identifiable 'black spots', where it seems staff shortages were endemic and long standing, it was evident from our findings that the problem was not simply one of inadequate numbers. Problems of 'staffing shortfall' often resulted from the unpredictability of the work demands. Over half of our sample found that unexpected fluctuations in workload caused considerable staffing pressures. Indeed, a minority of respondents, some 17 per cent, found that at times the problem was 'work underload', i.e. having to look busy during slack periods.

This problem of determining optimum staffing levels requires a solution which reflects patient needs and is yet flexible enough to match the changing demands of the total workload. A number of interesting approaches to the quantification of the demands of the various types of patient care have been developed. Hearn (1979) has developed a 'package' for calculating the staffing of geriatric wards. This approach was directly based on prescriptions of the nursing-care needs of each patient and specific standards of care. During trials, it was found that ward staff felt more able to give better care to patients and there was general agreement that the patient benefitted from the care given (although no quantitative measure was applied). Moreover, the nurses found great satisfaction in being able to design and implement care plans, and communication between them was improved by a formal planning mechanism.

More recently McGratty (1985) described a predictive system for matching nursing resources and workload, which she developed for the private sector in the UK. Making use of computer technology, the system reflects the demands on nurses and is quick and easy to operate. It is flexible enough to allow for daily changes in ward composition and patient movements. 'It now takes approximately ten minutes for the nurse on the floor to complete the worksheet and five minutes with the nurse manager to plan staffing for a ward for the next twenty-four hours . . . It can accurately predict one day in advance the nursing staff required to maintain each floor at maximum efficiency. The better matching of workload and resources means that nurses are being more efficiently deployed with a corresponding benefit in patient care and appropriate cost savings.' This approach and the detailed information it can provide concerning demand throughout the whole organization can provide the manager with the data needed to determine optimum staffing levels.

In addition, the pressures of inadequate staffing could be alleviated by exploring more flexible approaches to methods of employment. The possibilities of some staff transfer across unit boundaries (even across hospitals) in order to respond to fluctuations in demand and to ease the situation in the most problematic areas, could be explored; perhaps even the creation of a nursing 'task force' made up of individuals with wide experience who would be able to respond quickly to serious staff shortages across a whole Health Authority.

Difficulties with recruitment are becoming more and more problematic, particularly in specialized areas of care. The use of flexitime, jobsharing, etc., is well established in other occupations and deserves more consideration by the profession. More nurses who wish to work but are unable to offer a full-time commitment may be brought into the service by greater use of part-time contracts and pools of 'on-call' nurses. Another obvious area for consideration is the provision of supportive services in order that the nurse can devote her energies and attention towards the professional task. Remembering the words of Florence Nightingale, even a cursory examination of the day-to-day nursing task suggests that many activities simply do not make sense. They do not make sense professionally; nurses are trained 'in the care of the sick . . . not to act as water-carriers, beasts of burden, or steam engines.' Neither do they make sense economically; paying a ward sister or nursing officer to carry out domestic or clerical tasks is an inappropriate use of scarce resources and is just poor housekeeping.

In the final analysis, it may be the appeal to simple financial logic which will prove the most powerful force available to the nurse. The profession needs to utilize these economic arguments to convince the newly appointed general managers that there can be a direct payoff, not only from the provision of more supportive services, but also by responding to occupational stress in general.

Working conditions

Poor working conditions emerged as an important issue to many nurses. In discussion, specific difficulties, limited to certain work areas or locations, were often identified (these ranged from direction notices for patients, poor lighting, uncontrolled air-conditioning, to the lack of public telephones and an absence of changing facilities). Although not appearing serious in themselves, many of them were long-standing problems which were a constant source of irritation and pressure, and as such they seriously detracted from the quality of the workplace.

At a more general level it was possible to identify a number of areas of common concern. The value of 'breaks', from what is often an intensive work situation, was frequently commented upon by our respondents. Nurses require a 'stress-free' area to retreat to during their breaks—a rest area convenient to the work situation, but far enough removed to be free from interruption, to enable the nurse to 'switch off'. The lack of such facilities is all too common in hospitals—often rest rooms are too far away to be utilized except for longer breaks. The sluice room and toilets continue to remain the traditional places of retreat for many hospital nurses.

In the community, transport problems proved to be of particular concern. The possibility of a vehicle breakdown interfering with their work tended to be a constant source of anxiety. Access to an emergency pool of cars, perhaps shared with social service departments, would be a simple and cost effective way of dealing with this problem.

Again utilizing an economic argument, it is to identify a number of problem areas where even the outlay of modest financial resources would alleviate what are often seen as major sources of stress.

Home/work interface

Many of our nurse managers experienced the pressures of conflicting demands from home and work. As there are a growing number of married nurses in practice, their special needs should be recognized. Compared with other occupations, there is a dearth of child-care facilities available for nurses within the NHS. Many nurses with young children are obliged to reduce or change their hours of work because of the child-care problem. Some are forced to change jobs or even give up work altogether.

More workplace nurseries and crèches geared towards the unsocial hours often worked by nurses would help to reduce wastage within the profession as well as reduce the need of some nurses to absent themselves from work in order to cope with domestic problems. Furthermore, nurses who decide to have children would be afforded a more equal opportunity for further training and promotion.

TRAINING

The research findings raise a number of questions regarding professional training needs. These will be considered under four separate headings.

Stress awareness training

We have already noted that there are a number of established short courses on 'stress management' aimed at the 'caring professions' and which use well-proven techniques and methods of teaching. Following the same general pattern, a specific course catering for the profession and directed at the specific problems of nursing should be developed.

Basic training

Even at the level of basic training, there is a need to address the subject of occupational stress. Certainly, the fact that nursing is potentially a high-stress occupation should be recognized and discussed in order to raise the level of general awareness. In addition, students could be introduced to basic stress-reduction techniques appropriate to their level of understanding, and to the use of existing support systems (e.g. self-help groups, counselling facilities, etc.).

Post-basic training

At the post-basic level a more intensive programme should be made available for those with managerial responsibility. This might be provided by two- or three-day courses focusing upon the specific problems of the profession. Such a package would include the recognition of the signs and effects of stress in self, staff, and the organization. It would also introduce a variety of appropriate strategies aimed at the alleviation, or more positive management, of stressful situations in the workplace.

Training in management skills

In the light of the particular difficulties experienced by many respondents in fulfilling some aspects of the management task, training in this area needs to be re-examined. The development of 'interpersonal skills' and 'the ability to work effectively in team settings' were identified by our respondents as being particular areas of concern. These abilities are even more crucial with today's emphasis on the nursing process—an approach dependent not only upon individual nursing skills, but also upon an effective team approach. As Allen (1982) stresses, 'Today the nursing *team* is with us . . . Nothing could be more misleading than the idea that a team is brought into existence by simply selecting staff and saying now you are a team. There has to be some real interaction. Sharing with the clinical team is important and needs an examination of a common language for understanding to develop.' Training must keep pace with these needs and developments.

In spite of the recognition that the ward sister plays a key managerial role in the Health Service, the present system of management training, unlike that in the clinical areas, is both patchy and ad hoc. Individual Health Authorities often operate in total isolation. Courses are planned and mounted at local level and there is the ever-present danger of 're-inventing the wheel', of using scarce resources to duplicate what has already been developed, tried, and tested in another part of the country. Alternatively, staff are sent to established courses in Institutes of Further and Higher Education—courses that are often conceptually and professionally removed from the real world of the nurse manager.

A national review?

All aspects of nursing require some expertise in the basic management skills of planning, directing, and controlling. Our research leads us to suggest that often the profession tends to undervalue these abilities, concerning itself primarily with nurse/patient interaction and questions of clinical performance. Skills of nursing care will always be paramount, and our findings show that nurses are confident in their training and performance in this area. However, the quality of care is also determined by the management of the ward or unit, and this management task is recognized by many nurses as being more problematic, and gives rise to considerable degrees of anxiety and stress. Consequently, adequate training in this area is crucial.

Some review of the content and teaching methods used on current management courses seems to be called for, to ensure that their level and approach is appropriate for nurse managers. In particular, more attention should be paid to interpersonal skills training, dealing with the demands of change, and team development. More opportunity and support should be given to nurse managers to develop these managerial skills through appropriate in-house training. Finally, there is a need for a fundamental review of management training at this level and for a national standard to be set for all courses to meet the needs of nurse managers.

Specific role training

Twenty years ago, Virginia Henderson, in her classic 'The Nature of Nursing', pointed out that there was no clearly defined statement of the nurse's role. She believed that whilst this degree of 'unfinished business' existed then conflict between nurses and other supporting professionals would be both inevitable and costly. Sadly, this lack of role clarity is still with us today and is an on-going source of confusion and uncertainty. It is evident that many of the problems identified by our respondents were seen to be a direct result of the conflicts and ambiguities which often surrounded their post. This situation could be alleviated by more training aimed at preparing the nurse for the expectations and demands of the specific work situation.

The recent recommendations of the National Staff Committee for Nurses and Midwives (1983) for more 'role-based training' reflects this concern. They see the need for training aimed at 'helping the individual function more effectively in the role which she currently occupies by providing her with an opportunity to gain greater understanding of that role and the skills and knowledge needed for its successful occupancy.' Such induction and training programmes do already exist in a number of Health Authorities and are proving very successful. A somewhat different approach, in that it is 'pro-active', is the UK Ward-Sister Preparation Programme developed under the auspices of the King's Fund. The aim of the course is to prepare registered general nurses to develop the skills and expertise needed in the ward-sisters role. The six-month course is based in the 'real-life' situation and uses experienced ward sisters as role models. Its aim is to enable the nurse 'to explore, study and develop skills in the different and complex aspects of the ward sister's role—as manager, clinician, teacher and as the lynch-pin of the caring team co-ordinating the delivery of care to the best advantage of the patients.' Such an approach, with its emphasis on role modelling and action learning, could also be adapted to provide short preparatory training packages aimed at specific managerial levels and nursing specialisms, e.g. nursing officers and community-based staff (see King's Fund 1982).

The management of death and dying/bereavement counselling

If I cannot face my own death it is conceivable that I can't accept my patient's death. Each time we dare to get truly involved with our patients and reach a stage of acceptance it will help us come a step closer towards acceptance of our own finiteness. (Kubler-Ross, 1982)

It is apparent from our results that this is one of the few areas of clinical practice that was of general concern to the majority of the sample, and one in which they felt vulnerable and threatened.

Training and support

Improvements in training and in the provision of on-going support are called for. We can do no better than reiterate the recommendations of a recent study into the problem which highlighted the need for 'more teaching on the care of the terminally ill, and more support for nurses who are upset about a patient's death'. (Whitfield, 1979) Recognition of the problem and the provision of 'first-line' support should be provided through the general supervisory role of senior staff. Our research indicates that this support is not always forthcoming and, as we have suggested elsewhere, the whole question of professional support needs to be re-examined in some detail.

In addition, there seems to be the need to provide, within the organization, a specialist member of staff. Ideally, she would be a skilled counsellor or specially trained nurse clinician, who would provide the necessary support for those staff who experience more pronounced anxiety and stress in the care of the dying patient.

Although long recognized as a cause of professional anxiety, preparation and training in many Health Authorities seems minimal. More in-service courses in coping with death and dying and training in bereavement counselling need to be provided and made accessible to nursing staff of all grades.

Good practice

Again the profession should be more outward looking, identifying examples of 'good practice' and building upon these. One of the most interesting and exciting developments in health care over the last decade has been the growth of the hospice movement. Developments, not only in methods of direct patient care, but in approaches to nursing the terminally ill and appropriate methods of staff training and support, provide a pool of knowledge and expertise which has been largely ignored by the profession.

SUPPORT

The importance of a positive system of support in reducing occupational stress has been identified in many research studies (Caplan, 1974; Pines and Aronson, 1981). The main theme of the 'human relations' approach to the workplace emphasizes the crucial role played by social relationships in creating a satisfying and supportive work environment. There is growing evidence that the extent and quality of an individual's 'support network' can offset the negative effects of stress, including coronary heart disease (Cooper and Payne, 1978). Research carried out in Japan suggests that existing cultural norms, which encourage strong group dependence and provide effective social support, play an important part in decreasing the incidence of stress-related disease. 'Stress can be effectively managed if a meaningful social group is available through which the individual can derive emotional support and understanding.' (Matsumoto, 1970)

Within the 'caring professions', the support of colleagues and seniors is essential, as this support can provide an effective buffer against the more negative aspects of work pressure. An American study into the effects of burnout concluded that 'one of the most crucial elements determining the quality of staff morale . . . is whether they had a good working relationship with their colleagues.' (Cherniss, 1980) It was found that members of professional groups having a supportive environment, i.e. where day-to-day responsibilities and difficulties were shared, experienced far less stress than colleagues in less supportive group settings. However, the overwhelming evidence is that while stress levels are high in nursing the support available to cope with that stress is minimal (Marshall, 1980; Parkes, 1980a,b).

It is not surprising that this project has also identified lack of support, from both colleagues and senior staff, as being an important 'stressor'. It proved to be the cause of a considerable degree of anxiety to many of our group of nurse managers. From the interviews of Phase 1, it was apparent that different situations call for very different kinds of support. Overall respondents identified the need for two types of support. On the one hand, there was a need for career and professional support, and, on the other, a need for support at the emotional/personal level, though obviously, in reality, there is a considerable overlap between these two categories.

Career and professional support was seen as involving someone who can give advice and direction about work-related problems in a constructive way. Someone who can simply listen, when appropriate, and who is prepared to provide honest feedback on professional performance when it is needed. It was suggested that ideally all nurses should have a 'mentor'. A person who can *listen openly* (and will not try initially to solve the problem for you), *challenge constructively* (in order to allow professional growth and creativity), and *guide supportively*.

The second type of support is emotional. All 'caring professions' are emotionally demanding, and nursing particularly so. It is important for the individual to have this emotional support whether it is provided by a partner, by friends or by a professional service. 'It is important to know that someone is in your corner . . . Sharing your perception of reality with someone, and knowing that person is listening . . . can be a very effective stress preventer. You need people with whom you can share your ups and your downs, people who listen to your trivial everyday incidents, as well as your triumphs and your pains or frustrations. These people add the dimension of sharing as part of a support system. Who are the two people in your life who listen well to you and/or you can check out reality with? If you have difficulty naming people who provide these types of support for you, take note that your support system is not solid.' (Lachman, 1983)

The provision of professional and emotional support for all staff is crucial, and appropriate action is called for at both individual and organizational level to ensure that a system of support is available to all in the profession. In particular, three areas are identified for further consideration:

1. The availability of a general counselling service.
2. The encouragement of 'self-support groups'.
3. The provision of on-going professional support and supervision as part of the organizational structure.

Counselling

Lazarus (1980) makes the point that successful coping with some external stressors may only be achieved by the individual adjusting more effectively to those things which are beyond his control, '(so) an enormous amount of successful coping is emotion-focused . . . For many serious sources of stress in life, there is little or nothing that can be done to change things. If so, you are better off if you do nothing except take care of your feelings.' (Lazarus, 1980)

Counselling is a well-established method of helping the individual cope more effectively with the demands of living. Counselling is a shared activity in which, through a supportive relationship, individuals are helped to explore thoughts, feelings and behaviour in order to achieve a clearer understanding of themselves and their situation. As a method of dealing with stress it has three potential advantages.

(1) As it is based upon a sharing relationship it immediately engages the active help of another person; it widens, or in some cases establishes, the 'support network' recommended as essential by most writers on stress management.

(2) The very activity of verbalizing and sharing the problem is often accompanied by feelings of relief and a lowering of anxiety levels. Marks (1975) comments that, 'Subjects often experience great relief simply by talking about their problem, a confessional act that so far has not been subject to scientific study and which should be brought under experimental control if we are to understand it further.'

(3) Perhaps of greatest importance, counselling is also a means of personal learning and of increasing self-awareness. Counselling can be seen as a positive problem-solving activity. It is a coping method based upon the sequence of data gathering, followed by reflection and increased understanding, culminating in action and change. The counselling process aims to build up the strengths and problem-solving abilities of the individual in order to enhance appropriate decision making, coping actions and response to change. As Lightbody (1981) remarks, 'For counselling is about change. Change is a matter of an individual producing adjustment, either in themselves or in their environment.'

Counselling in the workplace

Counselling as a method of allieviating stress in the workplace has long been recognized in the USA (see Warsaw, 1979). In this country, the use of counselling has been slower to develop. However, the last ten years has seen the introduction of various forms of counselling by a number of large commercial and industrial organizations. Imperial Chemical Industries were one of the first to initiate a scheme in 1971 to train employees in general counselling skills (Hopson, 1973), and the Natural Environment Research Council followed suit in the same year (Watts, 1977); Shell Chemicals appointed the first full-time counsellor in 1974. Writing six years later, the Shell counsellor commented upon the extent of his work: 'I have been in personal contact with some 8 per cent per annum of all employees. I have accepted as clients for the service a figure equal to 5 per cent per annum of all employees, of whom half have been simple advice cases and half have been true counselling . . . clients have generally exhibited signs of having difficulty in the management of anxiety.' (Lightbody, 1981) The Trustee Savings Bank have recently established a similar service to cope primarily with stress-related problems in the workplace. In the private health sector, BUPA, at their new Behavioural Science Unit in London, provide a widely used individual counselling service as part of their stress-management programme.

Counselling in nursing

The need for a counselling service within the profession was stressed most strongly by the Report of the Parliamentary Committee on Nursing (the Briggs Report). It saw 'the creation of a comprehensive counselling service as an *urgent top priority*' (author's italics) (para. 580, p. 176), and devoted over 23 paragraphed references to a justification of the need for such a provision for all nurses.

Two RCN national conferences led to the setting up of a working party in October 1975 to further examine the issue and to make specific recommendations. 'Counselling in Nursing' (the report of the working party) was published early in 1978 and reiterated the need for a counselling service for the profession.

Writing a decade later on 'Counselling—a forgotten responsibility', Bailey (1981) comments, 'It is therefore quite unacceptable that so little has been achieved since the publication of the Briggs Report nearly ten years ago. Only two fully functional, independently appointed nurse counsellors closely approximating the Briggs proposals, are currently in post, both of whom are based in London, one at Guy's Hospital (Hughill, 1975; Annandale-Steiner, 1970a,b) and the other at St Thomas' Hospital (Stone, 1979).'

In spite of the recommendations of Briggs and the initiative of the RCN the implementation of counselling services within the NHS has been, with a few notable exceptions, minimal. Nationally only a few appointments were ever made. Indeed, the picture is even more depressing for in the recent times of financial stringency it has often been the counselling service which has been one of the first to suffer.

Alternative strategies for counselling provision

A wide variety of alternative models for the setting up of a counselling facility are possible and a useful review of a number of options is made by Watts (1977)

External This will depend on extending the use of already existing services:

1.   At the national level the expansion of and a closer contact and cooperation with such schemes as CHAT (the UK counselling service for nurses).

Internal A number of responses are possible depending upon the resources available. These could include,

1.   The creation of a specialist counselling post, either on a full-time or part-time basis. This could be a separate and discrete service (e.g. Bristol and Weston have one of the few full-time nurse counsellor posts), or as part of a larger more general service (Bloomsbury's proposed plans to establish a joint counselling and careers advisory service).
2.   Expanding the role of existing specialist staff—occupational health, personnel, tutors, welfare officers, etc. to include a counselling role.
3.   Creation of a voluntary team using existing staff who would undergo appropriate training (one Health Authority is exploring the possibility of using a group of ex-nurses to operate a telephone-based service).
4.   Creating a joint/shared service with other local agencies. Most education institutions have either full-time counsellors or well-established voluntary systems (e.g. Nightline, etc.). A Director of Social Services, writing in the nursing press, highlighted a similar need amongst his own staff and raised the possibility of cooperation between the services: 'The case seems inescapable for organizations like social service departments and hospitals to provide expert counselling for both staff and students, placing the job away from the hierarchical functions of line management and giving the

job the facilities and resources which allow workers to admit to their needs and seek help without stigma.' (Smith, 1978)

5. More informal approaches can be explored. Peer-support groups using 'co-counselling' techniques are well established in several parts of the country, and can involve individuals from a wide range of the caring professions.

Staff support groups
A number of support groups have been formed in both the hospital and community setting (see Townsend and Linsley, 1980). Many are run to include other professional groups within the hospital. Others are formed outside the organization and cater for members from a wide range of caring professions. Walton (1984) emphasizes that an important strategy for all nurses is to consciously review and, if necessary, develop one's own personal support system. He suggests that a useful way to do this is to take stock of your own network by making a note of those who can help you in the different aspects of your job or life and asking the key question 'Have you got all the support you might need?'. (See Figure 10.1)

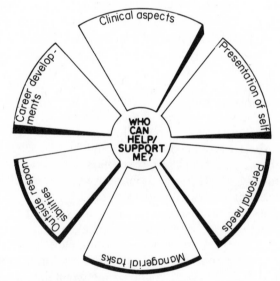

Figure 10.1 'Who can help support me?' From Walton (1984).

Quality circles

Origin

Health care organizations, possibly because of their size and structure, are not very outward looking. New ideas are often treated with suspicion and with a degree of resistance. However, one of the most interesting and potentially useful techniques imported from outside of the profession is the growing use of 'quality circles' within the health services. Quality circles originally developed in Japanese and American industry, and were used mainly to tackle problems of quality and production in a wide variety of settings.

True, ideas or new techniques cannot be naively transferred without careful thought and consideration of the very special needs of the service. But valuable lessons can be learned from the practice of other professions, and from commerce and industry. After all, the problems seem very similar: How can we improve service delivery? How best to reduce costs yet maintain standards? How can the quality of the working environment be improved? As a leading exponent of quality circles in this country remarks, 'Quality consciousness need not refer exclusively to the production line; indeed patient care requires quality analysis and solutions as much as any manufacturing or service agency.' (Hyde, 1984.)

What are they?

Although originally designed as short-lived groups, set up to tackle specific work related problems, they can also provide an exciting medium for staff development and support. Quality circles are composed of six to twelve employees from the same department or unit who meet regularly, perhaps one hour each week, to systematically work together on the solution of a common problem. As such quality circles cannot be said to be revolutionary, radical, or even new! Many health care organizations will say they already have them, but call them departmental meetings, etc. But quality circles are different, they can be radical, and they should be revolutionary, as they are grounded in a philosophy which holds that members are drawn from across the established bounderies which criss-cross the NHS.

So the aim of the quality circle is to include members of all involved professions. In this way, it can cut through the organizational hierarchy, drawing where appropriate upon the specialized skills and experience of a whole range of people from nursing officer to student nurse. Quality circles provide the opportunity whereby staff at every level of the organization can work together as a team, for a fixed length of time, in order to improve the quality of the service and the work environment. As such they provide at the same time a means of more participative management and a way of improving service delivery.

At the individual level they can provide an opportunity for direct worker involvement in the decision-making process, while at the same time encouraging the practice and development of a range of managerial skills, such as communication, team work, problem solving, etc. At the group/organizational level they can encourage closer collaboration across disciplinary boundaries via the solution of common problems. Finally, but perhaps of greatest importance to the organization, they can lead to increased efficiency and the more effective use of limited resources. (*Nursing Times*, 1984; *Nursing Mirror*, 1985)

A number of Health Authorities are now using quality circles to good effect and a leading exponent of the method has published a useful guide—'Quality Circle Developments within North Warwickshire Health Authority' (NWHA, 1984). This contains a full account of their experiences since setting up their first circle in 1983, and a description of operation of 16 such circles presently in use which range across a wide variety of settings. Problems tackled have included,

— the reduction of the accident level in a specific ward,
— the research and trial of Macadbeds,
— the development of a programme dealing with incontinence in mentally handicapped and elderly patients,
— improving the quality and presentation of patients' meals,
— developing care of the elderly courses with a local further education college,
— improving existing duty rostas,
— developing a scheme of family involvement in the treatment of elderly hospitalized patients.

It seems the use of quality circles as a well-tried method of involving the nurse in shared decision making and problem solving has much to recommend it. The NWHA reports 'benefits in changed attitudes, the devleopment of a problem solving ethic, improved leadership performance and increased participation among a wide range of staff.'

CONCLUSION

Finally, two general conclusions emerge from the study. The first revolves around the nature of occupational stress itself, and the implications for stress management strategies, and the second concerns the role of the individual and the profession in bringing about change.

Stress a multi-dimensional phenomenon

It is important to reiterate that stress takes place, and is the result of pressures, at a number of levels. A fuller understanding must involve a consideration of the personal, interpersonal, and organizational factors of the 'stress equation'. It is not the individual who cannot cope. Nor is it simply the overwhelming demands of a particular job. It is not even the constraints of the organization. Rather it is a complex interaction—an equation in which the individual, interpersonal, and organizational elements are in a dynamic relation one with the other, the 'person/environment fit'.

The exact pattern of such an interaction is often unclear, and as Maslach remarks, 'We do not yet know the relative importance of each dimension to answer such questions such as "Does the nature of the job have a greater impact than the individual's personality, or vice versa?" Nor do we know just how one dimension influences the other' (Maslach, 1982). All we do know is that a greater understanding of the phenomenon must encompass and incorporate all these dimensions.

Similarly attempts to deal with occupational stress must also be multidimensional. They must be able to deal with problems at the individual, group, and organizational level if they are to be truly effective. At the same time it should be remembered that solutions to these problems are inherently limited, since stress and strain are component dynamics of all organizational functioning. The ultimate aim must be to explore in detail the dynamics of the particular situation, so that 'dis-stress' can be identified and alleviated. Indeed, the systematic identification of the factors and symptoms of stress, the first stage of the problem solving process, is seen by researchers as providing the foundation of effective intervention. To use a medical analogy, 'The effectiveness of treatment is determined by the accuracy of the diagnosis'.

Individual

What of the individual dimension of this stress equation? What do we know of the causes, effects and solutions at this level? Research findings tell us that stress is more likely to have negative outcomes 'If the person is younger, less mature, and less self confident; is impulsive and impatient; has no family commitments but needs other people who can provide approval and affection; has goals and expectations that are not in tune with reality.' (Maslach, 1982). At the individual level the costs of stress can be both physical and psychological. Symptoms can range from mild disallusionment to the full blown 'burnout syndrom' (see Maslach, 1982) and can include exhaustion and illness, depression and irritability, and may result in the increased use of alchohol and drugs.

However, as we have seen the individual can take a number of positive steps to combat the problem. These coping strategies are aimed at bringing about personal change. Change, both in individual styles of working, and in the responses to the pressures of the job.

Interpersonal

At this level the focus turns to the part that other people play in the process. How does the nature of the involvement with colleagues and clients ease or exacerbate the individual's experience of stress? The inherent strain of the 'caring relationship' coping with the pain and apprehension of the patient and their families, difficulties with colleagues and co-workers, and the lack of support from supervisors are all factors which are likely to increase the individual's vulnerability to stress.

Effects at this level are seen most clearly in relations with patients and co-workers where a distancing may take place. There is likely to be a loss of quality in these relationships leading to an overall deterioration in standards of care and caring. In addition we can see from the research how the negative effects of problems with interpersonal relationships at work can spill over into the nurse's private life and may prove harmful to both family and friends.

Change at this level includes developing coping techniques that are aimed directly at improving the quality of interpersonal relationships in the work-place. This will include an examination of one's own strengths and weaknesses, particularly in the area of interpersonal skills and abilities; providing the opportunity for closer cooperation and interaction in a variety of ways; and increasing the quality of the support you seek for yourself—and provide for others.

Organizational

The organization is often held to be the major cause of occupational stress. 'If only the organization would change this . . . or provide more of that . . . then the problem would be solved.' Although many of these comments have a degree of validity there is the ever present danger of simply projecting all of the ills of the profession onto the organization. This is not only naive and inaccurate but dangerous. It removes the ultimate responsibility from the individual nurse and the profession onto 'them' or 'it', and, by doing so, it denies that the individual has any power, or right, to control their own situation. It is the classic route to alienation. Of course, the organization has much to answer for—it is the nature of the beast. But let us not lose sight of the fact that organizations are created by and made up of individuals. In the final analysis *we* are the organization.

However, there are a number of ways the institution can be seen to contribute directly to occupational stress. The very nature of formal organiza-tion with its structural patterns, is hierarchy and inherent rigidity will have a profound effect on the nature of the workplace. A range of problems are likely to be found, including excessive workload, management which is out of touch, bureaucratic procedures and controls, the lack of support structures, etc. Organizational indicators of the problem are to be seen in high rates of absenteeism and wastage and a poor quality of service delivery.

At this level there are a number of organizational strategies which can be used to bring about change. They range from reviews of organizational policy, the re-design of jobs, changes in staffing policy, establishing more flexible procedures, involvement of staff in decision making, providing supportive services and implementing appropriate staff training programmes.

Helplessness and hopelessness: change and control

Stress and burnout are more likely to occur, and will have greater negative impact, when people feel powerless. Being at the mercy of the situation, or the organization, or even the profession, can lead to feelings of helplessness, and prevent growth and change (Cooper and Hingley, 1985).

Echoing Menzies' findings of a quarter of a century ago, researchers have noted that there is still a high degree of ambivalence within the profession surrounding the problem of occupational stress, and a tendency either to deny its existence or to attribute it to the personal failings of the individual. Yet, at an individual level nurses are much more open to discussing the difficulties they experience, and the frustration and helplessness they feel in their role as carers in a large, and often impersonal, bureaucratic system. Although as a profession, and as one of the largest professional groups in the country, they are potentially very powerful, it seems that nurses have not yet found a common voice. As Lachman (1983) comments of their American counterparts, 'The time has come for nurse to give up the three S's of subservience, self sacrifice, and submissiveness'.

So, much will depend upon the individual, as a member of the profession, to make his/her voice heard. For in the final analysis it is up to the individual nurse, the health authority, and the profession to work together to provide opportunities for growth and development. Both organizational health and individual well-being reflect the nature of the relationship between the organization and the individual, and as Wright (1975) suggests,

> The responsibility for maintaining health should be a reflection of the basic relationship between the individual and the organization for which he works, it is in the best interests of both parties that reasonable steps are taken to live and work sensibly, and not too demandingly.

If that relationship is a negative one the levels of 'dis-ease' and 'dis-stress' will be high, and if the process continues unchecked then the very nature of work for the nurse is in danger of degenerating to the level reflected in the comments of a leading American observer, who suggests that,

> Work, is, by its very nature, about violence—to the spirit as well as to the body. It is about ulcers as well as accidents, about shouting matches as well as fistfights, about nervous breakdowns as well as kicking the dog around. It is, above all (or beneath all), about daily humiliations. To survive the day is a triumph enough for the walking wounded among the great many of us. (Terkel, 1972).

In the final analysis nurses must ask themselves this question: If, as a profession, they are unable or unwilling to care for themselves, can they in all honesty be expected, or even trusted, to care for others?

REFERENCES

Allen, H. (1982) *The Ward Sister*. London: Bailliere-Tindall.

Annandale-Steiner, D. (1979a) Unhappiness is the nurse who expected more. *Nurs. Mirror*, Nov. 29.

Annandale-Steiner, D. (1979b) The nurse counsellors role at Guy's. *Nurs. Times*, Aug., 1345–1349.

Aydelotte, M. and Tener, M. (1960) *An investigation of the Relation Between Nursing Activity and Patient Welfare*. Iowa: Univ. of Iowa.

204

Bailey, R. (1981) Counselling services for nurses—a forgotten responsibility. *J. Br. Inst. Ment. Hand.*, **9**: 45–47.
Bond, M. (1986) *Stress and Self Awareness: A Guide for Nurses*. London: Heinemann.
Byrnes, M.A. (1982) Non-nursing functions: the nurses state their case. *Am. J. Nurs.*, **82**: 1089–1097.
Caplan, G. (1974) *Support System and Community Mental Health*. New York: Behavioural Publishers.
Cherniss, C. (1980) Staff Burnont: *Job Stress in the Human Services*. London: Sage.
Cooper, C.L. and Payne, R. (eds) (1978) *Stress at Work*. Chichester: Wiley.
Harris, D.H. (1970) Staffing requirements. *Hospitals (JAHA)* 44. Ap 16. 64–70.
Hopson, B. (1973) Career development in industry and the diary of an experiment. *Br. J. Guidance Counselling*, **1**: Jan.
Hughill, J. (1975) Nurse counselling. *Nurs. Mirror*, April 10, 58–61.
Hyde, P. (1984). Something for everyone. *Nursing Times* Nov 28. 49–50.
King's Fund (1981) *Project Paper No 27: The Preparation of Senior Nurse Managers in the NHS*. London: The King's Fund.
Kubler-Ross, E. (1982) *Living with Death and Dying*. London: Macmillan.
Lachman, V.D. (1983) *Stress Management: A Manual for Nurses*. New York: Grune and Stratton.
Lazarus, R.S. (1980) Coping by thought and feeling. *J. Occup. Med.*, **22**: 13.
Lightbody (1981) Counselling in organisations. In Marshall, J. and Cooper, C.L. (eds), *Coping With Stress at Work*. Aldershot: Gower.
Marks, I. (1975) Modern trends in the management of morbid anxiety. In Spielberger, C.D. and Sarason, S.B. (eds), *Stress and Anxiety*. New York: Wiley.
Marshall, J. (1980) Stress amongst nurses. In Cooper, C.L. and Marshall, J. (eds), *White Collar and Professional Stress*. Chichester: Wiley.
Maslach, C. (1982) *Burnout—The Cost of Caring*. New Jersey: Prentice Hall.
Matsumoto, Y.S. (1970) Social stress and coronary heart disease in Japan. *Millbank Mem. Fund*, **48**.
McGratty, P. (1985) Confidence with practice. *Nurs. Times*, Sept. 11.
McFarlane, J. (1980) Essays on nursing. *King's Fund, Project Paper No. RC2*. London: Kings' Fund.
National Staff Committee for Nurses and Midwives (1983). *Report 1979–83*. London: HMSO.
Nursing Mirror (1985) Circles of wisdom. *Nurs. Mirror* July 17.
Nursing Times (1984) Four-part series on quality circles.
Something for everyone. Developing the quality of care.
A team approach to care. The American experience. *Nurs. Times*, Nov. 28–Dec. 19.
North Warwickshire Health Authority (1984) *Quality Circle Developments*. Nuneaton: NWHA.
Parkes, K.R. (1980a) Occupational stress among nurses. 1. A comparison of medical and surgical wards. *Nurs. Times*, Oct. 30, 113–116.
Parkes, K.R. (1980b) Occupational stress among nurses. 2. A comparison of male and female wards. *Nurs. Times*, Nov. 6, 117–119.
Pines, A. and Aronson, E. (1981) *Burnout: From Tedium to Personal Growth*. New York: Free Press.
Report on the Committee on Nursing (Briggs Report) Cmnd 5115, 1972, London: HMSO.
Rhys-Hearn, C. (1979) Staffing geriatric wards: Trials of a 'package'. 1 and 2 *Nurs. Times*, Occasional Papers **75**:
Royal College of Nursing (1978) *Counselling in Nursing*. London: Royal College of Nursing.
Smith, J. (1978) How nurses can help themselves. *Nurs. Mirror*, Nov. 9.

Stone, J. (1979) The nurse counsellor's role at St. Thomas's. *Nurs. Times*, Aug, 1343–1344.

Terkel, S. (1972) *Working*. New York: Avon Books.

Townsend, I. and Linsley, W. (1980) Creating a climate for carers. *Nurs. Times*, **76**: 1188–1190.

Walton, M. (1984) *Management and Managing: A Dynamic Approach*. London: Harper and Row.

Warshaw, L. (1979) Stress Management. Reading, Mass: Addison Wesley.

Watts, A.G. (ed.) (1977) *Counselling at Work*. London: National Council of Social Services.

Whitfield, S. (1979) A descriptive study of student nurses' ward experiences with dying patients and their attitudes towards them. *Unpublished MSc Thesis*, University of Manchester.

Further reading

The following annotated bibliography lists some of the books which you may find useful.

General

1. Cooper, C.L. (1982) *Stress Research.* London: Wiley.
Stress-related illness is on the increase and therefore the last decade has seen a tremendous growth in the amount of research into many aspects of stress. In this book, Professor Cooper presents the most important parts of current work and suggests directions for future research.

2. Cooper, C.L. (1981) *The Stress Check.* New Jersey: Prentice Hall.
'Coping with the stresses of life and work.' An invaluable guide to improved personal health that gives the reader an important insight into the various factors that can lead to debilitating stress at work and at home. The Stress Check explores the nature and origins of stress, how it affects individuals, organizations, communities and society. The book also gives specific methods and strategies that can help reduce the amount of stress felt, thus enabling the reader to cope more successfully.

3. Cox, T. (1978) *Stress.* London: Macmillan.
Stress, claims the author, is a threat to both physical and psychological well-being and to the quality of life itself. This book is a wide-ranging introduction to the subject and covers both the nature of stress and its effects, as well as its management. Dr Cox draws upon many disciplines including psychology, medicine, community health, and human engineering.

4. Dobson, C.B. (1982) *Stress: The Hidden Adversary.* Lancaster: MTP Press.
Intended as a comprehensive introductory text, this book attempts to cover the topic of human stress from many perspectives. The wide ranging effects of stress on physical and mental well-being, are examined in the young person as well as in the adult world.

5. Speilberger, C. (1979) *Understanding Stress and Anxiety.* London: Harper and Row.
An easily read, well-illustrated general guide to stress and anxiety. A useful introduction for the student nurse to the nature, causes and effects of psychological stress and strain. This book discussed the positive as well as the negative aspects of stress and suggests guidelines for learning to live with it.

Stress in nursing

6. Claus, K.E. and Bailey, J.T. (eds) (1980) *Living with Stress and Promoting Well-being.* St Louis: C.V. Mosby.
June Bailey, a leading writer on stress in the US nursing profession, has co-edited this

'Handbook for Nurses'. With contributions by leading figures in the stress field this book examines the nature of stress, describes the results of a major study of stressors in intensive care nursing, and offers strategies for dealing with stress.

7. Jacobson, F. and McGrath, H.M. (1983) *Nurses Under Stress*. New York: Wiley. This book presents proven techniques to prevent, diagnose and manage the stresses that nurses experience. Coverage includes the various levels of stress and practical strategies for reducing them, the problem of stress in specific roles, professional and organizational dynamics and how these relate to stress.

8. Lachman, V.D. (1983) *Stress Management*. New York: Grune and Stratton. A very comprehensive and rewarding book written especially for the practising nurse, the nurse educator and the nurse manager. 'This manual is designed to help nurses improve their careers so that the responsibilities and the problems don't drive them out. Several chapters are focused directly on the work climate, others address skills needed to function effectively and happily in their careers and homes.'

9. Marshall, J. (1980) Stress amongst nurses. In Cooper, C.L. and Marshall, J. (eds) *White Collar and Professional Stress*. London: Wiley. Concerned with the personal cost to the nurse of providing patient care, Judy Marshall reviews a substantial section of the available literature. This chapter raises many interesting speculations and poses important questions about stress amongst nurses. Particular attention is given to intensive care nursing.

Burnout

10. Cherniss, C. (1980) *Staff Burnout*. California: Sage. As Cary Cherniss points out, 'Before 1974, the term burnout had not appeared in print.' This book examines the nature of this concept and discusses the reasons why it has become a major source of concern in the caring professions.

11. Edelwich, J. and Brodsky, A. (1980) *Burnout*. New York: Human Science Press. This book portrays the four stages of disillusionment—enthusiasm, stagnation, frustration, and apathy—that constitute the 'burnout syndrome'. Based on extensive interviews with social workers, psychologists, counsellors, teachers and other professionals the authors explore the causes of burnout and propose constructive intervention methods for individuals and organizations.

12. McConnel, E.A. (1982) *Burnout in the Nursing Profession*. St Louis: C.V. Mosby. This anthology was compiled for the purpose of bringing together the information currently available about the burnout syndrome in nursing. It includes coverage of coping strategies for preventing burnout, signs and symptoms of burnout, potential causes of burnout (personal and organizational), and the costs of burnout. The narrative of each chapter is followed by selected readings and an annotated bibliography that augments the chapter content.

13. Maslach, C. (1982) *Burnout—The Cost of Caring*. New Jersey: Prentice Hall. Christina Maslach is a leading researcher on burnout. In this book she uses illustrative examples and first-hand accounts to identify the causes of emotional exhaustion and suggests methods to prevent and cure the situation. Written for professional and informal caregivers, this guide endeavours to give the reader an understanding of burnout, thus re-motivating them in their role.

14. Paine, W.S. (1982) *Job Stress and Burnout*. California: Sage. Burnout stress syndromes, the consequence of high levels of job stress, personal frustration and inadequate coping skills have major personal, organizational and social costs—which are increasing. Understanding and intervening in these syndromes is the focus of this book.

Coping

15. Bailey .R.D. (1985) *Coping with Stress in Caring*. London: Blackwell Scientific. Addressing nurses and allied health care providers, this book aims to promote an understanding and awareness of stress and to introduce techniques for successful stress management. A number of 'practical stress check schedules' are included which can be used in combination with stress control techniques.

16. Bond, M. and Kilty, J. (1982) *Practical Methods of Dealing with Stress*. Department of Educational Studies, University of Surrey.
This report is intended to serve three main purposes:
1. To be an aide memoire and additional resource for participants of (stress) workshops;
2. To provide a modest resources for anyone wishing to extend their range of ways of dealing with stress or to help others to do so;
3. To stimulate others to creatively design similar activities by providing examples of ways of organizing such workshops.'

17. Eagle, R. (1981) *Taking the Strain*. London: BBC Publications.
Though it has become popular to blame stress for many of our troubles, we can do a great deal to prevent ourselves falling victims to the unpleasant stresses of life. 'Taking the Strain' tells the reader how to recognize the physical and mental signs of stress and how to cope with them. Experienced teachers and therapists describe techniques the reader can learn to use: music relaxation, meditation, biofeedback, etc.

18. Garland, L.M. and Bush, C.T. (1982) *Coping Behaviours and Nursing*. Virginia: Reston Publishing Co.
This book is designed to provide nurses with a conceptual approach for identifying and responding to frequently encountered coping behaviours. The authors distinguish between adaptive and maladaptive coping mechanisms and discuss psychological and physiological stressors and responses includes implications for education, consultation and research and can be of use to nurses at all levels.

19. Which? (1982) *Living with Stress*. Hertford: Consumers Association.
Stress can cause illness and illness can cause stress. This book looks at the physical and emotional harm that can result unless stress is kept under control. It outlines the right and wrong ways to counteract stress and helps the reader to identify sources of stress in their own life.

Appendix

INTRODUCTION TO THE QUESTIONNAIRE*

You will see that we have organized the questionnaire to save you as much time as possible. In most cases you will only be asked to either circle the appropriate answer or place a number in a box.

There are five separate sections in all dealing with different aspects of behaviour.

Section I – covers relevant personal and background details
Section II – focuses in some depth upon the sources of occupational stress
Section III – examines how individuals cope with stress in their work
Section IV – looks at certain patterns of individual behaviour and beliefs
Section V – is concerned with how you generally feel and act and also gives you the opportunity to give your views about stress at work

Interspaced throughout are a number of blank sections labelled 'comments'. We have provided these as we would value your opinion about specific sections of the questionnaire or about the project in general.

Finally don't spend too long on any one section but do please ensure that *all the questions and sections are completed*.

SECTION I

Background information

For purposes of statistical analysis *only*, please answer the following questions about yourself. Your answers will remain *anonymous and strictly confidential*. However, this biographical data is *crucial* to the study.

Most of the questions below are answered by placing the appropriate number in the right hand column. e.g. Q 1 What is your sex? If you are female you would enter *1*, if you were male you would enter *2*.

1. Name (optional) ....
   Location (optional) ....

2. What is your sex? (please enter 1 or 2 in the right-hand column)
   Female   1   Male   2

* Reproduced by kind permission of the King's Fund.

Please enter
code number

3. Year of birth. Please complete the last two digits. $\boxed{1}\boxed{9}\boxed{}\boxed{}$

4. Were you born in the British Isled (i.e. U.K. & Eire)?

Yes   1   No   2

5. If *no* how long have you lived in this country?

Under one year	1	Between 5 & 10 years	3
One to 5 years	2	Over 10 years	4

6. Are you: Single   4

Married	1	Divorced/separated	5
Re-married	2	Widowed/widower	6
Living with partners	3	Other, please state	7

7. Number of children living at home (e.g. if 2 enter 02, if 10
   enter, 10 etc.)
   Please insert 00 if this does not apply to you.

8. Age of children: Please enter appropriate codes.

Not applicable	1	Post-school age	4
Pre-school age	2	Others, please	5
School age	3	state	

9. What is the highest educational level (if applicable) you have
   obtained, other than your nursing qualifications?

GCE 'O' Level/CSE	1	Postgraduate Diploma	4
GCE 'A' Level/	2	Higher degree, MA/Msc	5
Ordinary National		PhD	6
Diploma		Other – please specify	7
Higher National	3	....	
Diploma or equivalent		Not applicable	8
degree			

10. What was the first professional qualification you obtained?

SRN   1   ONC   2   RSCN   3   RMN   4

Others (please state) ....

11. Do you have any post-professional qualifications? (e.g. SCM)

Yes   1   No   2

If yes please indicate what qualification(s) you hold and the
year obtained.

....

....

12. How many years have you spent in nursing, including training?

Less than 10 years	1	20–25 years	4
10–15 years	2	More than 25 years	5
15–20 years	3		

Please enter
code number

13. Please specify your job title and exact work location (e.g. Ward
    Sister – Male Surgical Ward).
    ....

14. Are you employed:
    Full-time   1   Part-time   2
    Others, please specify ....
    If part-time approximate hours/week ....

15. Please indicate the main pattern of your work.
    Full-time (day only)   1   Part-time (day only)   4
    Full-time (shift)   2   Part-time (shift)   5
    Full-time (night only)   3   Part-time (night only) 6
    Others, please specify   7

16. How long have you worked for this authority?
    Less than one year   1   5–10 years   4
    1–3 years   2   More than 10 years   5
    3–5 years   3   Others, please   6
                                  state......................

17. Did you move to this authority from another area?
    Yes   1   No   2
    If yes, from ....
    Why did you move? Please identify the most important
    reason only.
    Promotion   1   Better living conditions 4
    Better working   2   Others – please state   5
    conditions   ....
    Partners work   3

18. Approximately how many people do you supervise (i.e. how
    many staff *in total* are directly or indirectly under *your*
    management)?
    Please state your answer in the form of a number.
    ....

19. Which of the following most closely describes your working
    environment (i.e. the area in which you carry out your work)?
    Central administration 1   Operating theatres   5
    /Planning   Outpatients or clinics   6
    Community-based   2   Wards or special units   7
    services   Others, please state   8
    Nurse education   3   ....
    Accident and   4
    emergency dept.

212

Please enter
code number

20. Please indicate your nursing grade.

District Nursing Officer level and above	1	Clinical Nurse Managers level	3
Director of Nursing or Midwifery Services level	2	Sister/Charge Nurse level	4
		Others – please state	5

....

21. If the majority of your time is spent in one hospital setting please indicate its approximate size.

| Under 100 beds | 1 | 301 and over beds | 3 |
| 100–300 beds | 2 | | |

22. If the majority of your time is spent in one hospital setting please indicate what type of hospital it is.

General hospital	1	Rheumatoid diseases hospital	5
Community hospital	2		
Geriatric hospital	3	Hospital for the physically handicapped	6
Psychiatric hospital	4	Hospital for the mentally handicapped	7

Others, please state 8

23. If the majority of your time is spent in the community is it in a mainly rural or urban area?

| Rural | 1 | Urban | 2 |

Approximately what is your average case-load? Express your answer as a number.

24. Do you consider that your work is in a generally recognized high-stress area (e.g. ICU, theatre, etc.)?

| No | 1 | Yes | 2 |
| | | Give details | |

....
....

Comments:

SECTION II

Occupational stress

Would you please circle the number that best reflects the degree to which that statement is a source of pressure at work. Pressure is defined as a problem, something you find difficult to cope with, about which you feel worried or anxious. The *greater* the pressure the *higher* the number, i.e.

1. causes me *no* pressure
2. causes me *slight* pressure
3. causes me *moderate* pressure

4. causes me *considerable* pressure
5. causes me *extreme* pressure

Do not spend too much time pondering, as there are no right or wrong answers. You will find it easier to complete this section fairly quickly.

Remember
Circle the correct response.

For office use only

	No pressure	Slight pressure	Moderate pressure	Considerable pressure	Extreme pressure
1. Time pressures and deadlines	1	2	3	4	5
2. Work overload	1	2	3	4	5
3. Work underload (needing to look busy)	1	2	3	4	5
4. Tasks outside of my competence	1	2	3	4	5
5. Fluctuations in workload	1	2	3	4	5
6. Unrealistically high expectations by others of my role	1	2	3	4	5
7. Coping with new situations	1	2	3	4	5
8. Uncertainty about the degree or area of my responsibility	1	2	3	4	5
9. Security of employment	1	2	3	4	5
10. Involvement with life and death situations	1	2	3	4	5
11. Coping with new technology	1	2	3	4	5
12. Exposure to death	1	2	3	4	5
13. Staff shortages	1	2	3	4	5
14. Poor physical working conditions	1	2	3	4	5
15. Lack of support from senior staff	1	2	3	4	5
16. Lack of privacy	1	2	3	4	5
17. Shortage of essential resources	1	2	3	4	5
18. Poor quality of supporting staff	1	2	3	4	5

	No pressure	Slight pressure	Moderate pressure	Considerable pressure	Extreme pressure	For office use only
19. Unsocial hours	1	2	3	4	5	
20. Lack of specialized training for present task	1	2	3	4	5	
21. Lack of participation in planning /decision making	1	2	3	4	5	
22. Difficult patients	1	2	3	4	5	
23. Dealing with relatives	1	2	3	4	5	
24. Bereavement counselling	1	2	3	4	5	

end of record

REMEMBER – the *greater* the pressure the *higher* the number.

Please circle correct response.

For office use only ☐ ☐ ☐ ☐ ②

25. Playing a leadership role	1	2	3	4	5
26. Bringing about change in staff/organization	1	2	3	4	5
27. Low professional status	1	2	3	4	5
28. Lack of job satisfaction	1	2	3	4	5
29. Lack of promotion prospects	1	2	3	4	5
30. Relationships with colleagues	1	2	3	4	5
31. Relationships with subordinates	1	2	3	4	5
32. Relationships with superiors	1	2	3	4	5
33. Fear of appearing weak	1	2	3	4	5
34. Promoted out of the 'caring' role	1	2	3	4	5
35. Job versus home demands	1	2	3	4	5
36. Over-emotional involvement	1	2	3	4	5
37. Taking problems home	1	2	3	4	5
38. Trivial tasks interfere with my professional role	1	2	3	4	5
39. Deciding priorities	1	2	3	4	5

For office
use only

	No pressure	Slight pressure	Moderate pressure	Considerable pressure	Extreme pressure
40. I have too little time in which to do what is expected of me	1	2	3	4	5
41. Others' demands for my time at work are in conflict	1	2	3	4	5
42. I spend my time 'fighting fires' rather than working to a plan	1	2	3	4	5
43. Decisions or changes which affect me are made 'above', without my knowledge or involvement	1	2	3	4	5
44. I must attend meetings to get my job done	1	2	3	4	5
45. I lack confidence in management	1	2	3	4	5
46. Conflict between my unit and others it must work with	1	2	3	4	5
47. Management expects me to interrupt my work for new priorities	1	2	3	4	5
48. Others at work seem unclear about what my job is	1	2	3	4	5
49. I only get feedback when my performance is unsatisfactory	1	2	3	4	5
50. I must go to other departments to get my job done	1	2	3	4	5
51. Management misunderstands the real needs of my department	1	2	3	4	5

REMEMBER – the *greater* the pressure the *higher* the number.

For office
use only

Please circle correct response.

	Strongly disagree	Disagree	Undecided	Agree	Strongly agree
52. Difficulty in dealing with aggressive people	1	2	3	4	5
53. My nursing and administrative roles conflict	1	2	3	4	5
54. Avoiding conflict with superiors	1	2	3	4	5
55. Difficulty in dealing with passive people	1	2	3	4	5
56. I find problems allocating resources	1	2	3	4	5
57. Frustration with conflicting procedures	1	2	3	4	5

216

	Strongly disagree	Disagree	Undecided	Agree	Strongly agree
58. My professional expertise contradicts organizational practice	1	2	3	4	5
59. Feelings of isolation	1	2	3	4	5
60. Organizational change	1	2	3	4	5
61. Lack of emotional support at home	1	2	3	4	5
62. Relationships with administrators	1	2	3	4	5
63. Relationships with consultants	1	2	3	4	5
64. I expect too much of myself	1	2	3	4	5
65. I don't feel adequately trained for the job I have to do	1	2	3	4	5
66. Difficulties with transport	1	2	3	4	5
67. Keeping up with professional developments	1	2	3	4	5
68. Sexual discrimination at work	1	2	3	4	5
69. Domestic/family demands inhibit promotion	1	2	3	4	5
70. I need to absent myself from work to cope with domestic problems	1	2	3	4	5
71. My superiors do not appreciate my home pressures	1	2	3	4	5
72. Others – please state	1	2	3	4	5

For office use only

....

....

Comments:

Some jobs are more interesting and satisfying than others. We want to know how you feel about your job.

How far do these statements represent how you are feeling about your present job? There are no right or wrong answers. We would like your honest opinion on each one of the statements.

Please circle correct response.

	Strongly disagree	Disagree	Undecided		Strongly agree
1. I am satisfied with my job	1	2	3	4	5
2. There are some conditions concerning my job that could be improved	1	2	3	4	5
3. Most of the time I have to force myself to go to work	1	2	3	4	5
4. Each day of work seems like it will never end	1	2	3	4	5
5. I frequently think about finding another job	1	2	3	4	5
6. I frequently think about finding an occupation other than nursing	1	2	3	4	5

7. Looking back over the year what percentage of total stress in your life results from your job?

Less than 10%	1	Between 50% and 75%	4
Between 10% and 25%	2	Over 75%	5
Between 25% and 50%	3		

Comments:

SECTION III

Coping behaviour

The purpose of this section is to find out the kinds of situations which trouble people in their jobs and how they deal with them.

Take a few moments and think about the events or situations which have been stressful for you during the last three months. By 'stressful' we mean a situation which was difficult or troubling you, either because it made you feel bad or because it took effort to deal with it.

How do you usually cope with these situations?

Please circle correct response

For office
use only

☐☐☐☐☐ 3

1. Blamed myself	1 2 3 4 5
2. Kept my feelings to myself	1 2 3 4 5
3. Wished I could have changed what happened	1 2 3 4 5
4. Got mad at the people or things which caused the problem	1 2 3 4 5
5. Let my feelings out in some way	1 2 3 4 5
6. Just concentrated on what I had to do next – the next step	1 2 3 4 5
7. Talked to someone about how I was feeling	1 2 3 4 5
8. Didn't let it get to me; refused to think about it too much	1 2 3 4 5
9. Went on as if nothing had happened	1 2 3 4 5
10. Avoided being with people in general	1 2 3 4 5
11. You went over the problem again and again in your mind to try and understand it	1 2 3 4 5
12. Talked to someone who could do something about the problem	1 2 3 4 5

Which of the following people do you feel you could turn to, to talk about a personal problem or crisis: *Please tick correct response.*

For office
use only

13. Mother   ....
14. Father   ....
15. Partner   ....
16. Son   ....(If more than one, state how many ......)
17. Daughter   ....(If more than one, state how many ......)
18. Relative   ....(If more than one, state how many ......)
19. Friend   ....(If more than one, state how many ......)
    (outside of work)
20. Work colleague ....(If more than one, state how many ......)
21. Others please state:

For office
use only

Please circle correct response.

How often do you use the following measures to relax?

1. Take aspirin	1 2 3 4 5
2. Use tranquillizers or other medication	1 2 3 4 5
3. Drink coffee, coke or eat frequently	1 2 3 4 5
4. Smoke	1 2 3 4 5
5. Have an alcoholic drink	1 2 3 4 5
6. Use relaxation techniques (meditation, yoga)	1 2 3 4 5
7. Use informal relaxation techniques (i.e. take time out for deep breathing, imagining pleasant scenes, etc.)	1 2 3 4 5
8. Exercise	1 2 3 4 5
9. Talk to someone you know	1 2 3 4 5
10. Leave your work area and go somewhere (time out, sick days, lunch away from organization)	1 2 3 4 5
11. Use humour	1 2 3 4 5
12. Other	1 2 3 4 5

220

13. Over the past year, which of the following best describes
    your typical drinking habits? (*one drink* is a single whisky,
    gin or brandy, a glass of wine, sherry or port or a ½ pint of
    beer)

Teetotal	1	Regularly, 1 or 2 drinks	4
An occasional drink	2	a day	
Several drinks a	3	Regularly, 3 to 6 drinks	5
week, but not every day		a day	
		Regulary more than 6	6
		drinks a day	

14. If you are not teetotal, has the quantity of alcohol consumed
    increased or decreased over the past year?

Increased	1	Decreased	4
substantially		Decreased	5
Increased	2	substantially	
Remained the same	3	Stopped	6

15. Re: cigarette smoking. Which of the following statements is
    most nearly true for you?

I never smoke regularly	1
I have given up smoking	2
I am currently smoking	3

16. If you are currently smoking, please circle the number which
    constitutes your average daily consumption of cigarettes:

0–5 a day	1	20–30 a day	5
5–10 a day	2	30–40 a day	6
10–15 a day	3	40 plus a day	7
15–20 a day	4		

17. If you are a smoker has the quantity smoked increased or
    decreased over the past year?

Increased	1	Decreased	4
substantially		Decreased	5
Increased	2	substantially	
Remained the same	3	Stopped	6

18. Hours of physical exercise engaged in per week:

Less than 1	1	7–9	4
1–3	2	10–12	5
4–6	3		

19. Over the past year, approximately how many days absence
    have you had to take? Express your answer as a number.

    ....

For office
use only

20. Over the years, have you experienced changes in the level of
    stress experienced in your job? Indicate one.

Increased	1	Decreased	4
substantially		Decreased	5
Increased	2	substantially	
Remained the same	3		

end of record

Comments:

Please use this space to add any comments you wish:

SECTION IV

General behaviour

Could you please circle *one* number for each of the 14 questions below, which best reflects the way you behave in your everyday life.

For *example* on question 1: if you are always on time for appointments you would circle a number between 7 and 11. If you are usually more casual about appointments, you would circle one of the other numbers between 1 and 5.

▢▢▢▢▢4

1. Casual about appointments	1 2 3 4 5 6 7 8 9 10 11	Never late
2. Not competitive	1 2 3 4 5 6 7 8 9 10 11	Very competitive
3. Good listener	1 2 3 4 5 6 7 8 9 10 11	Anticipates what others are going to say (nods, interrupts, finishes for them)
4. Never feels rushed (even under pressure)	1 2 3 4 5 6 7 8 9 10 11	Always rushed
5. Can wait patiently	1 2 3 4 5 6 7 8 9 10 11	Impatient when waiting
6. Casual	1 2 3 4 5 6 7 8 9 10 11	Eager to get things done
7. Takes things one at a time	1 2 3 4 5 6 7 8 9 10 11	Tries to do many things at once, thinks what he/she will do next
8. Slow, deliberate talker	1 2 3 4 5 6 7 8 9 10 11	Emphatic in speech (fast and forceful)
9. Cares about satisfying himself/ herself no matter what others may think	1 2 3 4 5 6 7 8 9 10 11	Wants good job recognized by others
10. Slow doing things	1 2 3 4 5 6 7 8 9 10 11	Fast (eating, etc.)
11. Easy going	1 2 3 4 5 6 7 8 9 10 11	Hard driving (pushing self and others)
12. Expresses feelings	1 2 3 4 5 6 7 8 9 10 11	Hides feelings
13. Many outside interests	1 2 3 4 5 6 7 8 9 10 11	Few interests (out of work/home
14. Unambitious	1 2 3 4 5 6 7 8 9 10 11	Ambitious

This is a questionnaire to find out the way in which certain important events affect different people. Each question consists of a pair of alternative statements.

Please select one statement from each pair (*and one only*) which you more strongly believe to be the case as far as you are concerned, and *ring* your selection (i.e. 1 or 2).

Be sure you select the one *you actually believe to be more true* rather than the one you think you should choose or the one you would like to be true. This is a measure of personal belief; obviously there are no right or wrong answers.

Ring 1 or 2 of the following statements as being *nearest* to your belief.

I.	Many of the unhappy things in people's lives are partly due to bad luck.	1
	OR	
	People's misfortunes result from the mistakes they make.	2
II.	In the long run people get the respect they deserve in this world.	1
	OR	
	Unfortunately, an individual's worth often passes unrecognized no matter how hard he tries.	2
III.	Without the right breaks one cannot be an effective leader.	1
	OR	
	Capable people who fail to become leaders have not taken advantage of their opportunities.	2
IV.	No matter how hard you try some people just don't like you.	1
	OR	
	People who can't get others to like them don't understand how to get along with others.	2
V.	Heredity plays the major role in determining one's personality.	1
	OR	
	It is a person's experiences in life which determine what they're like.	2
VI.	I have often found that what is going to happen will happen.	1
	OR	
	Trusting to fate has never turned out as well for me as making a decision to take a definite course of action.	2
VII.	In the case of the well-prepared student there is rarely if ever such a thing as an unfair test.	1
	OR	
	Many times exam questions tend to be so unrelated to course work that studying is really useless.	2
VIII.	Becoming a success is a matter of hard work, luck has little or nothing to do with it.	1
	OR	
	Getting a good job depends mainly on being in the right place at the right time.	2
IX.	There are certain people who are just no good.	1
	OR	
	There is some good in everybody.	2

224

Remember
Select only one statement.

X.	The average citizen can have an influence in government decision.	1
	OR	
	This world is run by the few people in power, and there is not much the ordinary person can do about it.	2
XI.	When I make plans, I am almost certain that I can make them work.	1
	OR	
	It is not always wise to plan too far ahead because many things turn out to be a matter of good or bad fortune anyhow.	2
XII.	In my case getting what I want has little or nothing to do with luck.	1
	OR	
	Many times we might just as well decide what to do by flipping a coin.	2
XIII.	Who gets to be the boss often depends on who was lucky enough to be in the right place first.	1
	OR	
	Getting people to do the right thing depends upon ability, luck has little or nothing to do with it.	2
XIV.	As far as world affairs are concerned, most of us are the victims of forces we can neither understand, nor control.	1
	OR	
	By taking an active part in political and social affairs the people can control world events.	2
XV.	Most people don't realize the extent to which their lives are controlled by accidental happenings.	1
	OR	
	There really is no such thing as 'luck'.	2
XVI.	One should always be willing to admit mistakes.	1
	OR	
	It is usually best to cover up one's mistakes.	2
XVII.	It is hard to know whether or not a person really likes you.	1
	OR	
	How many friends you have depends upon how nice a person you are.	2
XVIII.	A good leader expects people to decide for themselves what they should do.	1
	OR	
	A good leader makes it clear to everybody what their jobs are.	2
XIX.	Many times I feel that I have little influence over the things that happen to me.	1
	OR	
	It is impossible for me to believe that chance or luck plays an important role in my life.	2

XX.	People are lonely because they don't try to be friendly.	1
	OR	
	There's not much use in trying too hard to please people, if they like you, they like you.	2
XXI.	What happens to me is my own doing.	1
	OR	
	Sometimes I feel that I don't have enough control over the direction my life is taking.	2

Would you now please fill in the attached *Crown Crisp Index* and then come back to answer the questions below. ☐☐☐☐☐☐

SECTION V

Finally we would value your comments on the following questions.

1. What suggestions would you make to alleviate stress in nursing?

2. Overall stress has been seen as a negative phenomenon. For you are there any positive aspects of stress?

3. If you had heard of the project before you received your questionnaire please ring appropriate answer.
   1. Newsletter   4. Word of mouth
   2. Meetings   5. Other means (please state)
   3. Newspapers

Thank you for completing the questionnaire. We hope that you have found it interesting and not too demanding of your time.

Index